MICROFORMS AND LIBRARY CATALOGS
A Reader

Microform Review Series in
Library Micrographics Management

1. Microforms in Libraries: A Reader
   Albert Diaz, editor
   (Weston, CT 1975)
   Cloth CIP ISBN 0-913672-03-3

2. Studies in Micropublishing: A Reader
   Allen B. Veaner, editor
   (Westport, CT 1977)
   Cloth Index CIP ISBN 0-913672-07-6

3. Microforms and Library Catalogs: A Reader
   Albert Diaz, editor (Westport, CT 1977)
   Cloth Index CIP ISBN 0-913672-16-5

4. Serials Management and Microforms: A Reader
   Patricia Walsh, editor
   Cloth Index CIP ISBN 0-913672-11-4

5. Microforms Management in Special Libraries: A Reader
   Judy Fair, editor
   Cloth Index CIP ISBN 0-913672-15-7

6. Government Documents and Microforms: A Reader
   Robert Grey Cole, editor
   Cloth Index CIP ISBN 0-913672-12-2

7. Developing Microform Reading Facilities
   Francis Spreitzer
   Cloth Index Illustrated CIP ISBN 0-913672-09-2

8. Microform Research Collections: A Guide
   Suzanne Dodson, editor
   Cloth Index CIP ISBN 0-913672-21-1

MICROFORMS AND LIBRARY CATALOGS
A Reader

Edited by
Albert J. Diaz

MICROFORM REVIEW INC.
520 Riverside Avenue ■ P.O. Box 405 Saugatuck Station
Westport, Connecticut 06880

Library of Congress Cataloging in Publication Data
Main entry under title:

Microforms and library catalogs.

  (Library micrographics management series)
  Includes bibliographical references.
  1. Library catalogs on microfilm. 2. Computer
output microfilm devices. I. Diaz, Albert James.
II. Series.
Z681.M56   025.3   77-10457

ISBN 0-913672-16-5

ISBN for Mansell edition   0-7201-0732-6

    Microform Review Inc.
    520 Riverside Avenue
    P.O. Box 405 Saugatuck Station
    Westport, Conn. 06880
    Printed in United States of America

Published outside North and South America by
Mansell Information/Publishing Limited, 3 Bloomsbury Place,
London WC1A 2QA, England

the entire catalog. Even though microfilm itself is relatively inexpensive, the process of filming a substantial number of cards can be quite costly. Thus, the value of these distributed catalogs was seriously compromised by their inability to remain current.

In 1958 the first element of a solution to these problems began to emerge. Stromberg Carlson successfully wedded data processing and microform technologies.[6] The result has become known as Computer Output Microfilm (COM). We shall return to this innovation after we consider a second major development that was necessary before COM would be of any value to a library; (a technique for computer display is obviously of only academic interest without a store of machine readable data.)

In 1968 the MARC* pilot project came to a highly promising conclusion, and in 1969 a redistribution service of LC cataloging in machine readable form began.[7] The hesitant, amateur efforts to develop automated library systems took on a new, and more professional tone. Large scale systems, intimately integrated into the technical services operations of many libraries, began to appear. As a result of the development of the MARC communications format, the structure for the conversion of full bibliographic records existed, and the potential for interchange of that data loomed eminently feasible. The net result was that in a short time many hundreds of libraries began producing substantial fractions of their cataloging records in machine readable form. Some libraries even initiated programs of retrospective conversion. Albeit, some of these retrospective conversion projects opted for abbreviated records that would support only a limited, location function. At any rate, the consequence is that well over 1,000 libraries in the United States and Canada have substantial machine readable files of cataloging data for their collections.

Ironically, the earliest automated cataloging systems were attempts to create alternatives to the card catalog. Most of these early attempts, concerned themselves with the production of book catalogs. Probably the earliest such effort was in 1951 when King County Public Library in Seattle, Washington used tabulating equipment, the precursor to modern computing systems to sort and print the individual lines of a book catalog.[8] Exactly twenty years later, in 1971, the most successful automated bibliographic project, the shared cataloging system of the OCLC,* caused attention once again to be turned back to card catalogs.[9] The great advantage to OCLC's approach was that it minimized the dislocation that attended the introduction of automation into its member libraries. As long as cards were still being produced, and each user had complete freedom to modify a record brought up on the CRT screen, many problems could be disregarded; for example, closing of catalogs, rigorous adherence to standards, mechanical control of a machine readable catalog, etc.

---

*MARC—Machine Readable Cataloging.
*OCLO—The Ohio College Library Center, a computerized network consisting in 1977 of some 800 libraries.

Now that libraries have overcome the first major hurdle—the introduction of an unfamiliar and unproven technology—they have become much more sensitive to the possibilities that technology can offer. The machine readable cataloging data bases created as a result of the use of computerized systems are gradually achieving a primary rather than ancillary role. Librarians are becoming increasingly aware of the significance of the simple homily, "catalog cards produced by computer do not file themselves." Further, as the general level of understanding of the capabilities of the computer becomes increasingly widespread, librarians are beginning to muse more often on the potential offered by computers for *catalog maintenance*.[10]

The major limitation to catalog maintenance is posed not by the computer, but by the card catalog itself. It does little good to completely reorganize a machine readable file of cataloging data if there is no mechanism available to reflect the results of this reorganization in the card catalog. The only effective solution is to maintain identity between the contents of the library catalog and the machine readable file supporting it. Within the context of technology as we know it today, the ideal solution seems to be offered by an on-line system that offers a "window into the machine file." This, as a solution, seems about five years away for large research libraries, and at least a decade away for intermediate and small libraries.[11] The eventual solution may not even take the same form for each of these types of libraries.

Regardless of the eventual solution, it does seem that a system that can provide a static snapshot of the contents of a machine readable file—or rather a continuing series of such snapshots—will figure prominently. This brings us back to the first element of the solution to the problems of updating microfilmed catalogs that of necessity lay dormant until the advent of MARC. The fundamental problem in that case stemmed from the great cost involved in producing new cumulations, and cumulative supplements with great frequency; this is clearly the analogate of frequently displaying the contents of a machine readable file.

Computer Output Microfilm (COM) is a technique for translating information from digitally encoded form directly into microform. In a literal sense it offers a technique for making a 'snapshot' of a machine readable data base. The virtual lack of need for human intervention after the machine readable data base has been created makes this a relatively inexpensive process. The image being highly reduced, all of the economic advantages of microfilm also accrue.

The very low cost of COM makes it possible to take the required snapshots of a machine readable data base frequently enough to ameliorate the problem of lack of currency inherent in any static display. Further, a COM display in many copies can be created in a small fraction of the time it takes to produce an equivalent display in more traditional forms.[12] For example, the Santa Cruz campus of the University of California, has found that a catalog of modest size (250,000 titles growing at a rate of 20,000 titles/year in 1975) was taking as long as six months to print with a computer line printer, and reproduce in 20 copies electrostatically.[13] A similar catalog could be produced on about 186 42X microfiche in a matter of days with COM.

Although one cannot expect the currency of representation of new accessions that is possible with a well maintained card catalog, or the instantaneous access to all activity against a file possible with an on-line catalog, with COM we can, nonetheless, take advantage of the facilities provided by a computerized system for catalog maintenance and large scale reorganization not possible with a card catalog, and a distribution of access facilities that would prove prohibitive with an on-line system.

It should be painfully obvious that the enormous power of computing machinery to manipulate and rearrange data remains effete unless we provide a mechanism to display the effects of the action of this powerful instrument on a data base. Library systems are generally characterized by the prodigious amount of information that must be maintained and displayed. Thus, in a library application the extremely low cost of COM and the capabilities of computers form a uniquely symbiotic relationship—COM is the product of computer technology, but by the same token it may itself prove to be the means by which more effective use can be made of that technology.

This is the real promise of COM, not just the economies it can effect. The potential derives, albeit, from the magnitude of the expected savings. These savings can be large enough to provide adequate margin for innovation, and creativity in addition to economy.[14] In order to make this potential more concrete, let us consider the catalog of medium sized library, i.e., one which contains 250,000 titles to which 20,000 titles are added annually. Let us assume that a book form catalog is cumulated annually, and supplemented monthly with cumulative supplements. If such a catalog were to be produced with a computer line printer, the listing reduced, and duplicated by photo-offset into 100 copies, printing and binding alone for three years could cost $420,000. If this catalog were to be produced on 42X microfiche, employing the full ALA character set, and if we allow ten hours each month ($15,000) for the additional machine time needed to produce a cumulation rather than a supplement, we could have a complete cumulation each month, pay for 100 readers and still realize a $24,000 saving at the end of three years. If on the other hand we chose not to change the nature of the service, we could pay for 100 readers and effect a saving of over $366,000 in the same three years. Viewed from another perspective, a library that could not afford to spend $420,000 might easily be able to justify $54,000 in three years (about 2 clerical positions/yr.) as the result of staff savings (card filing, filing revision, and catalog maintenance could be eliminated, each service unit could have its own copy of the catalog thereby eliminating a journey to the official catalog), and improve service to its readers (the catalog could exist in nearly 100 separate physical locations.)

Hopefully, the preceding exercise should have demonstrated the efficacy of an inexpensive display medium, and perhaps the practicality of even seemingly radical innovations it permits. With the passage of time radical ideas gradually become transformed into conventional wisdom. Even today the two major commercial book catalog vendors, Autographics and Science Press, are producing microform catalogs for their customers in which they have dispensed with supplements entirely. For example, the Clark County (Nevada) Public Library now receives a new, completely cumulated catalog every other month rather than a supplement—COM has created the possibility of a "disposable catalog!"

When discussing the possibilities offered by COM, we should not lose sight of the most fundamental property of microform—its great compactness. For example, a catalog of 250,000 titles would require approximately 1,200,000 cards. If we permit some room for expansion, we would need 1,200 card trays (20 card cabinets) to house that many cards. In many libraries where space is at a premium reclamation of space by containing the catalog in a few cubic feet would clearly prove an intrinsic asset. Further, we have talked about the benefit of distributing catalog access. This is only feasible if the necessary space can be found. A few cubic feet of space can obviously be found almost anywhere.

We have also discussed the economic advantages of an inexpensive display medium, and the service benefits that can be considered within the substantial margin of savings that can be effected. Our discussion has thus far only concerned itself with frequency of production of a traditional catalog, and the number of copies of that catalog that can be provided. We could also use the potential savings to advantage by displaying additional information, or providing additional access points in a microform catalog. For example, by converting from a printed to a microform catalog, we have indicated that a saving of about 87% is possible. Some of this saving could be foregone in favor of more information provided with each entry, or entries duplicated under many more access points. The possibilities and permutations are enormous. Probably the only definitive statement that can be made is that the economic latitude provided by microform and COM technology is so great that the possibility for professional creativity is virtually unbounded.

Since the major advantages of COM are in its potential, one cannot help speculating on what the future will hold. It seems obvious that the current trend in which libraries are increasingly entrusting their cataloging data to a computerized system will continue. Developments other than technical advances will cause libraries to begin replacing their card catalogs with machine based catalogs. Certainly the accumulation of a sizeable fraction of cataloging by many libraries in machine readable form will serve as a stimulus in this direction. The implementation of a new cataloging code, which has been characterized by the chairman of the ALA committee that helped draft it as resulting in the closing* of existing catalogs, will surely provide an additional impetus. AACR II is scheduled to be implemented in 1980.

Finally, the closing of LC's catalogs in 1980 will, without doubt, serve as the signal to research libraries to do likewise.

It does not seem likely that technology will develop quickly enough to provide a complete on-line replacement for the card catalog by 1980; hence we can expect that closing of catalogs will begin with their replacement with some form of machine produced, static catalog. The use of computer produced microform catalogs seems the most viable interim step toward on-line catalogs. The economics are such that investments in such equipment can virtually justify themselves in three years. Hence, if completely on-line catalogs are likely in five years, timing would be almost ideal. Whatever the pace of development, investments in microform facilities will not be completely gainsaid by the development of on-line catalogs. It would seem impractical that a sufficient number of terminals can be provided to service all of a library's users at times of peak demand. A microform catalog would, therefore, provide a highly effective means of extending catalog access at very low cost. Many locations will exist where the presence of a catalog would prove useful, but its expected use would not justify the expense of an on-line facility. Finally, a static catalog produced at reasonably frequent intervals would provide a highly inexpensive form of insurance against a system failure.

A major problem to be faced by large research libraries, when they close their catalogs, will be the disposition of their retrospective catalogs. As these catalogs are closed, various procedures will be implemented to freeze and to cease maintaining them. At that time it will prove highly desirable to film them, dismantle them, and make them available in microform. Retrospective data conversion seems highly unlikely because of the cost involved, and is made even more unlikely by the implementation of a new cataloging code in 1980. Retrospective conversion under these circumstances would require a great deal of recataloging—a prospect no librarian cherishes.

The situation as it will affect libraries of intermediate size is somewhat more clear cut. It can be expected that they too will increasingly be reliant on computer produced cataloging products, but it can be expected, for a variety of reasons, that considerably more time—probably 10 years—will pass before they begin to make widespread use of on-line catalogs. They will proceed through a much longer interim period in which computer produced, hard copy catalogs will play a major role. They too will be affected by LC's decision to close its catalogs, and will also follow suit. Those with non-archival collections will find it most advantageous to delay conversion to an on-line catalog, as they can expect that collection turnover will make retrospective conversion more feasible as time passes. For these libraries COM catalogs will offer a solution to their immediate problems, and permit them to concentrate their attention to the machine readable data base, of which a COM catalog can be a current faithful representation. In this way

---

*Closing catalog means that one ceases to file cards into it, to be bound by its conventions, and possibly to modify entries in it. The catalog is, however, still available to the library's readers.

all of their efforts will contribute to the maintenance of that which will eventually constitute their catalog.

The very smallest libraries will not be able to afford the facilities required to input their cataloging data into machine readable form. They will probably purchase services from commercial vendors with whom they will contract to maintain their cataloging data bases, and periodically provide microform editions of their catalogs.

Such is the potential of the present, and a brief prognosis of the future of the uses of COM and microforms in libraries. The papers included in this volume will offer an enumeration, and analysis of some of the most significant microform experiments attempted in the last two decades. The successes encountered in these pioneering efforts should point the way for more sophisticated ventures made possible by the current state of technology. The difficulties and limitations imposed on many of these pioneering efforts by the technology of their time will provide intriguing exercises for the imagination in the application of a more advanced technology to their solution. Many of the techniques discussed in the papers to follow, e.g., filming of existing card catalogs, have also gained a renewed importance in a different context. The staggering pace of development has lent a renewed poignancy to Santayana's observation that "those who cannot remember the past are doomed to repeat it." Thus, these papers are an important recollection of the successes and the limitations experienced in the past. They should serve as a valuable guidepost to the future.

S. Michael Malinconico,
Assistant Chief,
Systems Analysis and
Processing Office,
The New York Public Library

References

1. Maurice F. Tauber and Associates, *Technical Services in Libraries* (Columbia University Studies in Library Service, no. 7), New York: Columbia University Press, 1953, p. 393.

2. Allen B. Veaner and John Fraser, "Card Reproduction by Xerox Copyflow," *Library Resources & Technical Services*, 8 (Summer 1964): 279-84.

3. H. Matsumiya and M. Bloomfield, "A Working Microfilm Card Catalog," *Special Libraries*, 55 (March 1964): 157-59.

4. Oliver P. Gillock and Roger H. McDonnough, "Spreading State Library Riches for Peanuts," *Wilson Library Bulletin*, 45 (December 1970): 34-57.

5. Katherine Gaines, "Undertaking a Subject Catalog in Microfiche," *Library Resources and Technical Services*, 15 (Summer): 297-308.

6. William Saffady, *COM Recorder Hardware and Software: The State of the Art*, Paper prepared for the ALA/RLMS, 1977, p. 4.

7. Henriette D. Avram, *MARC: Its History and Implications*, Washington, D.C.: Library of Congress, 1975, p. 9. (Originally published in *Encyclopedia of Library and Information Science*, v. 17)

8. Joseph Becker, "The Rich Heritage of Information Science," *Bulletin of the American Association for Information Science*, 2 (March 1976): 11.

9. Frederick G. Kilgour and Philip L. Long, "The Shared Cataloging System of the Ohio College Library Center," *Journal of Library Automation*, 5 (September 1972): 157-83.

10. An excellent and insightful discussion of the importance of this aspect of cataloging can be found in: Frances Ohmes and J. F. Jones, "The Other Half of Cataloging," *Library Resources and Technical Resources*, 17 (Summer 1973): 320-29.

11. Kenneth John Bierman, "Automated Alternatives to Card Catalogs: The Current State of Planning and Implementation," *Journal of Library Automation*, 8 (December 1975): 277-98.

12. S. Michael Malinconico, "The Economics of Output Media," *Proceedings of the 1976 Clinic on Library Applications of Data Processing: The Economics of Library Automation*, ed. J. L. Divilbiss, Urbana-Champaign, Illinois: University of Illinois Graduate School of Library Science, 1977, 145-62.

13. Bierman, op. cit., p. 285.

14. S. Michael Malinconico, "The Display Medium and the Price of the Message," *Library Journal*, 101 (October 1976): 2144-49.

INTRODUCTION

My earlier book on libraries and microreproduction (*Microforms in Libraries*, Microform Review, Inc., 1975) dealt with various aspects of libraries' traditional use of microforms—the reproduction of materials necessary for research, such as books, journals, newspapers, and government documents. This use of microforms is motivated by a number of factors, foremost among which are: (1) access to materials otherwise unavailable; (2) conservation of space; (3) in the case of journals, the replacement of originals instead of binding them.

This book deals with microforms in relation to library catalogs. It is divided into three sections. The first covers microforms as an intermediate step in printing catalog cards; the second deals with the reproduction on microfilm of existing card catalogs; the third, last and most extensive section covers computer-output-microfilm (COM), that is, the use of COM to create microform library catalogs.

There is uncertainty as to when microforms were first used to reproduce library catalogs. Stuart-Stubbs notes, "The catalogues of many Canadian libraries were filmed in the early nineteen fifties by the National Library of Canada as a step toward the creation of the existing union catalogue; although most of the resulting film has been converted to prints for filing, films of the catalogues of some major libraries have not been printed and are still searched in their present form."[1]

Regardless of when the first filming of a library catalog took place, marked interest in such filming began in the 1960s when, largely as a result of campus and other civil disturbances, libraries felt a need for back-up, microfilmed copies of their catalogs in case of vandalism, theft, or fire.

In the mid-sixties, there also developed a need for a number of institutions, or various locations within one institution, to have access to an existing card catalog and this need was in many cases met by microfilming the catalog.

The sixties also saw the use of microfilm as a means for printing both book catalogs and catalog cards, primarily through the use of the Xerox Copyflo.

Finally, with the emergence of COM, which permits printing directly onto film from magnetic tape, interest shifted to the direct creation of microform library catalogs, not as a replacement for, or copy of, a card catalog, but as the library's sole catalog.

In the last decade there has also emerged a number of firms providing microform catalog services of two types.

One is a data retrieval system which supplies Library of Congress cataloging data in microform, usually microfiche, along with a full-size, continually updated index, which locates the data for a given title on the appropriate fiche. Some of these systems have been the subject of critical evaluations, including an eighty-one page survey of five systems issued in May, 1975, by Library Technology Reports.[2]

The other type of service involves the design and installation of a customized microform catalog system, usually based on large (e.g. 500 feet) reels of COM-produced 16mm microfilm housed in special reading machines which include quick retrieval features, so that it is possible to reach a given entry within a few seconds. Updating is done by replacing the entire reel.[3]

The catalog data retrieval systems are primarily for use by technical services departments. The cataloging information is taken from the microform, either by making an enlarged print-out or by copying the information off the reader screen by hand or typewriter. These systems do not replace the card catalog but rather are a means for obtaining cataloging information and for making catalog cards. The customized systems are replacements for the card catalog and are used primarily by library patrons as they would use the card catalog or a book catalog.

The reasons for using microforms for library catalogs are many and varied. Among them: (1) to conserve space (i.e. the space taken up by the card catalog); (2) as a result of deterioration of the card catalog; (3) to provide a greater number of access points to the library's collection; (4) reduced costs; (5) to permit easy exchange of bibliographic data. In addition to these reasons, COM offers special advantages which will be discussed later.

In most instances the use of microforms for library catalogs has resulted from problems encountered with card catalogs, such as those identified by Elrod[4]: (1) size—the larger the file the more costly to maintain; (2) deteriorating editorial condition due to changes in descriptive cataloging, subject headings, etc. which make much of what is in the card catalog obsolete; (3) physical condition of both cabinets and cards; (4) vulnerability to mutilation, damage or loss of cards; (5) staff considerations—sorting, filing, and revision are not attractive tasks; (6) revision of subject headings, such as the change from ELECTRONIC-CALCULATING MACHINES to COMPUTERS; (7) space limitations—i.e. no more room for catalog cabinets; (8) upkeep costs—Elrod notes that at the University of British Columbia, it takes 5,500 hours (approximately 800 working days) to file in the main catalog alone; (9) the catalog is in one place only. As *Library Journal* noted in reviewing a session at the 1976 ALA convention, "Librarians are looking with increasing interest at the possibility of replacing their bulky, expensive, labor-intensive card catalogs, with either an on-line system or a microform catalog updated at regular intervals."[5]

This is not to say that a microform catalog will solve all problems associated with card catalogs. Keyes Metcalf, former librarian at Harvard University and now a consultant, has pointed out that the largest amount of space is taken up, not by card cabinets but by the people using the catalog, particularly in academic libraries.[6]

Frederick Kilgour, executive director of the Ohio College Library Center (OCLC), has been quoted as saying that a COM catalog is never up to date and requires a visit to the library to use, and thus combines the worst two features of the printed catalog.[7]

Nevertheless, COM-produced library catalogs have proliferated since the Technical Information Center of Lockheed Missiles and Space Company reported a 16mm COM cartridge catalog system in 1966.[8,9]

Among those with COM systems are: Council of Research and Academic Libraries (CORAL), a library consortium of the South Texas area (union catalog of monographic holdings of eight research and academic libraries/microfiche/42X/60,000 titles/36 author and 45 title fiche); Black Gold Library System, California; Temple University Libraries (periodical holdings/microfiche); Eastman Kodak technical libraries; Fairfax County Library System, Virginia (microfilm/48X/167,000 titles); Raisin Valley Library, Michigan; Huntington Beach Public Library; Westminster City Libraries, England; Los Angeles County Public Library; University of Cambridge; Yale University; Cheshire County Library, England; El Centro College, Dallas; Tulane University; Baltimore County Public Library; Northern Virginia Community College Libraries; Georgia Institute of Technology; University of British Columbia; University of Toronto; Birmingham University Library, and the British Library.

In addition to the advantages previously cited for microreproduced catalogs, what are the advantages of COM-produced catalogs? COM offers: (1) speed (10 to 20 times faster than a line printer); (2) low cost; (3) manipulation of data; (4) fast updating; (5) continuous cumulating; (6) inexpensive exchange of bibliographic records; (7) availability of many characters (i.e. type faces and sizes). In essence the primary advantages over all three forms of widely used catalogs (card, book, microreproduction of cards) are manipulation of data, fast updating, and continuous cumulation.

In establishing a microform catalog, whether it be through COM or simply the filming of an existing catalog, there are a great many choices that must be made: fiche or roll film; cassettes or open reels, positive or negative images; reduction ratio, format (arrangement of the images on the reel or fiche), how will updating be done, and so forth.

The purpose of this book is to give both practicing librarians and students a basic understanding of how microforms are being used *vis-à-vis* library catalogs. It includes information on procedures, alternatives, prices, equipment, and user reaction. The emphasis is on what has been done and reported to date, rather than on the theoretical, and on presenting readers with various views which will permit them to draw their own conclusions, as there is not one answer to any of the questions referred to above.

Albert J. Diaz

References

1. Stuart-Stubbs, Basil, *Developments in Library and Union Catalogues and the Use of Microforms in British Libraries*. Ottawa: National Library of Canada, 1973 [processed] , p. 6. [Excerpts from Stuart-Stubbs' study are included in this book].

2. The following articles evaluate catalog retrieval systems: Dagnese, J.M., "Catalog Retrieval Systems on Microfiche, a Preliminary Evaluation," *Special Libraries*, 61:357-61 (September 1970); Madison, Dilys E. and Galejs, John E., "Application of the Micrographic Catalog Retrieval System in the Iowa State University Library," *Library Resources and Technical Services*, 15:492-98 (Fall 1971); Ready, W. B., "Catalogue Retrieval; a Library Economy," *Library Resources and Technical Services*, 14:439-44 (Summer 1970); Swinburne, Ralph E., Jr., "Microfilmed Catalog Services," *Journal of Chemical Documentation*, 10:17-20 (February 1970); The Library Technology Report, *Microform Catalog Data Retrieval Systems* ($20.00, American Library Association) covers systems available from Information Dynamics Corporation, Information Design, Library Processing Systems, LISCO, and Information Handling Services. Not included is the Marcfiche system (Marc Applied Research Company, Washington, D.C.). The LISCO and Information Handling Services products are not systems *per se*: LISCO provides a computer-produced index by LC card numbers to the National Union Catalog, and Information Handling Services provides a microfiche reprint of the Library of Congress and National Union Catalogs. A short summary of the LTP survey by Allen Veaner will be found in *Microform Review*, 5:7 (January 1976).

3. Among the firms presently supplying customized microform catalog systems are: Auto-Graphics Inc., 751 Monterey Pass Road, Monterey Park, California 91754; Information Design, Inc., 3247 Middlefield Road, Menlo Park, California 94025; Science Press, Ephrata, Pennsylvania 17522.

4. Elrod, J. McRee, "Is the Card Catalogue's Unquestioned Sway in North America Ending?," *Journal of Academic Librarianship*, 2:4-8 (March 1976).

5. *Library Journal*, 101:1707 (September 1, 1976).

6. *Ibid*.

7. Napier, Paul A., "Developments in Copying, Micrographics and Graphic Communications, 1975," *Library Resources and Technical Services*, 20:247 (Summer 1976).

8. Kozumplik, W. A., "Computerized Microfilm Catalog," *Special Libraries*, 57:524 (September 1966).

9. Kozumplik, W. A. and Lange, R. T., "Computer-produced Microfilm Library Catalog," *American Documentation*, 18:67-80 (April 1967) [Included in this book] .

ADDITIONAL READINGS

Elrod, J. McRee, "Is the Card Catalogue's Unquestioned Sway in North America Ending?," *Journal of Academic Librarianship*, 2:4-8 (March 1976).

Hayes, Robert M. and Becker, Joseph, *Handbook of Data Processing for Libraries*. 2nd ed. Los Angeles: Melville, 1974.

The Library of Congress Card Catalogue: An Analysis of Problems and Possible Solutions, Washington: Library of Congress Processing Dept., April, 1972.

Rather, John C., "The Future of Catalog Control in the Library of Congress," *Journal of Academic Librarianship*, 2:5-10 (May 1975).

MICROFORMS AND LIBRARY CATALOGS
A Reader

I □ REPRODUCTION OF CATALOG CARDS UTILIZING MICROFORMS

CARD REPRODUCTION
BY XEROX COPYFLO

by Allen B. Veaner and John Fraser

The factors governing the choice of a card reproduction system have been described many times in the literature and can be summarized briefly as follows: the quality requirements, the number of copies needed, delivery time, the available means of presenting both Roman and non-Roman alphanumeric information, the percentage of Library of Congress cards applicable to the library's collection, and, finally, local cataloging policies insofar as they affect creation of the original card, the card format, and the insertion of variable data on the cards.[1]

The Preliminary Card System
Combined with Offset Printing

Over a period of years Harvard has developed an informal system of cataloging based on "preliminary cards" prepared by typists working from books and searching reports. These preliminary cards are edited by professional catalogers and retyped as necessary. Where little or no editing is required, the preliminary card is designated as the main card for the Official Catalog, and the balance of the set is typed. The possibility of mechanical reproduction of cards was always kept in mind, but the number of cards required for each title had not been considered sufficient to justify the equipment. During the middle 1950s, the need for increased production, combined with the difficulty of recruiting typists, made it urgent for the Library to abandon the typing of each card in a set.

In choosing a reproduction method, a primary objective was to preserve the preliminary card system, since it involved no worksheets and kept typewriters out of the cataloging room. A secondary objective was to make the system available to all units of the University Library, regardless

Reprinted from *Library Resources and Technical Services*, 8: 279-84 (Summer 1964).

of their separate cataloging policies and differing card formats. Offset printing from separate masters onto individual, pre-cut cards was finally selected. Besides fulfilling the above major objectives, this choice offered several other important advantages to Harvard: it eliminated the collating step associated with reproducing several cards at a time on a larger master; it required no cutting or punching equipment; and, finally, it permitted retaining the maximum of bibliographic detail on the official card, while limiting the information given on secondary cards, since the typist prepared an offset master from an edited original. A disadvantage was that Library of Congress cards could not be reproduced without typing a master.

In its early stages, the offset method functioned quite well; but as work from departmental libraries increased in volume, the system inevitably began to fall behind owing to the fixed capacity of the offset press when working with a single 4"x 6" master.

Change to Xerox Copyflo Printing

Just as this was happening, a visit to the Library of Congress Photoduplication Service drew the Library's attention to the Copyflo method. Besides offering speedy delivery, good quality, and an enormous capacity for expansion of the work load, the Copyflo system featured two unique advantages: it could produce exactly as many cards as were required and it could print on demand a single copy of any card file.[2] In the course of studying the Copyflo method, we also visited three commercial firms carrying out card reproduction work, but found the Library of Congress method to be the most highly automated and consequently the most efficient.[3] Although this system had been reported in the *Annual Report of the Librarian of Congress* and had been described in several journal articles, it appeared to have received little attention from librarians.[4-7] In January 1961 the Library Technology Project issued a brief statement on the Copyflo method, but this was only in reference to commercial Copyflo operators, many of whom are now actively soliciting the library card reproduction market.[8]

The minimum annual production required to support a rented Copyflo machine was figured at about 500,000 cards, and since production at Harvard approached a million cards annually, the method did seem practicable. After further discussions with the Library of Congress Photoduplication Service and submission of a detailed proposal to the Xerox Corporation, it was decided to adopt the Copyflo method in place of offset. As the Library was already purchasing Copyflo service from a commercial contractor, it also became apparent that the combination of card reproduction and Copyflo printing might result in savings over existing costs. Accordingly, arrangements were made through the Chief of the Photoduplication

Service at the Library of Congress for the laboratory supervisor at Harvard to familiarize himself with the operation of the Copyflo printer. The machine itself was installed at Harvard in April, 1963. After several months' experience with regular Copyflo work, pilot production of cards was begun in the summer, and by September the photoduplication laboratory was in full card production. The normal work schedule provides for daily operation and the completion of all incoming card work within 72 hours. We have found that one person doing all phases of the job can produce up to six thousand finished cards in a seven-hour day.

The basic steps in the production of Copyflo cards are: (1) pre-sort the original workcards according to the number of finished cards required, (2) microfilm the cards, (3) process the film, (4) print the cards onto a roll of card stock, (5) cut the cards to size, and (6) punch the holes. The purpose of pre-sorting is to enable the camera operator to take pictures as fast as possible; the operator takes as many exposures as cards are required. The pre-sorting is done by the libraries which use the service. The microfilming is done on a jig designed to assure precise registration of each card; this jig is underlighted to eliminate shadows around the edges of the cards and at the hole. After processing, the film is enlarged onto continuous card stock with the Copyflo printer. Cards are separated from the roll of stock with an Alves automatic cutter. Following this rough cutting, the cards are precision cut on a power cutter and then drilled. A complete technical explanation of the process may be found in the author's article "High Speed Reproduction of Library Cards," to be published in the *Proceedings* of the National Microfilm Association for 1964.

The approximate time required for handling a daily work load of six thousand cards is as follows: Microfilming about two hours; processing, one hour; printing, one hour; cutting and drilling, one hour. These figures are conservative and include setup time for each machine. The remaining two hours in the day are devoted to other Copyflo work and to maintenance of the various machines. Since the beginning of full-scale production in September, 1963, the Copyflo system has been able to maintain without interruption the announced 72 hour service, despite daily variations in the work load; and recently, owing to a special rush project, the system experienced a 30% overload with no delays in delivery time. No upper or lower limits are imposed on unit libraries regarding the number of cards which may be requested.

Advantages and Disadvantages

No system is perfect. The system selected for use at Harvard features some advantages and some disadvantages; it is a matter of weighing the one against the other, and maintaining the awareness that some disadvantages arise regardless of the system chosen. Perhaps the principal advantage to

Harvard of the Copyflo system is that it enabled an inherently inefficient unit production process to be batched into a fast, smooth-flowing continuous process.[9] Among the other advantages of Copyflo card reproduction are the following:

1. A single copy of any card file can be created at a reasonable price.
2. Any characters—Japanese, Hebrew, Arabic, etc.—may be reproduced and no retyping is required if existing copy is available in the form of Library of Congress cards or proof sheets.
3. Very few unwanted cards are reproduced.
4. Service is rapid.
5. Cost of the service is substantially less than the same service purchased from commercial sources.
6. The system has enormous reserve capacity.
7. The number of different machines and processes in use for card reproduction within the University has been minimized.
8. The University Library was enabled to install a Copyflo printer and obtain the benefit of its use for purposes other than card reproduction.

Among the disadvantages can be listed the following:

1. Individual libraries must spend time pre-sorting cards in preparation for microfilming.
2. A certain amount of collating may always be necessary to bring together the original card and the copies.
3. Secondary headings must still be typed manually.
4. Variable data are not readily masked or removed.
5. From time to time there are variations in the print density.
6. Considerable preventive maintenance is required to avoid objectionable xerographic "background" appearing on the finished cards.
7. As an internal operation, Copyflo is probably limited to those libraries requiring 500,000 or more cards per year.

It is apparent from the above that the Xerox Copyflo method of card reproduction—like any other method—cannot be endorsed or recommended out of context. *The decision to use a given method must flow from the institution's needs and not merely from the merits of the process itself.* No library should undertake the Copyflo method unless there is certainty that the method matches the need.

Only one other method was considered—offset printing from photographically generated masters containing at least eight card images. This method is recommended by the Library Technology Project for libraries cataloging 15,000 or more titles each year.[1] While offset printing is without doubt a highly satisfactory method in certain applications, it was turned down at Harvard for the following reasons: Waste was too great—

50% to 100% in the numerous instances where only four or five copies of
the card were needed; there was no economical way of creating larger editions of cards without cumulating (and hence delaying) cards from several
libraries and possibly getting cards from various libraries mixed up; editions of one, two or three could not be produced; the press would have
had no other uses in the library; and, most photographic masters had to be
printed immediately or could not be readily stored. Finally, the offset
method would have made it necessary to continue purchasing regular
Copyflo service at greater cost from an outside contractor.

Costs

A cost/volume study in the area of document reproduction usually produces a rule of thumb relating the process, the volume of work, and the
size of the editions. In the present case the justification for not following
the rule of thumb was a basic decision to concentrate on using the fewest
possible processes to produce the widest variety of results. Thus, one combination of machines is used for library cards, paper prints, and offset
masters. This decision permitted the elimination of some equipment, service contracts, and supplies, and reduced the need for trained personnel.
    Machine rental is currently $800 per month. Basic rental provides up to
1,000 minutes of operation, or 20,000 feet of finished copy at the rate of
20 feet per minute. A monthly production of 100,000 cards accounts for
nearly ninety percent of the minimum monthly commitment, and provides
a unit cost of about $.02 per card, counting Copyflo time, supplies, and
depreciation of auxiliary equipment, but not including labor, overhead,
utilities, and equipment installation costs. For 50,000 cards per month,
the unit cost would be about $.03 per card.
    On the few occasions where many copies of a card are required, the
Xerox Copyflo system is apparently used uneconomically; the incidence
of such use at Harvard is, however, so small that it is insignificant in comparison with the savings on overhead, depreciation and other costs associated with the maintenance of an additional process. If, for instance, thirty
or forty cards are needed, it is simply cheaper to go ahead and make them
with the established system than to spend time searching for an offset
printer to do the job.
    Beyond the minimum rental there is an overcharge at the rate of $.24
per minute of running time. If the machine can be used for any other purpose, such as reprinting books and articles or creating offset masters, the
the unit costs will fall as machine time rises. The decline of cost with increased Copyflo volume is much more rapid than for the Xerox 914; hence
real advantage accrues if there is any reasonable prospect for total volume
exceeding the minimum.
    The rapid progress of technology in the generation and copying of docu-

ments is demonstrating several important effects on the Library's equipment budget and its capacity to serve its clientele. It is no longer necessary to justify costly equipment on the basis of a long period of amortization, say ten or twenty years. The rapid growth of leasing and lease/purchase plans now permits libraries to take advantage of up-to-date equipment without tying up capital funds. What is perhaps more important, when a process becomes superseded, one need no longer carry on with the obsolete process. The lifetime of the present system of card reproduction is anticipated to be three to five years. The next advance in the production and use of catalogs, book, card, or other format, is expected to stem from the progressive installation of computers in libraries.[10-12]

References

1. Library Technology Project. *Catalog Card Reproduction Study: A Summary*. Chicago, 1963. 7 p. Mimeographed. In 1961 The Library Technology Project commissioned George Fry & Associates, Inc., to conduct a full-scale investigation into the matter of catalog card reproduction. As of this date the full report has not yet been published, but a number of the more important criteria for process selection may be found in this brief summary and in Mr. Treyz's article elsewhere in this magazine.

2. The Library Technology Project's summary report mentioned that Copyflo reproduction of cards "is subject to delays and the cards are often of poor quality." However, the quality of . card reproduction achieved by the Library of Congress Photoduplication Service left little to be desired. It was also felt that delays could be eliminated if, with its own equipment, the Library was not dependent upon outsiders who might have other more attractive commitments.

3. The problem of card reproduction attracted the attention of the Library of Congress Photoduplication Service from its beginnings. The Service's first report issued in the 1938 *Annual Report of the Librarian of Congress*, p. 312, voiced the hope "that a satisfactory automatic library card reproducing unit will be designed and built during the year."

4. *Annual Report of the Librarian of Congress*. Report for 1959. p. 70; for 1960, p. 15 and 57.

5. LaHood, Charles G. "Microfilm as Used in Reproduction and Transmission Systems." *Library Trends*, 8: 455. January, 1960.

6. LaHood, Charles G. "Production and Uses of Microfilm in the Library of Congress Photoduplication Service." *Special Libraries*, 15: 68-71. February 1960. See especially p. 70-71.

7. Holmes, Donald C. "Electrostatic Photoreproduction at the U.S. Library of Congress." *UNESCO Bulletin for Libraries*, 15: 18-20, 24. See especially p. 20 and 24. "Reproduction of Catalogue Cards."

8. Library Technology Project. "Some Comments on Reproducing Card Files by Microfilm and Copyflo." Chicago, January 1961. 1 p. Processed.

9. In computer usage, the more work which can be batched for machine handling in a single pass, the more efficient the process will be. The most inefficient operation possible is the batch of one, where each step of the operation is carried out individually in fixed sequence without cumulation or batching of like steps; for card reproduction the analogue is typing individual cards one after another. For this comparison I am indebted to R. L. Patrick, author of "So You Want to Go On-Line," in *Datamation*, 9: 25-27. October 1963.

10. Lipetz, Ben-Ami. "Labor Cost, Conversion Costs, and Compatibility in Document Control Systems." *American Documentation*, 14: 117-122. April 1963.

11. Fasana, Paul J. "Automating Cataloging Functions in Conventional Libraries." *Library Resources & Technical Services*, 7: 350-365. Fall 1963.

12. A collaborative project is currently underway by the medical libraries of Columbia, Harvard, and Yale to enter first onto punched cards and then into a computer currently cataloged monographs having 1960 and later imprints. A major purpose of the project is to experiment with mechanized retrieval of catalogue card information concurrently with the usual usage of the card catalog to see which type of retrieval system works best for which type of inquiry.

CATALOG CARD SETS—A MICROFILM FIRST?

by John M. Carroll and Alice D. Hackett

Although librarians are aware of the growing role of the computer in information retrieval and processing of library records, there are still steps in the processing of catalog information in both small and large libraries which do not have access to a computer, where the cost of reproducing catalog copy invites exploration of possible economies of time, money, and manpower. Great strides have been made in the use of microfilm and photoduplication in reproducing exact copy of catalog cards inexpensively. This has been done successfully by a number of firms and libraries. The photographic processes reproduce only the unit card and require further steps to convert a unit card to sets—either the added headings have to be run in after the unit cards have been reproduced, or copy for the complete set has to be prepared and each card in the set reproduced individually.

The Boston Public Library, as far back as November, 1963, began to explore the possibility of using photographic techniques to eliminate the need for running in headings after the main card was reproduced in quantity or preparing copy for a complete set for later reproduction. The Library experimented with transparencies to superimpose the added entries on the main card. Cut-outs were devised. It was a generally discouraging experience. Finally, through the cooperation of a commercial contractor, the General Microfilm Company of Inman Square, Cambridge, Massachusetts, a method was devised to run off from *one catalog card* a complete set or multiple sets of catalog cards, with the headings incorporated. Thus we have eliminated need for further manual processing of the unit cards for running in headings, the operation which raises the cost of every card purchased or prepared locally because of the manpower and additional materials or equipment needed to complete the sets. Multiple sets of cards can be provided from one card and one formula card regardless of the number of subject or added entries required for each title.

Reprinted from *Library Resources and Technical Services*, 10: 387-91 (Summer 1966).

Essential in the process is a "formula card" developed jointly by the contractor's representative and the Coordinator of Cataloging and Classification, Boston Public Library. The size of the formula card is 3 x 4 inches, custom designed for the processes involved. It serves a dual purpose. It indicates the required subject and added entries, typed on the 4-inch edges, using both sides of the formula card, or two or more formula cards, if necessary. (See Figure 2.) It provides the information on the number of cards to be duplicated in each category with the totals tallied on each side. The headings on the formula card are superimposed by overlay and photography, using standard microfilm equipment.

Since the cards produced can be no better than the original copy, good copy is essential. The catalog card stock provided by the contractor is one hundred percent new linen rag stock. The contract sets very specific standards for the card stock. There may be a slight shadow reflected in the area where the headings are added to the original copy, but the process provides *the complete set*, from one card, prepared and delivered for immediate sorting and filing. This seems to be a first in this kind of card service. In addition to saving the salary of the typists to process unit cards or to cut stencils, we have eliminated the cost of stencils, maintaining duplicating equipment, etc. It is expected that six typists positions can be eliminated by attrition and inroads still made on backlogs as a result of this innovation. The cost per card of 4½ cents to the Boston Public Library is a realistic price for this service. Although a smaller volume of orders might result in a higher unit cost, it would still appear to be a most efficient and economical method of making sets of cards.

This process can be adapted in various ways, particularly by the use of an LC slip, a clip from *Publishers' Weekly*, etc., instead of cataloger's typed copy. Any trained typist can prepare the formula card as well as the typed copy. Experience shows that copy typed on an electric typewriter reproduces better than copy prepared on a manual machine. The possibility of typing errors occurring after the copy has been prepared is completely eliminated. Additional copy for book card or cross references, apart from catalog cards, can be incorporated in the order and processed simultaneously.

To summarize, the preparation of copy for the Home Reading Division of the Boston Public Library includes:

1   main card typed with subject or added entry as heading (Figure 1)
1   formula card, indicating any additional subject or added entries and the number
    of cards needed for each run (Figure 2)
1   book card (optional)
1   copy for cross references if required for any title (optional)

In the experimental phase five test runs were made representing approximately 5,000 cards (1,000 cards in five lots), each title varying in its requirements, some only requiring 20 cards for four sets, some requiring 150 to 200 cards for 20 to 30 sets, depending on the number of branches or departments acquiring the title. Copy was returned ready for use within a week after being picked up by the contractor's messenger.

These experimental runs took place between May and July 1964. Provision for contracting for such a service was included in the 1965 budget requests. By July 1965, the Boston Public Library was able to begin using the method after the budget was passed, public bidding was held, and a contract was awarded. The system is now operating on a weekly schedule, with as many as 32,000 cards being processed in a peak week. The normal weekly flow is 11,000 cards.

CATALOGER'S COPY

```
709
B814p        EUROPE-DESCRIPTION AND TRAVEL-GUIDE BOOKS.

             Braider, Donald, 1923-
               Putnam's guide to the art centers of
             Europe.  N. Y., Putnam, c1965.
               542 p.  20 cm.




             Art-Europe.
             Europe-Description and travel-Guide books.
             Europe-Galleries and museums.
             Title.
```

FIGURE 1

FORMULA CARD

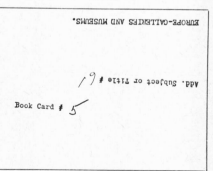

RECTO   VERSO

FIGURE 2

SHELFLIST CARD

ACCESSION	WITHDRAWAL	ACCESSION	WITHDRAWAL

709
B814p

Braider, Donald, 1923-
    Putnam's guide to the art centers of
Europe. N. Y., Putnam, c1965.
    542 p. 20 cm.

Art-Europe.
Europe-Description and travel-Guide books.
Europe-Galleries and museums.
Title.

FIGURE 3

UNION CATALOG

709
B814p

AD	BI	CON	FAN	LM	MTP	OSC	SCH	WV
ALL	BRI	DOR	HLS	MAT	NE	OSY	SB	WE
AV	CHA	EB	HP	MEM	OH	PH	SE	WR
BK	CSQ	EGL	JP	MTB	OS	ROS	UC	

Braider, Donald, 1923-
    Putnam's guide to the art centers of
Europe. N. Y., Putnam, c1965.
    542 p. 20 cm.

Art-Europe.
Europe-Description and travel-Guide books.
Europe-Galleries and museums.
Title.

FIGURE 4

REPRODUCED SET

709
B814p

  Braider, Donald, 1923-
  ▲ Putnam's guide to the art centers of
  Europe. N. Y., Putnam, c1965.
     542 p. 20 cm.

  Art-Euro
  Europe-I
  Europe-(
  Title.

709
B814p   ART-EUROPE.

             Braider, Donald, 1923-
               Putnam's guide to the art centers of
             Europe. N. Y., Putnam, c1965.
                542 p. 20 cm.

709
B814p   EUROPE DESCRIPTION AND TRAVEL-GUIDE BOOKS.

             Braider, Donald, 1923-
               Putnam's guide to the art centers of
             Europe. N. Y., Putnam, c1965.
                542 p. 20 cm.

709
B814p   EUROPE-GALLERIES AND MUSEUMS.

             Braider, Donald, 1923-
               Putnam's guide to the art centers of
             Europe. N. Y., Putnam, c1965.
                542 p. 20 cm.

709
B814p   Putnam's guide to the art centers of Europe.

             Braider, Donald, 1923-
               Putnam's guide to the art centers of
             Europe. N. Y., Putnam, c1965.
                542 p. 20 cm.

             Art-Europe.
             Europe-Description and travel-Guide books.
             Europe-Galleries and museums.
             Title.   O

FIGURE 5

A REGIONAL APPROACH TO CATALOG CARD REPRODUCTION USING MICROGRAPHIC AND ELECTROSTATIC TECHNIQUES

by Samuel M. Boone

Introduction

Electrostatic copying equipment is known and used by libraries throughout the country for the reproduction of catalog card sets. The University of North Carolina Library used this approach as early as 1961 and pioneered in the development of techniques for the process. It soon became evident, in spite of improved techniques, equipment, and procedures, that the needs of increasing work load were not being adequately met in this fashion. We were aware of a refinement in electrostatic copying of catalog cards which had been developed by the Library of Congress for the provision of out-of-print cards. This technique involved a combination of microfilm and continuous-flow electrostatic printing. It had been successfully modified and adopted for use at Harvard University as well as a few of the other larger libraries in the country. North Carolina's decision to use this L.C. system was made in 1965.

The equipment necessary is expensive and requires well-trained technicians to operate it. The cards produced are of high quality and unit cost is low, provided a high volume of cards is made. To become economically feasible, annual output should not be less than a half-million cards.

When the system was installed at the U.N.C.-Chapel Hill Library a number of neighboring institutions requested that their cards be produced for them. Since the admission of other libraries to the system sent the volume up, and unit cost down, an informal pattern of regional service soon developed.

Description of Process

1. *Card preparation.* Input for the system is based on access to the

Reprinted from *Current State of Catalog Card Reproduction*, Joseph Z. Nitecki, compiler. Philadelphia, 1973 (RLMS Micro-File Series, vol. 1, 1973). Fiche 4 of 5, pp. 193-199. Available on microfiche from the Photoduplication Service, Library of Congress.

Library of Congress depository card file, with secondary input from a variety of sources; original cataloging, enlarged copy from printed catalogs, and microfiche printout systems.

The L.C. depository file is first searched for current imprints: i.e., for the current year and the previous two years. If copy is found, then cataloging information is added to it along with a legend designating the number of cards needed for a set.

For older materials and recent materials where cards are not found in the depository file, one of the secondary sources is used. Enlarged copy from printed catalogs can be made on one of the office copiers having adjustments in the optical system for producing enlargements of approximately seventy percent. These copies must be trimmed and stripped onto standard size catalog cards.

Some libraries in the system have access to the National Union Catalog on microfiche (Information Dynamics). Printouts from this system must also be affixed to cards. While copy quality from these printout systems is generally acceptable, it must be remembered that these are secondary sources and results will be secondary in nature.

If copy from none of the above sources is available, then master copy can be prepared by typing. Typed originals can be reproduced faithfully with little or no quality deterioration.

Most of the libraries in the system have access to one or more of the above inputs on their own premises, and decide for themselves how their master cards will be prepared. Some of the smaller libraries prefer to have the U.N.C. Library of Chapel Hill use its depository file for furnishing the master copy. If demands of this sort are light, they are usually met with some degree of success.

When master cards have been prepared, they are sorted into batches according to the number of copies needed and sent to the duplication center.

2. *The copying process.*

a. *The microfilm camera.* The camera chosen for this process must be a modified version of a variable pull-down planetary camera, such as the Recordak MRD-2. Since the system depends upon a photoelectrically activated cutter as one of the final steps, the frames of microfilm must be slightly overlapped to prevent spaces between frames which would produce black marks and result in false cuts. This is accomplished by adjusting the pull-down ratchets of the camera to produce an overlap of about one-eighth inch.

Since the overhead exposure lamps of the camera will produce an unsightly shadow around each card, the camera must also be fitted with a sub-surface illuminator. A positioning jig, holding two cards, is permanently affixed to the plexiglass surface of the subsurface illuminator and positioned so that precise placement in the exposure area is assured. Black paper masks beneath the plexiglass prevent subsurface lighting from affecting the textual area of the cards. To produce a cutting mark for the finished cards, a black strip of tape is placed in the upper left corner of the exposure area on the plexiglass.

The operator places two cards on the exposure area and makes as many exposures as are required for the set. He can film about 600 masters per hour, his time varying according to the number of cards needed per set. A 100 foot roll of film will contain approximately 2400 frames, or 4800 cards. The camera is set for a reduction ratio of 9.75×. Lamp intensity is set to produce film density of about 1.1, with variations from 0.8 to 1.4 being considered acceptable.

A high resolution film, such as Kodak's AHU, will produce prints of optimum clarity. Since the film is discarded after completion of printing, residual hypo and other factors of permanence are not considered.

b. *Xerox Copyflo*. The Model 1, 11 inch, Copyflo with 20 ft. per minute operating speed was chosen for this system. Higher speed machines should not be considered since proper fusing of the heavy card stock will become a problem.

Processed film is placed on the Copyflo and the enlargement ratio set at 9.5×. Since the camera was set for a 9.75× reduction, it will be noted that a slight reduction in type size is achieved. The reduction is unnoticeable, but gives a slightly increased margin around the card which assures that information will not have bled off the margin nor affected the operation of the automatic cutter.

The fuse of the printer must be set at a sufficiently high temperature to assure proper fusing of heavy card stock. The card stock is supplied on rolls of 100% rag approximately 1000 feet long and 25 cm (the width of two cards) wide. One roll of card stock usually will contain the 4800 cards of one roll of microfilm, with some excess footage for positioning and line-up procedures. Printing time for one roll of card stock is about 50 minutes.

c. *Cutting and drilling*. Immediately after printing, the card pairs are separated with the Alves Model K cutter. The cutting mark shown in Fig. 1 serves to activate the photoelectric cell of the cutter providing a precise cut at the top of the cards. The card pairs are then stacked in order and "jogged" to the top edge. Stacks of 100 or so pairs may then be placed in the Challenge gang cutter for trimming off the excess at the bottom of the card and for separating the pairs into finished cards. Holes are then drilled and the cards are ready for delivery to the unit libraries. Turn-around time in the laboratory seldom exceeds 24 hours and on occasion may be eight hours or less.

Equipment

Those libraries which operate extensive microfilming operations will be assumed to already possess portions of the equipment necessary for this system. Those items which must be added will find many uses in addition to the card production system. Any large library, operating a variety of copying machines, will find the Xerox Copyflo to be useful in producing hard copy from their microfilms. The various cutters necessary may be used for such tasks as trimming uncut book pages, producing specially sized note sheets and a variety of other petty uses.

The basic equipment needs are as follows: Microfilm camera, Film processor, Xerox Copyflo, Alves Automatic Cutter, a power cutter and a power drill. Exclusive of the Xerox Copyflo, the total cost of the equipment, based on latest information available, is $14,405. The Xerox Copyflo may be purchased new for $60,800; however, most users prefer to rent this machine for $800 per month for a period of time until the system has proved itself. Outright purchase may be negotiated at a later date when a portion of the rental fees may be applied toward the purchase price.

In the table below, Copyflo rental will be shown as a precise element of the cost, while other equipment will be shown as an estimated amortization based on a ten-year depreciation schedule.

Costs

Figures in the table below are based on a 4800 card unit and give costs for supplies, labor, and machine rentals. The figures for equipment amortizations, equipment maintenance, and overhead are variables and are estimated on the basis of experience.

100' AHU microfilm	$ 6.70
1000' card stock, 100% rag	22.80
Copyflo rental	40.00
Labor	40.00
Equipment amortization	5.00
Maintenance and overhead	20.00
	$134.50

$$\frac{\$134.50}{4800 \text{ cards}} = \$0.028 \text{ unit card cost}$$

CATALOG CARDS FOR
SMALLER LIBRARIES

by Kenneth L. Eggleston

The problem of rapid procurement of Catalog Cards for smaller libraries is as acute as, if not more than, that of their larger contemporaries. Less available funds place the limited materials in a higher priority, since the user tends to view with impatience delays in availability of scarce items. A further problem area in card production for the smaller library lies in the cost of most systems for production of catalog cards "in-house." The budget usually will not tolerate such an expense.

A possible solution lies in cooperation ownership (Lease) of a card production system and machinery. A serious impediment to this solution is the notorious inability of separate entities to cooperate on any subject, for any length of time. Another possible solution finds one small library procuring the necessary system, then offering the service to any subscriber, hopefully at an attractive price, with a good degree of reliability, and with the expectation that sufficient demand will generate funds enough to amortize the cost of the system and the machinery.

The first essential is to identify available systems, and to then determine which is likely to be most satisfactory to the sponsor, and to his potential customer(s). This decision is further complicated by the fact that no single system is either completely up to date, or completely retrospective, in its single entity.

Pragmatically, then, the producer is faced with the necessity of starting his basic service, based on a compromise. (Compromises notoriously leave all patties in varying stages of dissatisfaction.) Further, not all cards produced under this compromise are going to prove aesthetically satisfying to the more fastidious librarian. . . . The librarian to whom the appearance of *The Card Catalog* is more important than the rapid processing of materials.

One such solution currently in use, and with sufficient usage to hold out hopes for survival, uses a combination of sources to provide basic materials

Reprinted from *Current State of Catalog Card Reproduction*, Joseph Z. Nitecki, compiler. Philadelphia, 1973. (RLMS Micro-File Series, vol. 1, 1973). Fiche 1 (of 5), pp. 26-31. Available on microfiche from the Photoduplication Service, Library of Congress.

in the production of catalog cards for a wide range of libraries, including Smaller Academic, Junior College, High School, Grade School, Seminary, Hospital, Theological, and a Governmental Agency. Not all of these use the full service; however some do, and the rest avail themselves of varying parts.

In describing the system, it is necessary to use trade or brand names, not for remuneration, but for clarity and identification. It is highly possible that some or all of these systems or machines have been superseded by others, newer, or better. Those named are simply the best known to the author at the time of writing. The combination used is described in some detail; in some instances, reasons for the decision will be given.

The basic system has as its base the MARC tapes. Beginning in 1968, Library of Congress transcribed cataloging on these tapes. CARDSET, subscribing to this service, reproduces the catalog cards from tape to film. Cards are produced from the film, printing directly from film to Card stock. The finished cards are ready for immediate filing in the catalog, *IF* the user accepts the LC class uncritically. If the Dewey class is preferred, the LC class may be masked out. All tracings are preprinted, regardless of class used, and may not be masked out. This system is relatively simple, as evidenced by the fact that all production is accomplished by students, under a minimum of supervision.

The step by step procedure follows:

The geographic location of a given set of cards must first be ascertained. This is done by searching on a mechanized Index Station, using either the LC number, or the title, as methods of access to the current reels of up-dated index film. (Updated every two weeks, assuring reasonable currency with current LC cataloging.) The Index Station is easily scanned, and provides the reel number, and the proper frame within the reel in locating the card to be reproduced.

The correct reel is selected from the carrousel holder, and positioned on the RAP/ID motorized drive, affixed to a Xerox 720 microprinter. The select line is positioned over the proper frame number, and the switch depressed, causing the reel to unwind to the selected frame. Minute positioning is done by hand, and when the proper focus has been selected, the print lever is depressed, and the card set is printed on six-up card stock.

The foregoing applies for all material on MARC tapes. This includes most material cataloged in 1968 and 1969, and all material cataloged since. For material cataloged prior to 1968, and for that material in 1968-1969 not available on MARC, an alternative method must be used.

The method finally selected in this instance is to utilize the NCR Sets of the National Union Catalog, on microfiche, from the beginning through 1969. With the microfiche, print-outs are made on a 3M "400" Reader-Printer, using the narrow sheet half sheet option to further cut costs. These printouts are cleaned, and trimmed to 3"x 5" size, affixed six at a time to a form, and cards printed out on six-up card stock utilizing a

Xerox 914 printer. Cards produced in this matter must have call numbers typed in, (may be done on the "printout" before printing), and tracings typed at the heading.

The process just described may also be utilized to produce cards from "typed originals," either from original cataloging, or from other sources. This additional option allows complete coverage of the cataloging spectrum, is simple, and economical. More importantly, it is rapid, being extremely responsive to immediate needs.

This process is not perfect. It is subject to all of the errors, or sins of omission or commission of anything associated with the humanoid. Some of the microfiche reproduced from the Library of Congress masters of the NUC are of poor quality, and produce a marginal card. Not all of the film in the CARDSET system is uniformly clear, and quality control in reproduction varies somewhat as a result.

Xerox machines appear to be subject to whims and whimsies, and eccentricities in operation from time to time. The initial nuptials of RAP/ID drive, Xerox, and Card stock are not immediately compatible, and require patience, tuning, and practice to cooperate smoothly.

Despite these shortcomings, the system described does provide *rapid* catalog cards for recently acquired materials. In cost, the service is less than that currently charged by L.C. In the factor of time, with over twenty current users, a minimum of one week return service is provided to the subscriber. The last two factors alone, price and speed, justify the occasional drop in quality, or the infrequent unattractive card.

The sole purpose of the card catalog is to direct the user to the geographic location of the material needed. *A call number*. Anything more is mere gilding the lily. Material in storage awaiting cards is material unavailable. Unavailability of acquired material, in a small library, is a sin of the first magnitude.

REPRODUCTION OF CATALOG CARDS UTILIZING MICROFORMS

Additional Readings

Arnold, R., "Extending the Use of Microfilm," *Australian Library Journal*, 19:269-71 (August 1970).

George Fry & Associates. *Catalog Card Reproduction*. Chicago: American Library Association, 1965. (Library Technology Project Publication Publication No. 9).

Hawken, William R., *Copying Methods Manual*. Chicago: American Library Association, 1966. (Library Technology Project Publication No. 11).

LaHood, Charles G., "Production and Uses of Microfilm in the Library of Congress Photoduplication Service," *Special Libraries*, 15:68-71 (February 1960).

Spreitzer, Francis F., "Card Reproduction in the University of Southern California Library," in, *Current State of Catalog Card Reproduction*, Joseph Z. Nitecki, comp. Philadelphia, 1973. (RLMS Micro-File Series, Vol. 1, 1973). Fiche 4 (of 5), pp. 200-205. Available on microfiche from the Photoduplication Service, Library of Congress.

Treyz, Joseph H., "Equipment and Methods in Catalog Card Reproduction," *Library Resources and Technical Services*, 8:267-78 (Summer 1964).

Turner, A. C., "Comparative Card Production Methods," *Library Resources and Technical Services*, 16:347-58 (Summer 1972).

Veaner, Allen B., "High Speed Reproduction of Library Cards through Microreproduction Techniques," National Microfilm Association, *Proceedings, 13th Annual Meeting, 1964*, pp. 159-63.

Williams, Harry D., and Whitney, Thomas, "Xerox-914: Preparation of Multilith Masters for Catalog Cards," *Library Resources and Technical Services*, 7:208-11 (Spring 1963).

II ☐ REPRODUCTION OF CARD CATALOGS ON MICROFILM AND MICROFICHE

A WORKING MICROFILM
CARD CATALOG

by H. Matsumiya and M. Bloomfield

Early in 1963 the Hughes Aircraft Company's Culver City Library opened a branch library some five miles away in the new Space Systems Division Building at El Segundo. One of the initial problems that confronted the branch was the duplication of the Hughes Aircraft union catalog maintained at Culver City, in which the holdings of the three major libraries of the company are listed. It should be noted that union catalogs are maintained at two other Hughes sites besides the Culver City Library. It was decided that the new branch library should have a copy of the catalog for it to do an effective job, and thus the problem was one of duplication.

After a casual approach to the problem, three possible methods of duplication were suggested: 1) a book catalog, 2) a regular card catalog, and 3) microfilm. With these three possibilities in mind, vendors were approached who could give their ideas about prices and feasibility. Whichever method was chosen, microfilming of the entire union catalog would be the first process, and if there were to be any cumulations, they would also have to be done initially by microfilming. This is the only practical way to start duplicating catalog cards. We would have preferred to use a method by which we inserted catalog cards at the rate of 1,000 a minute and have duplicated cards produced at the same rate for ten cents per 1,000 cards. This machine has yet to be invented!

Analysis of Three Possible Methods

The book catalog approach was felt to be the cheapest and most efficient method; however, almost as soon as some statistical studies were completed, a book catalog was found to be unwieldy, at least in the way it would have been prepared. A total of 160,000 cards had to be reproduced.

Reprinted from *Special Libraries*, 55: 157-59 (March 1964) by permission of the publisher. Copyright© 1964 by the Special Libraries Association.

With some reduction, 12 catalog cards could be placed on a single page. By simple division, this meant that the book catalog would be over 10,000 pages. The pages would have to be on fairly thick stock to stand the wear the catalog would receive, and it would have to be bound in many volumes. Once this was considered, the idea lost most of its appeal. The Library of Congress book catalog method was also considered. This would have entailed the additional cost of making an offset plate and then running only one page per plate, which would be very wasteful. The cost could have easily been blown up to $50,000 by this method, and the result would have still been unacceptable. The estimate received for microfilming the catalog and obtaining 8½ by 11 sheets in bound form was approximately $10,000.*

The second approach of using a regular card catalog seemed to be as logical as one could believe possible. By reproducing the card catalog, branch patrons were certain to be satisfied. To reproduce the catalog as it exists at the main library involved microfilming the cards, preparing duplicate cards from the microfilm, and purchasing furniture to house the catalog. Several vendors were requested to estimate the price for reproducing exact duplicates of the union catalog. The price generally was five cents for each card, including the microfilming process. With 160,000 cards to reproduce, the reproduction cost would be approximately $8,000. In addition, six 45 drawer catalogs would have to be purchased to house the cards. These six pieces cost about $800 each or a total of about $4,800. Thus the total cost rose to almost $13,000. Another factor considered, but not priced, was that a total of 54 square feet of floor space would be required in the branch. The branch was small enough without this additional space requirement.

The third method considered was using microfilm cartridges with the Recordak Lodestar reader. Since each process began with microfilming, we felt that the cheapest method would be one where the microfilm itself could be used as the catalog. The literature was searched to see if anyone had ever used microfilm for a working catalog, and nothing was found. We were sure that many catalogs had been microfilmed but did not find anything in the literature describing a working catalog used in microfilm form. One of the major Hughes libraries had microfilmed its catalog and provided microfilm copies throughout its facilities. Their success with this method swayed our thinking. However, this Hughes library has conventional catalogs for use in the library and their microfilm catalogs were not used by patrons. Our system would replace a conventional catalog in the library proper of the branch with a microfilm card catalog. We had seen a performance of the Lodestar reader-printer with microfilmed catalog cards and felt that it would be practical to use the Lodestar system. We believed microfilm would give us an effective method for reproducing the

---

*The prices quoted in this article will fluctuate from vendor to vendor and from area to area. They are included for comparative purposes only.

union catalog, although microfilm was not considered for the catalog of the branch's own collection.

It was our opinion that microfilm would also be the cheapest method. It was decided that the printer part of the Lodestar reader would not be necessary with a catalog, for we could not conceive of any occasion where someone would need to have a copy of the catalog cards. Our estimate was approximately $650 for the microfilming and about $1,000 for the Lodestar reader. This was $8,000 cheaper than using the book catalog and almost $11,000 cheaper than the full-size duplication.

Preparation of Supplements Studied

When considering which method to use, the process of preparing supplements to the catalog was investigated for each of the three methods. To keep a book catalog up-to-date, either weekly supplements would have to be prepared or cards could be held aside for a long period of time and then a fairly large supplement brought out. To prepare weekly supplements meant microfilming some 800 cards a week and then having some 65 pages reproduced. This would cost about $2,000 a year. Fifty-two supplements a year would have to be prepared and they present a formidable task to use. The alternative to weekly supplements would be to reproduce cards weekly and hold these cards for larger supplements. This would allow us to keep the union catalog up-to-date and let us prepare supplements to the main book catalog every two or three months. This method would increase the total cost by five cents a card or an additional cost of about $2,000 a year. Because the idea of having the initial duplication of the union catalog in book form was rejected, the means of preparing the supplements convinced us even more that the catalog should not be prepared in book form.

Next supplements were considered for a standard card catalog. Eight hundred cards a week would have to be duplicated. The delay in keeping cards out of the union catalog while the microfilm process took place was not felt to be a factor. The yearly cost of $2,000 to reproduce the 40,000 cards has already been calculated above. In addition to this, the cost of filing time and catalog trays had to be added. It takes an average of an hour to file 100 cards, and with this labor charge at about $2 an hour, the labor cost totals about $800 a year. We also calculated that it cost approximately $13 to house a thousand cards or a yearly cost of $650. This comes to a total of $3,450 a year for the maintenance of just one duplicate union catalog in conventional form.

After finishing these calculations, these two means of supplementing the catalog were compared with the cost of microfilming the complete catalog three times during the year. Instead of providing supplements, a new up-to-date catalog would be issued to the branch every four months. There would be no storage problem. There would be delay in the completeness of the catalog at the branch, but a four-month delay was felt to be acceptable. The cost of duplicating the entire catalog three times a year was three times $650 or $1,950. The microfilm catalog would have all the deletions removed. Deletions would be impossible to pull from the book catalog and would represent an increased cost to the standard catalog. The cost of microfilming will be kept at approximately $2,000 a year by lengthening the time between complete refilming over the ten-year period.

Ten-Year Costs

The three methods were then compared for ten-year costs. The book catalog would cost $10,000 initially plus at least $2,000 a year in maintaining it or a total of $30,000. The standard catalog would cost initially $13,000 plus about $3,500 a year to maintain for a ten-year total of $48,000. The microfilm catalog cost about $2,000 initially and will cost about $2,000 a year to maintain or about $22,000. Thus the microfilm catalog will save at least $8,000 over the book catalog and $26,000 over a standard catalog for a ten-year period. If the savings of the two other locations going from a standard catalog to a microfilm catalog were considered, the savings would be even greater. Additional microfilm catalogs made from a master microfilm catalog would not have the charge for the time spent in feeding the catalog cards to the camera. The single branch catalog would cost $2,000 a year to maintain, whereas if we were to maintain a second catalog at another location, the second microfilm catalog would cost only $600 ($200 per catalog times three).

Operation of System

With the foregoing cost analysis completed, the decision was made that a microfilm catalog would fill the needs of the Space System Branch, and microfilming begin.

The catalog was microfilmed and placed into 33 Lodestar cartridges. Microfilming took place in the library so that the catalog was available to both the library staff and library patrons during the four days needed to complete the work. The cartridges are four inches square and one inch thick and are placed in a convenient container occupying a table top area of only a foot by a foot and a half square. Each cartridge stores 100 feet of 16mm film and is self-threading. The microfilm reader and cartridges occupy only part of a standard desk top.

The Lodestar reader operates very simply. Cartridges are all labelled with the portions of the alphabet they cover. Once the proper cartridge had been selected, it is inserted into the reader, which automatically starts the reader. An advance switch transports the film across the viewer at variable speeds up to 600 feet per minute. Viewing speed may be held constant at any desired speed and sharp focus is easily maintained. When the film is removed, the reader automatically shuts itself off.

There are drawbacks to the microfilm. These drawbacks are not felt to be significant, but they are present. First, it is impossible for more than one person to use the catalog at a time, but since the branch is fairly small, it was felt that traffic to the catalog would not overload it. The second drawback is that of time of search. It takes longer to find something on the microfilm catalog than it does for the standard catalog. In a sample experiment, it took an average of about 20 seconds to find any card in the standard catalog, whereas it took an average of 40 seconds with the microfilm catalog. However, these drawbacks were not significant in our evaluation of a microfilm union catalog at the branch.

Since none of the patrons were familiar with the new method of providing a catalog, an educational task was necessary. The most effective way was to give actual demonstrations of the microfilm catalog system. Once users had been shown how to use the Lodestar reader and the microfilm cartridges, they became as adept at using the microfilm as they had been in using the standard catalog. The ease with which the system was inaugurated at the branch has been quite gratifying.

The advantages we felt we had gained by the use of the microfilm catalog system far outweigh its disadvantages. First of all, the microfilm system is cheaper than the other methods we had considered. Secondly, it takes up far less space than a conventional catalog. And thirdly, we feel that the microfilm catalog is almost as easy to use as the conventional catalog.

SPREADING STATE LIBRARY RICHES FOR PEANUTS

by Oliver P. Gillock and Roger H. McDonough

The $25,000 Micro-Automated Catalog System of the New Jersey State Library was designed by Kenneth W. Richards, head of its Archives and History Bureau, and grew out of a general concern for the safety of the card catalog. The project quickly developed from one of an archival nature to that of a multiple-copy microfilm catalog for placement in selected area and research libraries in New Jersey. As thus conceived, the MAC project was to: 1) allow area libraries to have immediate, specific, and directly accessible data on the holdings of the State Library; 2) reduce time and workload in processing interlibrary loans (ILL) requests at the area library level; 3) eliminate verification workload at the State level; 4) provide catalog data for New Jersey documents; 5) provide bibliographies; 6) test validity of MAC approach to substantiate desirability of similar service from all 17 area libraries to local libraries; 7) provide background for the possibility of a catalog-bank for all four research libraries in New Jersey (Princeton, Rutgers, Newark Public, and the State Library); and 8) provide an archival copy of the State Library's catalog for safe-keeping in the event of fire or other disaster.

Framework for MAC

The 1964 New Jersey State Plan, prepared by the New Jersey Library Association's Library Development Committee, and implemented with Library Services and Construction Act and State Aid funds, provides for three library service levels: local libraries (public, school, college, and special), area reference libraries (there are now 17), and research library centers. A primary responsibility of the area library is to provide interlibrary reference and loan to all libraries within its service area.

Reprinted from *Wilson Library Bulletin*, 45: 354-57 (December 1970) by permission of the authors and publisher. Copyright © 1970 by The H. W. Wilson Company.

In 1969, a further refinement of the State Plan was effected with the designation of the Newark Public Library as the Northern New Jersey Metropolitan Regional Library Center, providing interlibrary reference and loan service to the area libraries in its region. Newark's region embraces the three Standard Metropolitan Statistical Areas surrounding and including Newark and contains 4 million citizens and the majority of the public and school libraries in New Jersey. The New Jersey State Library continues to serve the western and southern portions of New Jersey.

The nine libraries selected for the pilot MAC project were made up primarily of those area libraries using the New Jersey Library directly, but also included the Newark Public Library to speed its regional ILL service, and the New Jersey State Library itself, to facilitate its telephone service.

Included in the State Library's dictionary card catalog at time of microfilming MAC were 600,000 author, title, and subject cards for the 200,000 titles in the various special collections—reference, archives, genealogy, Jerseyana, New Jersey, and U.S. law and documents—and in the general collection, where major emphasis is placed on the social sciences. Since fiction entries are not listed in the main catalog, the fiction shelflist was included in the MAC project as a supplement to the main catalog.

The 660 drawers of the State Library catalog were filmed, with an effective date of July 1, 1969, with little disruption of the normal operations of the library. Catalog cards were fed into the camera on their five-inch side, so that the resulting microfilm could be viewed easily without rotating the reader-printer head. This yielded only 5,000, rather than 7,000, images per roll of microfilm, but did not raise costs substantially. Because of the excellent technical work of the Microfilm Unit staff, the filming was completed in twenty-five working days with no retakes necessary. The cost of labor and supplies for producing the master film was $1,000, a small price to pay for the protection of the catalog and an initial investment which was to reap significant dividends.

Duplication of the master set of film to provide the nine sets for the participating libraries was contracted for, at a cost of $382 per set of 100 reels, or $3,438 total. Microfilm cartridges were purchased for $1.25 each, or $125 per set, $1,125 total. Loading the microfilm cartridges with processed film at the State Library at the rate of 45 cartridges per day entailed an equipment and labor cost of $540, the labeling and indexing of the cartridges being absorbed into the operational budget of the State Library. Thus, the total cost of duplicating, loading, labeling, and indexing the nine sets of MAC film came to $5,103, or $567 per set.

In addition, as part of the project, the State Library purchased the equipment required for the participating libraries. The equipment costs were as follows:

Quantity	Item	Unit Cost	Total Cost
9	Cartridge Reader-Printer, with ½ page print-out adapter	$1,795.00	$16,155.00
		64.25	578.25
9	Office Machine Stand	101.50	913.50
9	Desk-Top Cartridge File	86.00	774.00
		$2,046.75	$18,420.75

Inherent in the MAC project is the need for timely cumulative supplements on at least a quarterly basis. To keep MAC current, a duplicate set of catalog cards for every title added to the State Library collections after July 1, 1969, is filed in a MAC card supplement at a present cost of $10,800 per year. This labor is expensive, but it is felt to be fully justified in light of the benefits derived from making the catalog widely available.

The total cost of the pilot MAC project, including provision of an archival copy for the State Library came to less than $25,000, or 2,725 each for the nine installations.

Using MAC

The microfilm cartridge is self-threading and access to any entry on a reel of MAC film can be achieved in fifteen seconds, using the reader-printer's odometer. Because the catalog guide cards provide a natural index to the catalog, they were microfilmed in place and became the entries for the printed MAC index. The odometer location of each guide card was noted, to form a visible index for rapid access to the MAC entries, which are reduced to 1/24th actual size on microfilm.

At the participating library, ILL requests are checked against the library's holdings. If material is held and available, the area library fills the request directly. If not, the request is processed on MAC. After finding the proper cartridge and mounting it on the reader-printer, the operator checks the printed guide index to find the odometer number; the proper entry is located by advancing the film to the number. If a request slip is needed, the reader-printer generates a printout in six seconds at a cost of five cents.

The reader-printers and the other equipment were delivered in late 1969; the completed MAC film was installed in the participating libraries early in March 1970. The first MAC interlibrary loan request was received from the Trenton Public Library on March 9, 1970, approximately one year after MAC was conceived.

By March 19, the first mailed ILL requests on MAC printout arrived at the State Library and were filled on the same day. With new procedures, MAC requests are filled within four hours of receipt by the State Library and are taken to the mail room, where all ILL's are packed and shipped daily.

From March 19 to September 30, 1970, a total of 4,585 MAC requests were received in 137 working days (33.5 per day) from the seven area libraries and the one regional library.

Of these requests, 3,658 (79.8 percent) were filled immediately; 29 (0.6 percent) were non-circulating; 898 (19.6 percent) were not available at time of request, and of this last category, approximately one-third were later returned to the State Library for reserve.

From an interlibrary loan standpoint, MAC has meant that the requesting library knows what the State Library owns and, more important, what is does not own. It no longer has to type out an ALA interlibrary request except for new books too recent for the MAC supplement. Most important for improved service, however, the requesting library may search the State Library catalog by subject.

For the State Library, MAC has meant that the costly and time-consuming catalog search of ILL's has been eliminated for most requests from the MAC libraries. Replies to ILL requests have been rapidly accelerated without an increase in staff. Still to be improved is the speed of ILL delivery: van delivery or a parcel service may provide an answer to this problem.

Participating libraries are using the new system heavily not only for the ILL requests, but as a primary verification and cataloging tool. One library uses MAC as its first source for verification of ILL requests; another is using MAC in order to catalog its New Jersey document collection.

It would appear that the pilot phase of the MAC project has amply demonstrated the practicality of the system, which is now fully operational.

Future plans for MAC

Serious consideration is now being given to microfilming the 1,162,000-card catalog of the Newark Public Library in 1970-71 for its eight area libraries. In addition, a copy will be deposited at the State Library, and Newark itself will receive the master copy for preservation and safety purposes, and a copy for its internal use. The copy of Newark's catalog at the State Library will effect reciprocity between the State Library and Newark in filling ILL requests and will simplify provision of book locations State-wide.

Further refinement of the MAC system will depend upon installation of telecommunications among the MAC libraries and the other two research libraries in New Jersey. It is hoped that the combination of rapid delivery and instantaneous communication will overcome the constant delay of matching book with reader.

As the New Jersey State Library and the other MAC libraries have experimented with a microfilm catalog, the State Library has recognized the shortcomings of its main catalog. It is anticipated that as various separate catalogs (Library for the Blind and Handicapped, Juvenile, and Fiction) are brought up to date and edited, they will first be microfilmed as supplements to the existing Mciro-Automated Catalog. Subsequently, as interfiling of all separate catalogs into the main catalog is achieved, the main catalog will be refilmed, creating the second edition of MAC at the New Jersey State Library. This refilming is probably two years away and will be fully justified in saving search time at all MAC installations in New Jersey.

It is hoped that, in cooperation with the New Jersey Department of Higher Education, firmer ties will be developed with the area and academic libraries which are designing a computer-assisted acquisition, cataloging, circulation-control, and ILL system on a Statewide basis. It is also hoped that MAC film of all four research libraries can be deposited in the next few years in many New Jersey colleges and area libraries and be available for purchase elsewhere. However, these developments await funding beyond the present capacity of New Jersey's share of LSCA Title III.

Meanwhile, MAC itself has provided the means by which the New Jersey ILL network has made a quantum jump in one year with a simple, practical, and cheap medium which would appear to have wide applicability for other libraries which are at the center of network functions.

Not least of all, MAC has permitted the New Jersey State Library to "publish" its catalog in a form which allows recipient libraries to generate ILL requests by pushing a button.

UNDERTAKING A SUBJECT CATALOG IN MICROFICHE

by Katharine Gaines

The Ramapo Catskill Library System, Middletown, New York, developed a subject catalog of materials in the central library and the system headquarters. As a card catalog this tool assisted the system staff in finding subject material from books which are located within the system area. In an effort to better serve the individual in member libraries desiring this material, subject heading simplification was instituted, the subject catalog was filmed and placed on standard microfiche, and a set of the microfiche catalog was placed in each of the member libraries. A system grant was offered for the purchase of a microfiche reader.

In June 1970 Ramapo Catskill Library System initiated a subject catalog in microfiche form. This consists of 178 (4 x 6) microfiches including approximately 60,000 subject entries for books available throughout the Ramapo System. Each microfiche has at the top in eye-readable text the first and last subject heading included on that microfiche. The complete set of this subject guide takes up four inches of filing space. One set has been given to each of the forty-five libraries in the system free of charge.

The headquarters staff felt that a subject listing to Ramapo Catskill Library System (RCLS) area library books would provide not only quicker access to what patrons wanted but also would spur interest in other referred subjects. *Books in Print, Cumulative Book Index*, and other standard bibliographies with their thousands of entries can be self-defeating to many patrons. If the subject is all that is needed (not a particular book or author) and cannot be found in the local library, Interlibrary Loan Department time can be saved for more specialized tasks, since three vital conditions are met to expedite the filling of the request satisfactorily:
1. Item has been selected by the patron himself.
2. Automatic verification (copied from reproduction of Union Catalog record).
3. Availability in the area.

Reprinted from *Library Resources and Technical Services*, 15: 297-308 (Summer 1971).

Hopefully, an increasing percentage of TWX (teletype) items will no longer have to be diverted to the state or other institutions outside RCLS. This will result in future costs savings to the taxpayer, albeit proof of this claim would be improbable.

Throughout library literature of the 60s were found statements such as: "Initially microfilming was thought of as a technique for space reduction in some special libraries or in connection with the need for preservation of materials in scholarly libraries. This was true both for files that were going to be stored away for safekeeping and for the preservation of much more fragile documents, such as newspapers. However, microforms are now beginning to be used as a medium of communication, much as books and report literature are used."[1]

We at Ramapo are enthusiastic about microfiche applied to a subject catalog because:

1. It is a microform system designed and tailored for user requirements.
2. Our pattern of learning and knowledge from earliest childhood is divided into units or categories or subjects. This concept is easiest for us to handle. A unit microform merely adds a new technical dimension to aid us in switching, copying, or redistributing information.
3. A unit microform is a simple economical means of preparing and distributing technical documents where the unit is generally 5 to several hundred pages long.
4. Within the last year, major federal government technical information service and others, here and overseas, have standardized on microfiche to distribute technical report literature. They use a standard format recommended by the National Microfilm Association, and the COSATI group of the Federal Council for Science and Technology. The outputs of these agencies represent the greater percentage of technical report literature being distributed today. Continuity and compatibility will bring a greater availability of pertinent information, a wider range of good low cost using equipment.
5. Unit microforms are easily filed, easily found, and easily retrieved. They can be interfiled, regrouped for user convenience, used one at a time as a unit, and stored in a minimum of space. The user has a choice of copying the documents in a miniaturized form or full size. He can select and copy pages at will. Convenient equipment, including readers, reader-printers, hard copy printers of many manufacturers are available to make full use of the unit microforms.[2]

National Cash Register (NCR) has put it this way: "One 60-page report on one microfiche. No need to wind through 100 feet of film to find the report you want. No need to tie up 100 feet of film while you look at one report."[3]

In other words, once the machinery was available for the use of the microfiche catalog, the machine could be put to other uses in reading actual books and articles, and only limited by what the mushrooming micropublishers will be issuing, and of course, the capabilities of the machine itself.

It was felt, therefore, that the new catalog would be put to the most effective use if each library purchased a machine, which is called a reader, to be used exclusively for microfiche. The Atlantic F66 Microfiche reader, which we chose, had several definite advantages:

1. It is sturdy and simple to operate.
2. It enables the user to adjust the focal point in such a manner that it moves over the entire surface of the fiche vertically and horizontally at will, both backwards and forwards. Subjects could thus be easily searched, compared, and identified.

Some of the larger libraries wanted expensive machines which operate both microfilm and microfiche. The use of time-consuming attachments, i.e., a microfiche attachment to a microfilm machine, etc., was discouraged. Immediate access to a dependable microfiche reader was essential if proper use of the catalog was to be rewarding. Also, it was strongly felt that our libraries would particularly benefit from the economy of the low prices of materials on microfiche. Constant and ready accessibility to microfiche through a machine was of utmost importance.[4]

Throughout the project, which truly began in the middle of December 1969, many decisions had to be made under pressure. We set a deadline of April 15, 1970. We undertook the project with no extra filing or typing staff, but our staff did a magnificent job of filing 58,500 cards in the five and a half months while keeping other essential duties going. We logged 659 hours of filing including the revision of each card according to the second edition of *ALA Rules for Filing Catalog Cards*.

After considering the advantages and disadvantages of using negative or positive film, we decided on recommending negative film for the following reasons:

1. Articles definitely are easier to read on negative film because less light reaches the reader's eye and we felt that librarians should train patrons to feel comfortable with negative.
2. Presumably card catalogs seldom will be used for reading, instead they will be used for locating subjects quickly.
3. Scratches are distracting on positive fiche, particularly in the case of catalog card reproduction.
4. Negative replacements are quicker and cheaper to reproduce.
5. Most reader-printers are designed to work best with negative microfiche because black and white is reversed in printout.
6. Used by government agencies for distributing reports.[5]

Although it is true that positive film renders photographs easier to interpret and many people find positive easier to adjust to, we felt that the advantages outweighed the disadvantages of the negative.

Therefore, fifty sets of negative were contracted for. Five positive sets were ordered at a greater cost and the first five libraries requesting these received them. We feel that through system-wide discussion and debate we will have learned much in this area when we update the catalog in 1971.

This subject guide on microfiche is referred to when the patron of the library cannot find subject access in the library's own card catalog. (However, it should be borne in mind that this edition of the catalog is restricted to the selection of Central Book Aid (CBA) materials and 68-69 RCLS pool collection books plus three hundred selected holdings from member libraries which are not duplicated in the pool collection. Therefore, representation of many *popular* subject areas is excluded.) Depending on each library's decision, especially during the first months of getting acquainted with the actual physical use of this form of a catalog and the machine, the patron may or may not look for subjects on his own. In particular regard to this question (and other related matters), please refer to the results of a survey conducted among the member libraries and given in Appendix 1.

In making a search for subjects requested, the librarian goes to the microfiche file holder and simply selects the correct microfiche (i.e., by looking at the index guide at the top) and inserts the sheet of film into a microfiche reader. The image of the original catalog card with its subject heading at the top of the card appears clear and enlarged on the screen (actually several cards are seen at once on the screen). Since microfiche is the fastest way of retrieving *so long as the filing is free of error*, an important step has been made economically in enabling the people in our communities to know immediately if any of these subjects can direct them to the material they need. If the catalog is heavily used, a cumulation will be planned in 1971; the goal is at least an additional 40,000 entries. The usefulness and value will be tripled because of the experience we have gained in producing this first catalog.

Filing integrity is not a serious problem with the short four inches of 178 subject guide fiche, each one of which is marked clearly: "1 of 178," "2 of 178," etc. However, when the library's files are increased to more than fifteen inches, a simple system of color coding will be introduced to assure with ease the accurate replacement of fiche in their holder cabinets.

By October it is hoped that library patrons can benefit from using the guide for themselves at certain times. The user is asked to fill out a brief charge slip. Upon return of the fiche to the desk, the slip is torn up and the fiche is immediately refiled by the librarian. However, if time is required to teach a patron how to use a reader during busy hours, it should be understood that he can use the card catalog and subject bibliographies in book form and be invited to come back when time can be devoted to introducing him to the use of microfiche. Also, during the busier hours, written requests for subjects could, of course, be put aside for the librarian to search at some more convenient time.

For easier and more direct subject access we are experimenting with truncated subject headings. The Library of Congress advocates abbreviated 17th edition Dewey classification numbers for certain libraries. To help libraries determine a shorter number without having to take time to think out the structure of the classification scheme of that number, the number is truncated by prime marks (i.e. 021'0095) on the Library of Congress card. A local library can then use the truncation mark as the cutoff point.

The computers of processing centers in reproducing catalog cards, as we understand it, can be economically instructed to stop at such a symbol and do one of the following:

1. Ignore what follows the mark in the printout (providing there is consistency in always wanting this to be done).
2. Overlook what follows the mark in the filing scheme.

We indicated our truncation of certain redundant subdivisions by utilizing a tiny dividing black bar inked on the card in front of the dash before an undesired subdivision. Thus we could consolidate subject areas for public library use. It was agreed that this consolidation is more essential than separating materials merely by the fact that it is a "popular work," an "introduction," or an "essay." Such subdivision especially becomes lost among essential subdivisions such as "—AFRICA"; "—BOSTON"; "—BIBLIOGRAPHY"; and "—HISTORY."

Knowledge and experience in the handling of materials, however, is essential to ascertain what subjects might *need* to keep selected subdivisions, which in most cases should be truncated for average public library use. For instance, literature works might best be kept separated by "—ADDRESSES, ESSAYS, LECTURES" when this subdivision applies to the work being cataloged (i.e., AMERICAN LITERATURE—ADDRESSES, ESSAYS, LECTURES, but there is little significance in using GEOLOGY—*ADDRESSES, ESSAYS, LECTURES*).

Following are examples of subject headings which include truncated subdivisions with the tiny black bar. Please note that these subdivisions are ignored in the filing order of the microfiche subject catalog.

1. —ADDRESSES, ESSAYS, LECTURES (as is illustrated in figure 1)
2. —POPULAR WORKS

Of what practical use is this differentiation to the public library catalog? This subdivision should be interfiled among the main headings GEOLOGY and not "lost" on another fiche among *fifty* necessary subdivisions of *GEOLOGY*. "Necessary" subdivisions are:

> GEOLOGY—BIBLIOGRAPHY
> GEOLOGY—CANADA
> GEOLOGY—HISTORY

3. —COLLECTIONS

Many people looking in a public library catalog can see no advantage in particularizing most subjects as "COLLECTIONS" or as "COLLECTED WORKS." Anthologies of poems or essays—yes! *AMERICAN POETRY—COLLECTIONS* is necessary to lead patrons to anthologies.

4. —INTRODUCTIONS

Similar to the subject heading POPULAR WORKS, the above subdivision can serve to separate in the catalog an author's works (see in figure 2 the three cards having Karl Barth as the author). A sensible policy would be to rely on subtitles, annotations, etc., in browsing among catalog cards to find this aspect of a subject. In most cases this would not take long. (See illustration in figure 2.)

The truncation
sign before
"Collections"
has consoli-
dated the
filing of these
two works by
Bartlett on the
same subject.

> U.S.—FOREIGN RELATIONS
> 327. Bartlett, Ruhl Jacob, 1897–
> 73   Policy and power; two centuries of American
> Ba   foreign relations. [1st ed.] New York, Hill and
>   Wang [1963]

> UNITED STATES—FOREIGN
> RELATIONS ▌—COLLECTIONS
> 327. Bartlett, Ruhl Jacob, 1897–   ed.
> 73   The record of American diplomacy; docu-
> Ba   ments and readings in the history of American
>   foreign relations, edited by Ruhl J. Bartlett.
>   4th ed. enl.

This entry
would have
filed 200 cards
afterwards if
the truncation
sign had been
omitted.

> U.S.—FOREIGN RELATIONS ▌—
> ADDRESSES, ESSAYS, LECTURES
> 327. Bemis, Samuel Flagg, 1891–
> 73   American foreign policy and the blessings of
>   liberty, and other essays. New Haven, Yale
>   Univ. Press, 1962.

> U.S.—FOREIGN RELATIONS
> 327. Bemis, Samuel Flagg, 1891–   ed.
> 73   The American Secretaries of State and their
> Be   diplomacy. New York, Cooper Square Pub-
>   lishers, 1963—   [v. 1-10. c1928]

Figure 1

Furthermore, it is too much to expect cataloging consistency in these
particulars. The Library of Congress itself omits the subdivision "—Introductions" in the tracing for several titles even though there are clues to
this fact on the card, such as the subtitle reading "an introduction," etc.
For example, perhaps there is an obscure technical reason for omitting
"Introductions" in the subject tracing "1. Insects" for the work entitled
Entomology for Introductory Courses, 1951, by Robert Matheson. Nevertheless, public library cataloging should not have to involve itself in trying

This card
would have
been filed 50
cards after-
wards if the
truncation sign
had been
omitted.

THEOLOGY, DOCTRINAL
238.   Barth, Karl, 1886–
11   Dogmatics in outline. With a new foreword by
Ba   the author. [Translation by G. T. Thompson]
            New York, Harper [1959]

THEOLOGY, DOCTRINAL ■—
INTRODUCTIONS

230.   Barth, Karl, 1886–
081   Evangelical theology; an introduction. Trans-
Ba   lated by Grover Foley. [1st ed.] New York,
            Holt, Rinehart and Winston [1963]

THEOLOGY, DOCTRINAL
238.5 Barth, Karl, 1886–
Ba   The knowledge of God and the service of
            God according to the teaching of the reforma-
            tion, recalling the Scottish confession of 1560.

Figure 2

to be consistent with Library of Congress practice in tracing comparatively useless subdivisions.

Moreover, for the patron who is looking for "an introduction" or for the scholar who wants "collections" on a subject, the information is still there on the microfiche reader screen. The subdivision is simply not used in the filing order. However, as has been implied, we hope the Library of Congress offers the service of truncated subject tracings. The cards which are commercially produced will no longer show certain subdivisions in the heading at the top although the tracing at the bottom of the card would still be printed in and could therefore be used for its information value. For example, the subject at the top of the card might read as "POVERTY" but the tracing would still show as "1. Poverty ■—Addresses, essays, lectures."

On the microfiche project there were two subdivisions which were marked out (there was no time for either retyping or erasing) as being confusing and misleading. "Translations into English" was deleted, since this catalog is one of English works and is therefore completely redundant.

The second one is "Selections: Extracts, etc."; and "Collections" instead was preferred and added.

"Selections: extracts, etc." separates collections of works too particularly for most tastes, assumes too much knowledge of subdivision on the part of both patron and librarian, does not apply to many books, and is often too time consuming to verify for catalogers. What practical advantage can there be, therefore, in such a distinction?

We just did not foresee certain unfortunate results from filming the catalog cards in this manner. And although the usefulness of the catalog is not diminished, its critics can find the points described below irritating and time-consuming. Now that we have gained hindsight in the traditional trial-and-error way, we can promise far more effectiveness in the next edition by instructing the company on how to avoid these flaws.

First, the most serious time-consumer is finding the continuation of the same subject on a second fiche without any indication of its being continued; that is, it should have had on the lable: ARTHUR, KING (Continued on fiche 12). Since it is undesirable to have headings split in this manner, however, the next edition of the catalog will not have this drawback at all. It is true that often a main heading would have to be split, but one subdivision of that main heading (or subject) would be completely listed on one fiche before beginning on the next fiche with another subdivision of the same subject heading.

Included in the index labels were "see references." On fiche no. 19 the label.has: *BOOKS—HISTORY* to *BRIGHT CHILDREN see GIFTED CHILDREN*. The word "see" was fortunately typed in lower case but "see references" should never have been included in the labels at the top of the fiche (the part of each fiche that is in eye-readable print). However, once the confusion is explained "away," time can be saved since fiche no. 19, for example, does not have to be placed in the reader at all; that is, if one wants material on BRIGHT CHILDREN, one should extract fiche no. 64 which includes material about *GIFTED CHILDREN*. If this catalog is updated, "see references" will be omitted from the labels, notwithstanding the advantage just mentioned.

Naturally, inaccuracies in filing resulted but the error incidence is surprisingly low considering the rate of speed at which the filing was implemented in changing over to the new ALA rules. "AFL-CIO" is found mistakenly after "Afghanistan" instead of where it should be: the first card ahead of *AACHEN—HISTORY*. It is a peculiar rule to understand at first since periods are not used with the initials; i.e., AFL instead of A.F.L.

The print on the cards themselves was uneven. In some cases, it was very light; this resulted in uneven exposure because camera registration was set in such a way to keep labor costs down. Some of the fiche are thus difficult to read. Many are being turned in because they are blurred. However, the master copy renders legible copies and replacements are sent immediately to the member libraries.

Regrettably, there was not enough time on this edition to treat cancelled subject headings properly or give enough explanatory references. For example, do people know the distinctions Library of Congress makes between *MARRIAGE, MIXED* and *MISCEGENATION?* In a new edition of this catalog, we will treat cancelled subjects as illustrated in Figure 3.

One side effect that has not been mentioned is that small libraries will be able to catalog some of their holdings just as if it were a "cataloging-in-publication" (formerly "cataloging-in-source") service.

Since cross-referencing will be tailor-made for RCLS, all personnel in our libraries will probably begin to see the advantages of knowing about true subject access. One of our librarians wanted material on "Language Arts." Library of Congress does not recognize this as a "bonafide" subject heading but guidance is given in the following: "LANGUAGE ARTS, *see* COMMUNICATION, ENGLISH LANGUAGE, LITERATURE, LITERA-TURE—STUDY AND TEACHING, READING, SPEECH." The referred subjects are now listed in a column, but we receive most cross-references from commercial firms with each one separately printed, and we have to revise and edit them. Since hundreds of revisions are made by the Library

The present
microfiche
catalog has
only the
suggestion:
"See also."

FACTORIES—MAINTENANCE AND REPAIR
For works cataloged since 1966 see
PLANT MAINTENANCE

PLANT MAINTENANCE
For works cataloged before 1967 see
FACTORIES—MAINTENANCE AND REPAIR

Figure 3

of Congress each year in both subject and name headings, each New York State Library System headquarters should aid the member libraries in basic updating. All public libraries in a given area cannot be expected to keep up with the supplements to *Subject Headings Used in the Dictionary Catalogs of the Library of Congress*, 7th edition, and *Sears* does not keep up with language changes.

Introducing microfiche to libraries required further education and aid in gathering the right kind of materials. Effective implementation of the project necessitates many hours on the phone, and a personal visit to each member library was made by the cataloging and reference headquarters staff to demonstrate microfiche readers.

In order to insure the all-important integrity of filing of the fiche, a simple means of color-coding, using a permanent felt tip marker, will be introduced to each member library when it requests it. One member library is acquiring a sizable microfiche collection and we have already suggested a simple method of drawing straight lines diagonally on the bottom of a group of fiche. If a fiche is not found in its regular place or two or three places either way (and, of course, if it is not a numbered group as, for example, our subject catalog on microfiche), the group of usually three to seven inches is gripped together, turned upside-down, and the missing item shows up easily by the markings being out of line.

The opinions about the project from the directors of the member libraries are variable, but on the whole, this catalog is a successful and economical means of getting better subject access in the hands of our readers (cf. appendix 2). Meanwhile, at the system headquarters we are busy working on a bigger and better edition!

In closing, I wish to quote some choice statements from an article entitled, "Little Fiche Eat Big Librarians—One Whale of a Story," by Edward C. Jestes.

> Librarians are now drowning in the flood of paper produced by the polluting pulp mills. Our weakness is our meticulous record keeping. In the process of record keeping something rubs off—we have memories, and human librarians are the best information retrieval system in existence. Lack of information and its dissemination could be blamed for the very possible destruction of the delicately balanced life system of earth and atmosphere which took millions of years to evolve. Lack of information on how people might learn to be gentle and loving could make life miserable for our children. The world's information is channeled across the desks of librarians, and if some of this information can be put into machines and compacted to save space and time and permit more efficient retrieval, then librarians should be the most efficient candidates for the job.
>
> Librarians must flow over, under, around, and into the black boxes, put them to good use, and not let technology dehumanize anybody—librarians or patrons.
>
> It might help if librarians were given an hour each day to read about microfiche, systems analysis, programming, critical path analysis, use and control of media centers, and one's own subject specialty. How about it, administrators? Industry has been supporting continuing education of its employees for years.[6]

APPENDIX 1

This questionnaire was sent to RCLS Member Libraries. The answers which were returned are summarized on the right-hand side below.

Affirmative answers
(Approximate figures)

I. Subject catalog on microfiche
    1. Do you find this catalog useful?   84%
    2. Have you allowed the public to use this catalog
       by themselves?
       Comment *"They love it"—"We are still in process
       of educating"—"As setup permits"—etc.*   52%
    3. If you had an extra set, would you like to see the
       public use it in the same way a book or card catalog
       is used?   68%
    4. The new edition of the subject catalog will have at
       least twice as many entries. Are you looking forward
       to the ENLARGED edition of subjects?   94%

II. Use of the microfiche reader in your library
    1. Do you patrons use the reader for ERIC articles?   42%
    2. Have you ordered periodicals or other materials
       on microfiche?   36%
    3. How often is your subject catalog used each week?   ?:4;never:1; 1-5:6;
                                          6-10:6; more than 10:2.
    4. Do you have any plans to purchase other materials
       on fiche?   52%
    5. Has any attempt been made to help older people
       overcome objection to reading material in this
       manner?   21%

    The latest complete tabulated system report (1969) was used as the basis for eliminating certain small libraries from being included in the percentages on the preceding page. These "small" libraries serve less than 5,000 populations and/or are locally funded less than $15,000 a year. Eight of the fifteen libraries in this group sent in answers and only two of those eight answered I. (1) and I. (4) negatively. More bibliographic selection aid and personal visits will be required before the smaller libraries derive the most benefit from the microfiche project. In the aforementioned group of better funded libraries, 79 percent of these twenty-four libraries selected to be included in the table answered the questionnaire.

    The following three libraries were also excluded in the report: Newburgh, the RCLS central library (a complete CBA subject card catalog is housed there); Monroe (only recently received their microfiche reader); and Spring Valley (now withdrawn from the system).

APPENDIX 2

Cost comparison with the book catalog.
    CBA book catalog (printed by Data-Matic Systems Corp.)

			Entries	
1967	100 copies:	Author and Subject entries for each work	51,000	$11,264.00
1968	100 copies:	Author and Subject entries for each work	4,153	922.00
				$12,186.00

(Approximately 55,000 entries)

Subject Microfiche Catalog (1970)

Ordered		Quantity	Unit	Price
178	Masters 105 × 148 per 1,000 images	178	25.00	$1,467.97
8,900	Diazo Duplicates backed each 105 × 148	8,900	.13	1,157.00
890	Silver positives duplicates each	890	.15	133.00

$2,757.97
(58,720 entries)

(Approximately 60,000 entries)
Another way to put it:

50 sets (negative) $23.14 each	$1,157.00
5 sets (positive) $26.75 each	133.00
Basic costs of master set	1,467.97

$2,757.97

Microfiche holder cabinets

46 (Demco) with discount	$ 497.06
Money set aside for readers to each member library; (110.07 plus delivery) approx.	$5,535.00
Total for catalog sets, readers, and holders approx.	$8,790.53

References

1. Douglas M. Knight, ed., *Libraries at Large* (New York: Bowker, 1969), p. 622.

2. A. I. Baptie, ed., *Microfiche Planning Guide for Technical Document Distribution Systems* (West Salem, Wis.: Microcard Corp., c1965), p. 2.

3. NCR Microcard Editions, *Catalog 10. 1969-70* (Washington, D.C.: Industrial Products Division, National Cash Register Co.), p. 1.

4. The author wishes to express special appreciation to the following: Mrs. Joseph Gobolos, RCLS Reference Coordinator; Mr. Sumner White, former RCLS Assistant Director; and Mr. Joseph Kelley, Production Manager for the Atlantic Microfilm Corp. Also, Mr. James Connolly, Program Manager, Arcata Corp.

5. NCR Microcard Editions, *Catalog 10. 1969-70* (Washington, D.C.: Industrial Products Division, National Cash Register Co.), p. 2.

6. Edward C. Jestes, "Little Fiche Eats Big Librarians—One Whale of a Story," *Wilson Library Bulletin* 44: 650-52 (Feb. 1970).

THE USE OF MICROFILM IN RELATION TO THE RETROSPECTIVE AND PROSPECTIVE CATALOGS OF THE RESEARCH LIBRARIES OF THE NEW YORK PUBLIC LIBRARY

Introduction & General Summary

With the aid of a grant from the Council on Library Resources, The New York Public Library's Research Libraries conducted an experiment lasting from July 1971 through March 1972. The object of the experiment, which was in three parts or phases,* was to determine the acceptability of microfilm as a substitute for the public card catalog, the new book catalog, and the authority file for the new book catalog. Because many of the cards in the heavily-used public catalog are badly deteriorated and in need of replacement, various alternatives, including microfilming and book publication, have been studied. Part I of the experiment was designed to test the feasibility of the first of these alternatives. Parts II and III, involving the use of microfilm as a substitute for the authority file and the new book catalog, as it related to the Processing Division, are reported on by the Chief of that Division. Part III also involved public use of The Research Libraries new book catalog on microfilm. A report on this part forms the final portion of the report.

Any evaluation of the results of the experiment must be made with careful reference to the special needs and problems of The Research Libraries. For another institution, such an experiment might well result in a quite different set of recommendations. For example, a library with a less heterogeneous readership and with a public catalog which has suffered less through time and heavy use might find microfilm a more acceptable substitute than would be the case for the Research Libraries. On the other hand, The Research Libraries, because of their acute space problems and the rapid growth of their new book catalog, probably have greater need than most for a substitute such as microfilm would provide for the authority file.

This is a reprint of the New York Public Library report, *The Use of Microfilm in Relation to the Retrospective and Prospective Catalogs of The Research Libraries of The New York Public Library: a Report to the Council on Library Resources (CLR grant no. 516).* New York: New York Public Library, June, 1972. (ERIC ED 967 107).

The question of whether a catalog such as The Research Libraries' new book catalog is more useful in book form or in microform can be answered perhaps more clearly than the questions dealt with in the first two parts of the experiment. There would appear to be general agreement that a catalog in book format is easier and more convenient to use. For The Research Libraries, however, the factors of space and production costs must be taken into account. If they should eventually loom so large as to make continued publication of the catalog in book form impractical, the experiment demonstrates the feasibility of using microfilm as an alternative.

The Research Libraries are grateful to the Council on Library Resources for making this experiment possible. It has answered questions which have a most important relationship to the preservation and continued usefulness of The Research Libraries' catalogs. Insofar as libraries share similar problems wherever they may be, the experiment contributes to a fund of knowledge upon which all may draw.

*In the reports which follow, the words "part" and "phase" are used interchangeably.

REPORT ON MICROFILM CATALOG EXPERIMENT
(CLR Grant No. 516)

Part 1: The Use of Microfilm as a Replacement
for Part of the Public Catalog

Introduction

The following report was prepared at the request of the Chief, General Research Services, The New York Public Library, by the Microfilm Catalog Assistant, General Research and Humanities Division, The New York Public Library. It is intended to form part of the basis of a report to the Council on Library Resources of an experiment conducted in connection with that group July 26 to December 31, 1971. The report is based on activities recorded in the "Diary of the Use of the Microfilm Catalog in The Research Libraries," a daily record of each event related to the experiment or the Microfilm Catalog Assistant.

Background and Purpose

In 1971 The Research Libraries of The New York Public Library began the change from a traditional cataloging process to one using a computer and adaptor to systems used by the Library of Congress. For various reasons this necessitates the creation of two catalogs: a "retrospective" catalog of all holdings received before a specified cutoff date and cataloged according to the old procedures, and a "prospective" catalog of entries cataloged using the new procedures. After the cutoff date all new entries, including corrections and updating of entries in the "retrospective" catalog, were to go into the "prospective" catalog.

Thus the 10,000-tray Public Catalog would be "frozen," and no new entries added after the cutoff date. Some of the cards are so old (in some cases going back to 1857) that they are physically deteriorating. Therefore, it was decided that the "retrospective" catalog should be preserved in some more permanent form, either in book form, or on microfilm. Microfilm is less expensive to produce than books, but until recently the technical problems involved made the use of a microfilm catalog out of the question. However, the development of the Memorex 1642 Viewer, which uses cassettes instead of having to be threaded by hand and which has been found to be sturdier than other microfilm viewers, made the use of a microfilm system seem feasible. It was therefore decided to test this possibility by installing Memorex Viewers in the Public Catalog on an experimental basis.

The purpose of the experiment was to test the usefulness of microfilm reproduction of a segment of the Public Catalog in The Research Libraries of The New York Public Library. Among the factors to be considered are user acceptability, mechanical feasibility of the microfilm readers, and the means by which this service is to be administered by the staff. It was thus very much open-ended in terms of the specific problems to be investigated, as well as the methods of investigation to be employed.

Methodology

Equipment

Two Memorex 1642 Viewers, designed to use 16mm film mounted on cassettes and turned by a hand crank, were installed in the Public Catalog, Room 315 of the Central Building. They rested on tables used for filling out callslips, situated beside the catalog drawers.

Originally 20 catalog trays were filmed in an area thought to be representative of the entire catalog (Deutschland C - Dickson, 1), and divided between 2 cassettes. Later the next eleven trays (to Dilt) were filmed, making a third cassette, and a fourth was added from World War, 1935-1945 to World War, 1939-45—Evacuations (9 trays). The machines were located in the corner of the room next to the "D's." The drawers were taken out and stored in an area accessible to staff only, close enough to be consulted if necessary. No "rehabilitation" of old cards was done prior to filming, and it was assumed that some classmarks (call numbers) barely visible on cards might be obscure on film.

Signs were installed over the empty spaces left by the drawers. The one in the "D's" read: "Catalog cards for Deutschland C to Dickson, 1 (later Dilt) are available on microfilm only. For use of this part of catalog, consult technical assistant at microfilm reader in adjacent area, or librarian at Information Desk." The sign in the "W's" read almost the same, substituting "World War, 1939-45" to "World War, 1939-45—Evacuations" in the appropriate place and "northeast corner" for "adjacent area."

Personnel

The machines were under the supervision of a Library Technical Assistant 1, known as the Microfilm Catalog Assistant, whose duties were to "assist users of the microfilm catalog," "maintain the microfilm readers and cassettes in working order," consult the cards themselves if necessary to determine classmarks, and record the incidents related to the experiment in a diary. On lunch hours and coffee breaks, the assistant was relieved by clerks from the division. The catalog assistant had had no prior training in research methods, and was not a librarian. His previous experience had been as a catalog-card filer, so he was familiar with the filing system of the cards recorded on film. Relief personnel had not had this training.

In addition the assistant found himself answering routine questions not requiring the assistance of a librarian, locating cards in the card catalog for readers (and occasionally librarians) confused by the complex card-filing rules, and referring readers to the Information Desk nearby (staffed by librarians), other divisions of The Research Libraries, and nearby branch duties related to his previous training, and clerical duties related to the experiment.

Administratively, the assistant was part of the General Research & Humanities Division, the division in charge of the Public Catalog. However, most orders and arrangements related to the experiment came to him through the Chief of General Research Services, whose jurisdiction includes the General Research & Humanities Division, or directly from persons in the Photographic Services and the Processing Division. The Library's Microform Reading Room, in charge of older-model machines for reading books and newspapers, had no direct or advisory contact with the assistant or the experiment.

All filming of cards was done by The Library's Photographic Services. Preparation of cards for filming was done by the assistant and the Filing Section of the Processing Division.

Procedures

After the machines were set up and the drawers taken away, the assistant or a relief person stood or sat close to the machines at all times The Library was open. No attempt was made to solicit readers to use or comment on the machines, though staff members were notified of the experiment through that Library's *Staff News*, and some staff were solicited to give opinions and observations. Everyone who needed an entry in the part of the catalog on film had to use the machines and was noticed and nearly always approached by the assistant or relief person.

No standard questions were used and readers were generally not asked their opinion of the machines or the experiment when they used the machines. However, the nature and purpose of the experiment was explained to most readers using semi-standardized descriptions, and comments by readers made during conversations with the assistant or relief person were recorded afterwards. Readers generally knew they were participating in an experiment but were not told their comments would be recorded. Some staff were told the latter.

During part of the experiment, a record of the number of readers who glanced at the sign and/or the machines and then left was kept. For all readers notation was made of their approximate age: "undergraduate" (under 22), "graduate" (22 to 35), "middle-age" (35 to 65), "older" (over 65), as estimated by the assistant or relief person. No record was kept of name, race, sex, or other characteristics of readers. Original plans were to estimate relative amount of library experience of readers, but this proved unfeasible except in special cases where evidence was inadvertently provided by the reader. The reader's business with the library was interrupted as little as possible by data-gathering for the experiment and the latter was kept as informal and simple as possible.

Conversations and incidents related to the experiment and/or the duties of the assistant were recorded in the diary as soon after they took place as was convenient, based on the memory of the assistant or relief person. Other observations on the experiment were also included in the diary by the catalog assistant.

It should be pointed out that no control experiment testing the feasibility of retrospective book catalogs for comparison with the results of this experiment has as yet been conducted by The New York Public Library. Most of the readers who commented on the experiment were told that the planned alternative to the microfilm was a book catalog and some that the card catalog would eventually be eliminated altogether in the Public Catalog.

Results

As a result of the five-month experience with microfilmed portions of the Public Catalog, several sets of findings can be reported. They can be loosely classed as "technical," "social," and "administrative."

Technical Problems

The "technical" problems were the ones which the experiment was designed to illuminate, so the findings in this category can be stated with less caution than in the other categories.

Machinery. The cassettes were fragile for the use they are likely to receive by the public. One was dropped accidentally in the course of the experiment from a height about equal to the top of a desk. The hinges were both broken so that the cassette would not close tightly. It was replaced at a cost of $1.25 per cassette. The public did not have much of a chance to drop anything, since the cassettes were usually either already in the machines or inserted by the assistant.

Light bulbs had to be replaced once in the first machine (after 3½ months) and twice in the second. Once in each machine the chain for the focus knob came loose and had to be put back into place.

The machines were plugged into sockets connected to the lights used at the tables in the Public Catalog. The sockets were loose enough to cause the machines two or three times not to turn on when the cassette was pushed in.

Photography—Margins. At the very beginning it was found that in one cassette the film was so far over on the screen that the left margin was hidden. This was corrected by enlarging the window of the cassette slightly and by filming subsequent cassettes with a narrower space between the two columns of cards.

Focus. One of the biggest stumbling blocks to adoption of the microfilm permanently by The Library seemed to be the focus problem. Sometimes part of the screen was in focus; sometimes all of it was in for up to 40 seconds and then it would "jump" out of focus, or vice-versa. Sometimes it would be in focus until the crank was turned or as soon as it was touched. Personnel in the Photographic Services of The Library believe that the problem can be traced to the silver emulsion used in some of the film, which absorbs heat from the light bulb. However, if a solution is not found, the focus problem would be a major obstacle to the convenient use of a catalog on microfilm.

Rehabilitation. Before filming for either a book or microfilm, old cards will have to be rehabilitated. Old, heavily-used cards have darkened corners from decades of users' fingers. The edges may show up so brightly on the negative film that classmarks are difficult to read. Photographic Services has been able to overcome most of the problem here by varying filming techniques and type of film used, but at the cost of dulling the contrast of the images on the screen. On other cards the corners have broken off, and new cards will have to be made using cards from the Official Catalogs. In a few cases pencilled entries are all but invisible and would have to be corrected in the same way. A minor question also is what to do about the small percentage of cards where information primarily for staff use appears on the back of the card.

Use - The Searching Problem. Though some readers who used the machines for the first time said it was faster than the card catalog, nearly everyone who had experience using both for a while agreed that it takes longer to find an entry in the microfilm catalog than in the card catalog. Of course, most of the "experienced" people still had biases toward cards, and most still had not had a great deal of practice finding entries on microfilm. However, even one of the most vocal proponents of the microfilm said he did not claim it was faster, and the assistant, who had five months of practice finding entries on film, still thought it was slower than cards. No systematic comparison with books was made.

There are several possible reasons for this difference. First, whereas in a card catalog the tops of cards can be seen while flipping through them, it is necessary to stop periodically to check one's location while searching for an entry on film. Second, a cassette has ten times the number of entries in a tray: it is difficult to tell how far to turn the crank before stopping. The usual tendency for readers using it for the first time is to go too slowly, checking every dozen cards or so even when they're starting at Dewey and want to go to Dial, 4,000 entries away. Faster users still have trouble guessing when to stop, and readers in general seem to have trouble figuring out the difference between main and added entries quickly enough to tell where they are. Third, the nature of microfilm is such that, regardless of how fast the crank is turned, one still has to cover every inch of information while searching. With a card or book, one can start anywhere in the middle or the end, skip whole areas with a flip of the finger, and deal most of the time with only the edges of the cards or pages.

The Browsing Problem. Persons who need to "browse"—i.e. check a large set of entries to decide which, if any, may be of use to them—find that they take more time and are more likely to be confused than when using a card catalog. One reason for this may be the fact that guide cards (which contained instructions for the manner of filing) were not filmed;

it may also be due in part to lack of practice on the part of the user. On the other hand, more than one entry at a time can be seen with a film—and especially a book—catalog, which some readers say compensates to some degree. This problem is important, since "browsers" include scholars checking for an overview of the library's holdings on a particular subject, catalogers comparing editions, readers unsure of the exact form of an entry acting on hunches, and others with serious purposes. Again, no comparison with books was made.

The Theft Problem. Once during the experiment a fuse was found missing; the cap holding it in the machines is at the back (and therefore on one machine out of sight of the assistant nearly all the time), and clearly marked "fuse" with an arrow indicating how to remove the cap. A dab of paint might be all that is needed to avoid aiding someone who collects free fuses. The cassettes pose a more dangerous problem: they fit easily into a coat pocket or large purse. What's more, the film can be stolen out of the cassette—or even replaced, as one vicarious prankster has pointed out—and the cassette returned with no one the wiser for perhaps a long time. It was pointed out that it is easier to know what to replace if it is a large area than if just a few cards, but continuous replacement might be costly. Preventive measures such as magnetic tape placed inside with a detection device, or some sort of chain attached to each cassette or some sort of checkout system, might be costly or inconvenient to readers, or both.

Sight Problems. Quite a few readers complain of dizziness or headaches, some even after only a few turns of the crank. Others predict eyestrain or fatigue from more than a few minutes of use. One librarian from another division says a regular reader there claims to be unable to use their microfilm machines at all. The reader wears very thick glasses, None of these possibilities was investigated further, so there is as yet no evidence to indicate whether any of them might pose a major stumbling block to adoption of the microfilm catalog.

The Queuing Problem. It was thought at the beginning that tying up ten trays in one cassette would mean people would be standing in line to use the machines. Since only three or four people a day used the machines—sometimes none, at the Thanksgiving "rush" no more than eleven—people were kept waiting only a handful of times during the course of the experiment. Never was more than one person waiting at one time, and only once was the person kept waiting more than a few minutes: in that instance the reader was able to look up entries elsewhere while waiting. It is not anticipated that queuing would be a problem if duplicates are made for heavily-used cassettes and a sufficient number of machines are provided. (Incidentally, it will probably be necessary to have at least one machine by the telephone reference service and several at the Information Desk. One librarian with a telephone call was delayed by a reader who refused to yield the machine, and ended up "cheating" by using the cards. It has been suggested that machines—and perhaps cassettes—could be put in the special study rooms for scholars.)

Social Problems

"Social" problems were a secondary interest, but due to the informal methods of data collection, results here must be interpreted very cautiously. For one thing, the sample of opinion was slightly biased due to the ability of some scholars doing long-term research to postpone using location of reference books in the Public Catalog room, how to fill out a call slip correctly (including a few routine "verifies"), how to locate cards in the card catalog (especially periodical titles beginning with the same word as a subject), the nature of the supplementary catalog. The assistant was able to help librarians by finding entries filed in the card catalog according to unusual rules, correcting filing errors brought to his attention which otherwise would have had to wait until Filing Section was notified, and occasionally explaining the reason for a strange-looking but correct filing order. In a few cases the assistant was able to help a reader who had already seen one or more librarians but not been able to get a satisfactory answer. Sometimes the assistant was able to spot readers who appeared lost or confused and approach them with "Can I help you?" Sometimes the assistant would be seen behind the Information Desk and taken for a librarian; usually he found it unnecessary to refer the reader to someone else. In some cases in which the assistant referred a question to the desk, he told the reader how to formulate the question and sometimes even predicted the answer ("Tell them you're working on ——. They may refer you to ——.") In all cases the assistant felt unhurried (no lines of people as may be at the Information Desk) and could ask clarifying questions, follow hunches, and in other ways give readers individual attention often impossible to get from other staff. It may be that some readers asked questions of the assistant who would never have gone to the Information Desk, though there is no evidence to show this.

The usual problems of intra and inter-divisional relations expected in a large organization were complicated by the experimental nature of the project. Relations between the assistant and the librarians, especially regarding referrals and confirmations of answers given to readers, were easy to work out. However, at times there were borderline questions in which the assistant had to judge whether he could give a satisfactory answer—usually such answers were accompanied with a referral to the desk. In addition, often when the assistant gave a guarded answer punctuated with "ask the librarian to make sure," the reader would simply take the assistant's answer as correct and neglect to ask the librarian.

A few cases did arise in which conflicting orders from different supervisors had to be resolved. Usually the assistant simply made a temporary decision in consultation with whoever seemed most knowledgeable on the question, and a permanent decision (often reversing it) would catch up later after confirmation by the Chief of General Research Services.

Relief. By providing relief for the assistant, the General Research & Humanities Division lost over 1½ man hours per day to the experiment. Training consisted of a single explanation by the assistant at the beginning of the experiment, plus a few comments from time to time when, for example, a visit by someone from Photographic Services or Memorex was expected. Communication between the assistant and the relief personnel was minimal, primarily because they worked, of course, at different times. Experience gained by the assistant and resulting changes in emphasis or recording techniques were not transmitted as a rule to relief, and vice versa. Consequently, some benefits gained from varying the person attending the machines were not gained.

Memorex. The repairman was called only three or four times during the five-month period. Twice the focus problem was brought to his attention, and once the fact that one of the machines did not light. In each the section of the catalog included in the experiment until after the experiment was over, and the ability of librarians to bypass the machines and go directly to the place where the drawers were hidden. A few cases of each were noted by the catalog assistant, but it is obviously impossible to tell how many others there were. For another thing, some aspects of the experiment which affected readers would not be present were the entire catalog to be filmed, e.g. older cards with entries difficult to read would be rehabilitated.

Use. Ability to use the machines varied by age, previous experience with similar machines, previous library experience, and attitude toward the experiment. Older readers tended not to "play" with the machines as often as younger ones when no one seemed nearby, or to be as willing and able to use the machines after being shown how by the assistant. Younger readers not infrequently would already be operating it by the time the assistant came over to them. Readers who had used microfilm or cassette-operated machines before had little difficulty teaching themselves how to use the machine. Those with long experience using card catalogs were often frustrated by the time factor and could become confused by the filing order of the entries even though it was the same as when the entries were on cards. Those opposed to the experiment had more difficulty adapting to the machines' problems; in a few cases they would interrupt the assistant as he tried to explain how to cope with them. Very few people, even those who figured out all other aspects of the machine's operation, could eject the cassette without instruction.

It should be noted that, due to the way the experiment was conducted, there were many things which the reader was not left to puzzle out on his own. He was told to consult the assistant before using the machine, so the assistant found it difficult not simply to find the proper cassette himself and insert it. A few times he would even find the entry for the reader, or at least help when the reader appeared lost. Thus a whole set of problems which might have caused the reader trouble (e.g. which way to insert the cassette) never came up for most readers.

Attitudes: Scholars and Regular Users. Those for whom the library was designed and those to whom the library caters are precisely the persons who expressed the most persistent opposition to the machines. In terms of numbers, the group was small, and the vocal opposition within it even smaller, but their criticisms and problems were important—and sometimes dramatic. These are the readers who do "serious browsing" through the catalog, who sit for long periods of time with a single set of entries comparing editions or taking an overview of a subject, who skip back and forth within a large group of entries to follow a "hunch" as to how a book may be entered. These are the readers who complain that the time factor significantly handicaps them in their work and who voice stronger complaints of inconvenience to the administrative office. Some scholars and regular users foudn the microfilm catalog acceptable or even desirable, some merely asked about it in order to be prepared if it were adopted, but those who needed it for their own use at the time generally found it undesirable.

Attitudes: Staff. These users were somewhat less opposed than the scholars. Librarian-level staff from public divisions (especially librarians in the Public Catalog) tended to be strongly opposed, while those in Preparation Services were more often neutral or in favor. This may be due to the fact that Preparation Services is more directly affected by mechanization of the cataloging process and are having to make major adjustments anyway, whereas this experiment was perhaps the first aspect of a mechanized cataloging process that directly affected a public service division. In any case, criticism from both sources ranged all the way from simple expressions of stubbornness to very sophisticated and relevant comments. Young librarians tended to favor strongly, older ones a little more likely to oppose than favor.

Non-librarians had less to say one way or the other, and, surprisingly enough, though the head of the section had no comment, most of the

readers of the Filing Section seemed to like the machines. No one
directly connected with the experiment (Photographic Services, Systems Analysis and Data Processing Services) expressed outright opposition to the machines, but only a few appeared strongly favorable; the
rest appeared to prefer making sure the experiment ran well and reserv-
ing judgment until the results were in. The assistant fell into the latter
category. Microform Reading Room was never officially consulted for
an opinion. In general, Library staff were more opinionated than other
groups, and more often than not against the idea of putting the catalog
on film, whether or not they knew the alternative was a book.

Attitudes: Others. Businessmen tended to be more curious and receptive
than others the same age. Graduate students split among those in favor,
those neutral, and those opposed.

Attitudes: In General. Most readers had little to say about the machines
but in general attitudes tended to go along in the same direction as ability to use the machine—especially with regard to age. Younger people
tended to feel at home with the machines, and, of course, they are the
scholars and librarians of the future. If the criticisms raised by the older
readers can be answered or prove to be unimportant, public opposition
to the machines can be expected to decrease as older readers are replaced by younger ones, simply because younger readers have had more
experience with microfilm and cassettes in other areas of their lives.

Administrative Problems

"Administrative" problems which came up during the experiment were
never crucial to the decision whether to institute the microfilm on a permanent basis, but they did indicate possible areas to be explored if the decision is favorable—and, in some cases, areas which might be explored regardless of what the decision is.

The Catalog Assistant. Since only 20 to 40 of the nearly 10,000 trays in
the Public Catalog were on microfilm, the number of persons actually
using the machines was only about 3 or 4 a day during non-peak periods.
Therefore, the assistant found most of the questions asked were either
general questions about the machiens by curious readers not using the
machine, routine questions on call slip procedure or how to find an
entry or how to use the reference books shelved close to where the assistant was stationed, and a few reference questions referred to the Information Desk. The overwhelming amount of information given by the
assistant, either in answer to specific questions or volunteered where it
seemed appropriate, concerned the following topics: the nature of the
experiment and its relation to the automation of the cataloging process,

case the repairman claimed that the problem was caused by the fact that the machines are plugged into a socket shared with a light bulb, not provided with a socket of their own. Library personnel pointed out that the intensity of the light—the only factor which would be affected by a faulty electrical connection—did not vary when the image went out of focus, and the incident in which one machine failed to light was traced to the loss of a fuse. The Library did not change the electrical connections, and a few times the machines failed to light until the assistant adjusted the plugs in the sockets, but none of the problems brought to the attention of the repairman and blamed by him on the connections later proved traceable to that factor.

Flare Spaces. When the final two cassettes were filmed, flare spaces equal to about ten cards were left everytime a drawer was completed, and a "target" (sign) indicating the next entry was inserted. Two or three times within each drawer, that is about every 500 cards, there was another flare space, with no target. The spaces were inserted for the convenience of the Photographic Services, and the targets were thought to be of possible help to readers. In practice, they rarely were helpful, since even the slowest readers turned the crank too fast to see the targets. As a matter of fact, the flare spaces caused a few readers to think the reel was over when they had come to one of those spaces.

Physical Arrangements. The scope of the experiment did not permit the study of how large numbers of machines and cassettes would be installed and maintained. Presumably, after the card catalog is removed, there would be sufficient space for several machines to be placed on each table and several sets of cassettes in racks against the wall. However they would be arranged, it was assumed that page and clerk staff now engaged in reshelving card catalog trays would be able to handle similar duties in relation to cassettes, and could easily perform routine maintenance on the machines. Checkout systems, mentioned before, could not be tested.

Conclusions

Any decision by The New York Public Library to put the retrospective public catalog on microfilm will be based on information in at least two areas beyond the scope of this report: feasibility and desirability of book catalogs as an alternative to microfilm, and financial aspects of each of the alternatives. Therefore this report can draw no final conclusions but simply outline the pros and cons of microfilm discovered during the experiment and note areas which need further study.

It appears as though most of the technical problems connected with film can be answered, but there are two—the searching and browsing problems—which cannot be overcome using the machines tested in the experiment. If other microfilm machines are developed which cut down searching and browsing time without too large an increase in cost, then the most important technical problem connected with microfilm will be reduced. However, motorized machines and machines with index numbers or special call-up devices may have their own problems. Further experimentation—such as the test of motorized Memorex machines in the Cataloging Branch—would be necessary for each type of machine.

As people become used to the machines, and as older readers are replaced by younger ones, problems connected with user acceptability can be expected to decrease over time. However, scholars and regular users can be expected to continue at much the same rate their complaints that the searching and browsing problems cost too much in time and effort. Another problem has not been adequately researched in this experiment: the possibility that readers can become "dizzy" or even "sick" from using the machines for a long time or that their eyesight may be so bad that they cannot read the entries at all. Research would have to establish how many and what kinds of readers who now use the card catalog would be cut off from the microfilm catalog for one of these reasons.

Administratively, the microfilm catalog can be expected to fit into the structure of the Library with no new or insurmountable problems. It appears that they can be supervised by assistants below the librarian level, though problems may arise in connection with the fact that they will therefore be unable to provide the full range of information services. Further research, perhaps, and careful planning would have to establish the proper classification of the position, the training required, and the precise duties to be performed. Careful attention should be paid especially to the relationship of the assistant to the reader on the one hand, and the librarian on the other.

Librarians and scholars seem fond of claiming that it is easier to find a book at The New York Public Library than at Harvard or the British Museum or the Bibliotheque Nationale. It does not seem from their comments that adopting the microfilm catalog with its time factor would put us "behind" in that comparison—but it would cut our "lead" a little. The fact that this Library is more convenient than ones elsewhere would be no reason to make it a little less convenient.

Notes to Report

Presumably those who evaluate the experiment will read the diary in its entirety (including the "notes on methodology"—which explain, among other things, the abbreviations used in the diary—and the other material used in connection with the experiment). However, some examples drawn from the diary illustrate points made or alluded to in the report. Following are some incidents with the date and time given:

11-11, 1:20 - The incident ending in the 'Administrative Office.' A reader was talking to the librarian at the Information Desk, who turned and pointed in my direction. I got up as reader walked over. "Dickens, please. The catalog." I got the proper cassette, inserted it in machine #2, and turned the crank to the "Dickens" entries. "Are you going to look through it, or is there anything in particular you want?" Reader had pulled up a chair, "I want to look through it." I explained that the "Dickens" entries begin with all "Collected Works," then "Selected Works," then individual works by title, then "Letters," "Miscellany," "Poetry," "Selections," and then entries for things he co-authored or edited, followed by works about him. "Can you turn it backwards and forwards." "Yes. Also, here's the focus knob. It will go out of focus. Here's how you turn it off, and this is for light intensity—you don't need that."

While reader was at machine, I found the appropriate secondary (supplementary) tray. "Here are a few more. Any card with something typed in the upper left-hand corner for a book received in the last few years *might* be in here." "Thanks a lot."

Later I wandered over to the reader to make sure everything was all right. "I'd better check that entry. I think you need a number after that p.v." (Dickens, Charles. . . Selected Works (Charles Ludwig)). Reader said, "It should be 79, I think. Here it is down here." "Oh, yes." What looked like part of a classmark was repeated on another part of the card. "I'll check anyway; I don't have anything else to do." I checked the cards in the enclosure. "It's 79. You're right."

Half an hour later, reader was still there. "It's dreadful. Too time-consuming." "It's an experiment. They microfilmed 20 catalog trays to see whether or not to do it to the whole catalog. They're changing to a new cataloging system using a computer, so they're going to freeze this catalog and put it either on microfilm or in book form." (One of my "semi-standardized descriptions," usually abbreviated "Expl. experiment, old & new catalogs," in the diary.) Reader claimed to like cards better, mentioning the focus, browsing, and searching problems, and saying that in a book catalog it is possible to see more entries at once.

Shortly after, I went on my lunch hour, and a relief person was at the machines. Several of the reader's call slips were returned for "verifies" and a librarian came over to check the entries on the cards. The librarian was unable to locate the entries on film corresponding to those on the returned callslips, so after a while the librarian took the tray from the enclosure and located the entries there.

According to the librarian, there were two primary reasons for the inability to locate the proper entries on film. First the guide cards, which in this case contained filing instructions, were not filmed; this mistake was corrected when subsequent trays were filmed. Second, the librarian, who admittedly had had little experience with the machine, was unable to figure out quickly the organization of the entries by acting on hunches and skipping back and forth. The fact that the callslips were filled out in a confused way made no difference, since the librarian was able to match them with the appropriate cards in the card tray.

Reader left the area around 2:45, after having appeared disgusted with the machine and the amount of time it took, and commenting in addition that "it's bad on the eyes."

According to a staff member in Room 214, the reader then went there. (Room 214 is the Research Libraries Administrative Office, and complaints, among other things, are handled there.) Reader talked with Mr. Baker, a short while, describing the incidents which had just taken place. Reader claimed to use the library a lot, and that the machines would be a great handicap since they double the time necessary to perform tasks requiring the catalog. Mr. Baker listened, then said the incident and reader's complaints would be recorded by those involved in the experiment. The reader seemed satisfied.

One thought occurred to me later: what if a reader's objection was not to the machine but to me, or what if a reader for some reason decided I could not be trusted to give their opinion proper consideration, or what if a reader and I had a clash of personalities? If no one else was asked to record information on the experiment (e.g. librarians at the Information Desk, personnel in Room 214), valuable information could be lost.

Incidents concerning the Memorex repairman:

7-22, 12:45; 8-4, 4:05; 8-6, 10:10 & 11:45 & 1:45; 8-26, 4:15; 8-27, 10:45 & 1:50; 8-30, 3:45 (pp. 2, 27, 32, 33 75, 77-78, 81)

The first of the incidents concerning the Memorex repairman happened the first day of the experiment. He was called out and shown the focus problem. He was told that the film appears in focus at first, then jumps out after a few seconds. This problem was demonstrated to him. The repairman replied that the problem originated in the power supply and recommended that the Library tell its "electrician to put in another outlet for the machine rather than running it off the lamp." He said that what made him sure it was the outlet was the fact that the lamp was in focus and then jumped out; if it had not, the problem could have been something else. He was asked why the intensity of the light appeared unchanged, since problems originating in the power supply would logically affect light intensity. "You don't know a lot about these things, do you," he smiled. Then he repeated his explanation.

August 4, when machine #2 failed to light at 4:00 in the afternoon, I switched light bulbs with #1, and #2's bulb lit in #1. I asked a couple of people where there were spare light bulbs, but no one knew. Then I called Memorex; they said they'd be out the next morning. As I recall, the man again claimed the problem was the power connection. Two days later, Mr. Lorona said he would call Memorex again. In the meantime, Louis Falck discovered that the fuse in #2 was missing. We tried the fuse from #1, and it worked in #2. We told Mr. Lorona, who said he would call Memorex and arrange for some spare fuses and light bulbs. That afternoon the Memorex man arrived and said the salesman should have explained the procedure for getting new bulbs, and told Louis and me to get new fuses marked 250 watts, 2 amperes.

On August 26, the third incident began. I was instructed to call Memorex about the fact that in #2 the sides may be out of focus when the middle is not, or the top may be out when the bottom is fine, and the fact that the lines of type are closer together on the left side than the right. Also, the alignment on the left was off. I called Memorex the next morning, and described the problems to someone who took the message and promised to send someone right out. In the meantime Mr. Sajor fixed the alignment problem himself by adjusting the mirror and said he and Mr. Noble were working on the focus problems. The next working day Memorex had not shown up, but Mr. Lorona decided not to call again, since the problems were under control.

The only time anything about the "sight problem" was ever tested:

9-13, 12:15 (p. 107) - A friend of a staff member, who had been by to see the machines before, asked for help in finding an entry in the National Union Catalog close by. He had left his glasses downstairs by accident. I found it for him and then asked him to see if he could see the entries on microfilm. He had to stand a "normal" distance from the machine, i.e. he could not lean over and put his face close to the screen, but otherwise he had no trouble. I asked him to look at the cards in a tray: a little trouble, but he could read them. I showed him Volume 4 of the Berg Collection book catalog, a 15-inch high book with photographs of 21 catalog cards on each page. He could read them only with difficulty and only from a distance of slightly more than arm's length. Incidentally, while we were discussing the new catalog, I mentioned that entries in the prospective catalog would resemble those in the Mid-Manhattan catalog. He made a face, saying they had left out information he needed, which was that a book was for reference only.

REPORT ON MICROFILM CATALOG EXPERIMENT
(CLR Grant No. 516)

Part II: Use of Microfilm for Authority File

April 11, 1972

Part II of the Microfilm Project funded by the Council on Library Resources, the purpose of which was to test the feasibility of an Authority File on microfilm cassettes, came to a close on February 29, 1972. The experiment began on October 1, 1971, and was scheduled to the concluded on December 31, 1971. Since the extension of the project for an additional two months did not significantly increase the cost of the project, it was believed that extending the time frame would permit involvement of larger numbers of cataloging personnel in an experiment which might have significant implications for the introduction of new techniques in the automated book catalog system.

The Authority File consists of a dictionary listing of all headings established for use in the new book catalog. The entries represented in the dictionary listing are those usually associated with authority files, though some libraries choose to have a separate file for subject headings. Most of the headings represent Library of Congress form of entry. Entries include personal authors, corporate entries, topical subject headings (including every permutation of subdivision and regionalization used in the book catalog), geographical entries (including topical subdivisions), series entries (including cataloging decisions), an elaborate structure of cross references, catalogers notes for internal use, and scope notes included for the use of the public in the book catalog. The Authority File also lists language codes for each entry, filing forms, type of entry code, computer-produced control numbers for retrieval maintenance. All headings are fully delimited, wherever required.

When the project commenced in October 1971, the Authority File consisted of nine thick volumes (approximately 3400 pages); when the project was concluded the file consisted of fourteen equally thick volumes (5482 pages). The Authority File will grow very considerably within the next several months. The rate of growth will probably not begin to decline for at least two years. Proposals for the merging of all topical subject headings contained in MARC records would vastly increase the size of the file. There would be obvious advantages if these headings could be merged into the Authority File, though it would represent a considerable cost increase if these were included in computer printouts. The computer printouts provided by the Systems Analysis and Data Processing Office are photographically reduced before they reach Cataloging Branch. The Authority File is cumulated quarterly and updated by weekly cumulative supplements.

The Authority File is inextricably tied to the new book catalog, with interface between authority file data and bibliographical data in the book catalog. While the Authority File is an indispensable file for the generation of headings in the automated book catalog, the extent of its use by catalogers is not completely clear at this point. Now that MARC interface has been successfully implemented, it is no longer necessary to pre-check entries in the Authority File for the approximately 1500 records which are currently being input monthly by this method. Catalogers will depend on MARC proof for guidance in establishing headings which have not already been generated in the Authority File. Basic issues and monthly cumulative supplements of the book catalog are more accessible tools for quickly checking whether a heading has been established. These two alternatives for by-passing the Authority File are very significant, but it is too early to judge, with any degree of precision, how much consultation of the Authority File will be reduced. When the project was undertaken in October 1971 a total of seventeen sets of the Authority File (including two sets on microfilm cassettes) were deemed to be necessary. With the growth of the Authority File, however, it was decided to reduce the number of sets required to ten. It is highly unlikely that this number will be reduced in the future in view of the many access points required, e.g., locations within Cataloging Branch and in foreign language divisions.

When the project began in October 1971, the input of bibliographic records was still on an experimental and limited basis. Except for two para-professionals who were concentrating exclusively on the new system of cataloging, other catalogers were phasing into the new system on a more limited scale and were cataloging a far higher number of titles for the retrospective card catalog system. July 1, 1972, has been set as the target date for the complete phase out of the retrospective system of cataloging. Due to the training requirements of the new system of cataloging, there has been a careful phasing-in of the new procedures for each new group of catalogers. Until January 1972 the new system of cataloging was largely concentrated in Monograph Cataloging Section. Serial Cataloging Section did not become involved in the new system, and with the Authority File associated with the new system, until January 1972. The extent of use of the new Authority File on the part of serial catalogers was consequently limited during January and February. Serial catalogers, by the nature of serial cataloging requirements, would do less checking of topical subject headings than monograph catalogers. Towards the end of February, cataloging personnel of Jewish and Slavonic Divisions began training in the new system of cataloging. Their training had not progressed to the point, however, where they would be making extensive use of the new Authority File. A demonstration of the use of the Authority File on microfilm cassettes was held for cataloging staff of Jewish Division and Slavonic Division.

Evaluation of the microfilm project has been based on completed questionnaires distributed to nineteen (19) professional and para-professional catalogers. Approximately fifteen (15) additional personnel had been introduced to the use of the Authority File on microfilm, but it was not felt their experience had been extensive enough to enable them to make an evaluation of the new system.

Phase II of the Microfilm Project was limited to the use of two Memorex Readers, Model 1643 (automatic) and Model 1644 (automatic with a manual override). It was decided at the outset of the experiment, based on the use of manual machines in the first phase of the project, that manual machines would not meet the requirements of rapid checking of the Authority File.

Nineteen (19) questionnaires were completed, though some participants did not choose to answer some questions due to the limited time in which they had been involved in the project. A reproduction of the questionnaire is attached. Brief comments following each question have been made by the Chief of the Processing Division. The comments are posed, in part, on written comments and conversations with the Chief Cataloger who, with the Chief of Processing Division, have monitored the project.

QUESTIONNAIRE

1. Authority File data are more quickly necessible in the

    (A) Computer printouts: *16*
    (B) Microfilm Cassettes: *3*

    > The consensus of most users is that the computer print-out provides a more rapid check. The response from the three catalogers who found the microfilm cassettes as a accessible tool is surprising. Several time checks were made which demonstrated that zeroing-in on a particular heading frequently took up to a minute, while searching the name heading in the printout could usually be accomplished in less than 30 seconds. While this type of checking was limited to random time checks, it is hard to conclude that, with the equipment used, checking is more rapid on microfilm.

2. Which Memorex Header do you prefer?

    (A) Model 1643 (Automatic) *1*
    (B) Model 1644 (Automatic with manual override) *18*

    Comment: It is extremely difficult to zero-in on a specific heading with Model 1643. The manual override on Model 1644 represents a significant improvement over the earlier model and reduces the time required for locating a specific heading.

3. Indicate type of microfilm copy you prefer

    (A) Negative copy: *7*
    (B) Positive copy: *12*

    Comment: It is not believed these figures can be considered conclusive. Sometimes the quality of copy, whether negative or positive, was not consistently good. Failure to achieve the best quality of reproduction for either negative or positive was evident from time to time, so it is possible that participants were largely influenced by a poor negative while the positive of the same data may have reached standard requirements. From the standpoint of both legibility and focusing, second generation positives and third generation negatives were consistently of high standards. Catalogers traditionally work more frequently with positive copy and this conditioning may account for some bias on this question. If the proposal to accept the Authority File on microfilm is approved, further experimentation in the use of negative and positive copy would be recommended.

4. Focusing is better on

(A) Negative copy: *9*
(B) Positive copy: *8*

Comment: Two participants thought focusing on the different copies was insignificant. It was not until late in the project that it was felt that reproduction of both nega tives and positives achieved a high standard.

5. Did you find the line-guide attachment on Model 1644 useful?

(A) Yes: *6*
(B) No: *11*

Comment: The line-guide is an attachment of no great significance. It should be considered an optional attachment which catalogers might choose to use or to ignore. Most use of the Authority File is concentrated on data on the left side of the file, but the line-guide could possible be of some limited use when it becomes necessary to do some maintenance which would make lining-up of data on the right side of the file with that on the left.

6. Would you prefer placement of reader at

(A) Sitting height: *18*
(B) Standing height: *1*

Comment: No readers were placed at standing height. If suitable furniture and space becomes available, it might be advisable to have both types. Catalogers going from their desks to the readers to make a quick check might find a standing location faster to use. For individuals doing extensive checking, the sitting height is obviously preferable. If the proposal to accept the Authority File on microfilm is approved, experiment with reader placement may be recommended.

7   This project has been limited to microfilm on Memorex cassettes. If
     you have had experience in the use of other microform formats,
     please indicate which of the following you find most acceptable:

     (A) Cassette: *13*
     (B) Roll microfilm: *0*
     (C) Microfiche: *0*

     Comment: Six catalogers did not feel they had had enough experi-
                  ence with other formats of microform to reply to this
                  question. While microfilm on cassettes is not without
                  flaws, the experience catalogers have had with this for-
                  mat has probably been more responsible, than any other
                  factor, for overcoming many of the traditional objec-
                  tions librarians have to microfilm.

8.   Have you found obstacles in the use of the readers?

     (A) Yes: *13*
     (B) No: *6*

     Comment: See comments under 9 below.

9.   If your answer to the above question is yes, what was the obstacle to
     your use of the reader?

     (A) Queuing: 7
     (B) Reader malfunction: 7
     (C) Delay in filming of the Authority File: *3*
     (D) Other: Eyestrain (2) and jamming of cassettes (3)

     Comment: The experiment was limited to the use of two readers
                  and not infrequently to one reader (for reasons of reader
                  malfunction) so the problem of queuing was not unex-
                  pected. In the event the proposal to accept the Authority
                  File on microfilm is approved, enough readers to prevent
                  any undue queuing would have to be requisitioned. Ma-
                  chine malfunction was primarily due to the frequent
                  burning out of lamps. There was also jamming of casset-
                  tes. Servicing of readers interrupted use of readers. While
                  only three catalogers complained about the delay in the
                  filming of the Authority File, I believe this was one of
                  the most serious flaws in the experiment. Cassettes for
                  the latest weekly cumulative supplements were removed
                  when superseded by a later weekly printout. This forced
                  users to use the printout instead of the cassette. If we
                  were to adopt microfilm as a substitute for printouts,
                  however, catalogers would be handicapped if they did
                  not have prompt access to microfilm supplements. Dur-
                  ing the course of the experiment catalogers were always
                  able to fall back on the use of the printouts if micro-

film of the same data was not yet available. On at least three occasions the weekly cumulative supplement on microfiche did not arrive until *after* the following weekly cumulative supplement was available in the printout. The weekly cumulative supplement on microfilm was prepared by an outside firm (Xerox). The delay in receipt of the microfilm varied, the microfilm was received too late for use. If we are to use the Authority File on microfilm, it would be essential camera equipment would be made available within Photographic Service so we could be assured delivery of microfilm within 24 hours of receipt of computer printout by Photographic Service. In my opinion, delays encountered in the filming of the Authority File was the most conspicuous failure of the experiment.

10. With which system are you more likely to batch worksheets for Authority File checking?

(A) Computer printouts: *6*
(B) Microfilm cassettes: *10*

Comment: Catalogers working with worksheets accompanied by Library of Congress cataloging copy are more likely to batch their work than catalogers who are doing original cataloging. Since it is possible to remain in a seated position while checking a large number of worksheets against microfilm, I am not a little surprised that some catalogers found it more expedient to batch worksheets with computer printouts. Most individuals who did a large amount of batching worksheets preferred the microfilm cassettes over the computer printout. It is my personal view that batching of worksheets is a more likely prospect, if one could remain seated, and work with two or more cassettes, than to consult a dozen or more volumes of the printout. It must be conceded, however, that it takes less time to locate an entry in a printout than on microfilm.

11. Has the selection of the correct cassette been a problem?

(A) Yes: *1*
(B) No: *16*

Comment: Since the experiment never involved the use of more than three (3) cassettes, no problem was expected. In the event we accept the Authority File on microfilm, display racks or holders would be used. There is very little space for labelling contents of each cassette, but this is not a serious obstacle to acceptance.

12. How many readers do you believe would be required in your section
    if this system should be adopted?

    (A) Monograph Cataloging Section: *4* readers (average)
    (B) Serial Cataloging Section: *2*

    Comment: The Chief Cataloger and I agree that five (5) readers
                would be required for Monograph Cataloging Section.
                There is, of course, a higher production rate in Mono-
                graph Cataloging than in Serial Cataloging. Two readers
                should be adequate to meet the needs of Serial Catalog-
                ing. Not only is the prodcution rate lower in this section
                but there would be far less need to consult the Author-
                ity File for subject headings in this unit. One additional
                reader would be required for placement in Jewish Divi-
                sion and one in Slavonic Division. Oriental Division
                should be able to share the reader in Slavonic Division.
                A total of nine (9) readers would be necessary to meet
                cataloging requirements of The Research Libraries.

13. Should copies of the book catalog be located in the same work area
    where the Authority File is located?

    (A) Yes: *17*
    (B) No: *2*

    Comment: While 17 catalogers responded affirmatively to this ques-
                tion, in the opinion of the Chief Cataloger it does not
                seem likely that catalogers would be constantly checking
                back and forth between the two bibliographic sources.
                The new book catalog system is still such a new concept
                in The Research Libraries, it is perhaps premature to
                reach a conclusion about this question. I agree with the
                view of the Chief Cataloger, but if the microfilm system
                is accepted, experimentation in the display of biblio-
                graphical tools could be considered within space limita-
                tions.

14. The Authority File will grow very considerably in the next several
    months. Growth will continue through the years, though at a dimin-
    ishing rate. If adopted, a sufficient number of readers would be pur-
    chased to avoid queuing. The availability of other equipment, and
    other types of microform format, would also be considered. Consid-
    ering the factor of space saving, and the considerable cost savings of
    microfilm over computer printouts, would you find Authority File
    data in microform an acceptable substitute for the computer print-
    out?

    (A) Yes: *18*
    (B) No: *1*

Comment: The lack of space in Cataloging Branch is so critical that
it is difficult to overstate its seriousness. Long before the
Authority File reached its present size we realized we
would be confronted with space problems for the display
of this file as well as issues of the book catalog. Space
and cost factors have undoubtedly weighed heavily in
the affirmative response noted above.

Summary

Despite some of the flaws that appeared in the course of the experiment,
microfilm as a substitute for Authority File printouts appears to be acceptable to most catalogers. The use of cassettes, as opposed to roll microfilm, seems to have had the effect of overcoming some prejudices individuals may have had towards microfilm.

While authority file date may be more quickly located in the printouts,
and while more catalogers might prefer printouts for other reasons over
microfilm, it is encouraging to note that most catalogers agree that microfilm would be an acceptable substitute for printouts. All catalogers are
very much aware of space problems and the fiscal distress of The Research
Libraries, but it is doubtful catalogers would find microfilm an acceptable
substitute for these reasons alone.

Attached to this report is a paper prepared by Mr. Richard G. Noble,
of the Systems Analysis and Data Processing Office, relating to the costs
of printouts versus microfilm costs. It should be pointed out that Mr.
Noble's estimates are based on the production of seventeen (17) sets of the
printouts, but in the meantime it has been found possible to accommodate
present needs with ten (10) sets of the printouts. Mr. Noble's presentation
nevertheless makes a positive case for the acceptance of microfilm as an
alternative to printouts. Processing Division has submitted a request for
funds in the 1972/73 budget for the possible implementation of a microfilm system for the Authority File. It should be noted it is crucial that
funds would also have to be allocated for the purchase of camera equipment which would make it possible to make in-house microfilm copies of
the Authority File.

While there were certain flaws, or shortcomings, in the microfilm
project, I believe most would be subject to correction or improvement.
The consensus that microfilm is an acceptable substitute for computer
printouts is encouraging. As a result of this experiment, I recommend the
adoption of microfilm as a substitute for computer printouts for the Authority File.

The question of adopting microforms in other areas of Preparation Services should be explored or encouraged. The official catalogs, consisting of
several million cards and which duplicate most of the public catalogs, ex-

cept for subject headings and indexed items, occupy much valuable space
in Preparation Services which is needed very urgently for other purposes.
There will be a continuing need for the official catalogs although the use of
these catalogs will decline. Contained in the official catalogs are data not
represented elsewhere. The official catalogs will be heavily used in rehabili-
tating public catalogs which are scheduled for publication in book form. If
reader/printers could produce acceptable copy, the catalogs on microfilm
might be efficient tools for the rehabilitation project.

Allen J. Hogden
Chief, Processing Division

THE NEW YORK PUBLIC LIBRARY
LIBRARY MEMORANDUM

From: R. C. Noble   *Date:* November 23, 1971
To: Mr. Allen Hogden   *Re:*   Xerox versus Microfilm
                                          Costs

   Attached is a set of calculations estimating the cost of Xeroxing the Research authority list versus the cost of microfilming these lists. The calculations show that utilizing microfilms in the period from October 1971
through June 1972 would realize a savings of approximately $8,000. This
cost savings would mean that you could afford to purchase Memorex microfilm readers and produce the microfilm in that same period instead of
utilizing the Xerox copies. These cost estimates are based upon the
premise that the rate of accumulation for authority entries will continue
to be about the same as it is now.
   An increase in the number of bibliographic entries would mean a corresponding widening of the gap between the microfilm and Xerox costs.
These costs should be taken as estimates only, but barring drastic changes
in the input rate, or the cost of producing the microfilm, they should have
about a 10% accuracy. The cost difference is so large that it may even pay
to go to a much more expensive reader if this will make the difference between acceptance and non-acceptance of the microfilm by the catalogers
of Preparation Services. A mix of Xeroxing the small supplements (under
200 pages) and filming the larger supplements and reaccumulations could
also be accomplished.
   The cost of producing the microfilm is based upon the present cost to
us of going to an outside service and having the NYPL Photographic Services reproduce the film. If NYPL Photographic Services, were to do the
filming themselves, we probably could get the per roll cost to be less than
the $20 per 50 foot roll cost now charged by Xerox. The problem would

be to absorb the cost of the rent or purchase of a rotary camera. The rental cost of a rotary camera is approximately $160 per month. If the services rendered by an outside microfilm service are not timely enough, it would be worth our while to absorb the extra cost of a purchase of a rotary camera.

Another argument for utilizing the microfilm is that it is ecologically sounder than Xeroxing which produces mountains of waste paper. Economically it is sounder also since at the end of 8 months the Library would have 17 readers worth several thousand dollars instead of a mountain of scrap paper.

If there are any questions concerning the attached calculations, I will be glad to clarify them.

Dick Noble

DN:la

Microfilm & Xerox Costs

These computations are based upon utilizing the present system of printing the lists out on the computer printer then sending the listings to be copies. The cost of the original filming is based upon the charges to this office by the Xerox Corporation. These charges are higher than the costs that would be charged to us by the NYPL Photographic Services, if they had the proper equipment. The reason why Xerox was given the task instead of Photographic Services is because it would have been costlier to rent the proper camera to film the output than to have the Xerox Corporation film the output.

The basic costs for Xeroxing and binding the Xeroxed pages are as follows:

Cost to Xerox	0 - 50,000 pages	-	$.0216/page
	Next 50,000 pages	-	$.0136/page
Binding			$ .002/page
Misc. Costs (Covers, binders, etc.)			$.0014/page
		TOTAL	$.0250/page

The basic costs for microfilm production are as follows:

Original filming based on minimum of 50 feet of film at $20.00
Copy cost based upon minimum of 50 feet of film at $3.50

Cost per page of original	$ .020
Cost per page of copy	$.0035

Sample cost to produce October cumulations:

Xeroxing: 17 copies, Xeroxed, bound of 2,600 pages
            27 x 2,600 - 44,200 total pages
            Cost - 44,200 x $.0250 - $1,105.00

                        TOTAL COST $1,105.00

Microfilm: Cost to film 2,600 pages - 2,600 fit on 100 feet
            Cost - $40.00

            Cost to produce 17 copies - 17 x $7.00 - $119.00
            Misc. Costs (spooling, etc.) - $10.00

                        TOTAL COST $ 169.00

Project Costs - Microfilm

No. of Pages Reaccumulation	No. of Pages In Supplement	Cost to Microfilm Original @ $20 min.	Cost to Produce Copies ($5-7/copy)
2,600 10/30/71	Total 3245 - 8 weeks	$160.00	$ 640.00
3,231		40.00 (2 rolls)	238.00
	Total 3250 (9 weeks)	180.00	720.00
3,831 (2/1/72)		60.00	238.00
	Total 4620 (11 weeks)	220.00	880.00
4,501 (4/18/72)		60.00	238.00
	Total 3850 (10 weeks)	200.00	800.00
5,201 (6/22/72)		70.00	280.00
		$990.00	$4,034.00

Project Costs - Xerox
at Addition Rate of 70 Pages Per Week

No. of Pages Reaccumulation	No. of Pages Supplement	Cost to Xerox & Bind (17 copies) @ $.0250
2,600 (10/30/71)		

177

263	
318	
389	
426	
480	
561	
<u>631</u>	
TOTAL 3,245	$1.379 125
	$1,373.175

3,231 (2/1/72)

70	
140	
210	
280	
350	
420	
490	
560	
<u>630</u>	
TOTAL 3,150	$1,338.75
	$1,628.175

3,831 (2/1/72)

70	
-	
-	
-	
-	
11 weeks	
-	
-	
<u>770</u>	
TOTAL 4,620	$1,963.50
	$1,912.925

4,501 (4/18/72)

70	
-	
-	
-	
10 weeks	
-	
-	
<u>700</u>	
TOTAL 3,850	$1,636.25
	$2,210.425

5,201 (6/22/72)

$13,442.325

Part III: **A.** *Use of Microfilm as Substitute for Book Catalog*
by Preparation Services Personnel

Part III A of the Microfilm Project, the book catalog on microfilm, was
carried out by Monograph Cataloging Section, Serial Cataloging Section,
and Searching Section during the month of March. Due to the phasing in
of the new system of cataloging, Part II of the experiment, the Authority
File on microfilm, was extended to a total of five months in order to allow
for the participation of as many members as possible of the Cataloging
Branch staff. While the results of Part III A may, in many ways, be deemed
inconclusive, it is doubtful the results would have been otherwise had the
experiment extended beyond the duration of one month. A total of 44
staff members of Cataloging Branch participated in the project. Of this
total, 24 were professional librarians and 20 were para-professionals. Part
III of the Microfilm Project was not limited, of course, to participation by
members of the Cataloging Branch. The major part of this part was conducted at the Public Catalog in the General Research and Humanities Division over a three month period.

The basic volumes of the *Dictionary Catalog of the Research Libraries*
(January 1972) and the monthly cumulative supplement for the month of
March 1972 were used for the experiment. These parts of the catalog were
placed on the cassettes for each of three microfilm readers. The microfilm
readers used in the experiment were (1) Xerox reader with two-part cassettes, (2) Memorex reader (automatic), Model 1643, and (3) Memorex
reader (automatic with manual override), Model 1644.

The following is a summary of the results of 44 questionnaires completed by members of the Cataloging Branch. A copy of the questionnaire
is attached.

1. Except for three users, the Memorex reader, Model 1644 (automatic with manual override) was rated as the test reader.

   Except for three users, the Memorex reader, Model 1644 (automatic)
   was rated as second choice.

   Except for two users, the Xerox reader was rated as third choice.

2. Most readers found the Xerox reader to be unacceptable. While two
   users commented on the excellent resolution of this reader, most
   readers found this equipment unacceptable because of the difficulty
   of placing or removing the two-part cassette. The two-part cassette
   was extremely cumbersome to manipulate and the risk of damage to
   the film was always present. The Memorex reader, Model 1643 (automatic) presented many difficulties in zeroing-in on a particular entry.
   The Memorex reader, Model 1644 (automatic with manual override)
   was rated the best reader, but several users pointed out that it took
   longer, even under the best conditions, to locate an entry on micro-

film than in the computer printouts.

3. Forty-two (42) users responded negatively to the question whether there was any advantage in the use of microfilm over the printed volume.

4. Opinion on the question of whether microfilm would be an acceptable substitute for the printed book catalog, once the latter had grown to considerable size, e.g., 20 volumes, was evenly divided with 22 positive and 22 negative responses.

5. The question of whether microfilm for the monthly cumulative supplement would be an acceptable substitute for the monthly printed format. If the basic cumulation were made available in printed volumes, drew nineteen (19) positive and twenty-five (25) negative responses.

6. Twenty-four (24) users expressed the opinion they would find computer output microfilm (COM), if it were to become available, less acceptable than the photocomposed catalog with various type faces. Eighteen (18) users expressed the view that COM, if it were made available, would make no difference from the standpoint of acceptability. Two (2) users expressed the view that COM, if it were made available, would be a more acceptable format than the photocomposed catalog with various type faces.

7. Twenty-seven (27) users responded they would find microfilm a more acceptable substitute, for the authority file, while ten (10) individuals expressed the view that microfilm was a more acceptable substitute for the book catalog, including supplements.

While most participants chose not to make detailed comments on the experiment, the following comments by a few individuals are pertinent:

1. If supplements were placed on microfilm, catalogers would be more inclined to use the weekly cumulative bibliographic in-process list than they would supplements on microfilm.

2. The present book catalog format with constrasting type-faces would probably be easier to scan and search on microfilm than COM output would be.

3. A few users commented that when the printed book catalog had achieved considerable size, a single set would permit access to several readers at the same time, but that use of microfilm with much data

condensed on a single cassette would make purchase of several microfilm readers a necessity.

4. One participant made an observation on the size of the microfilm
readers, and suggested that more emphasis should be placed on miniaturization of readers. The exhibits at the recent meeting of the National Microform Association would indicate this development is
taking place. Severe space limitations in Preparation Services would
make it very difficult to place microfilm readers. If microfilm were to
be accepted as a substitute for the book catalog, or for authority files.

5. Several serial catalogers indicated that cataloging in this area was less
likely to be a mass production activity and the consultation of both
the book catalog and the authority file would be far less frequent
than it would be for monograph catalogers. Serial catalogers who expressed a view on this subject indicated a decided preference for the
printed book catalog over a microform substitute.

6. Several catalogers commented on future space savings in the use of
microfilm over the printed catalogs and authority files. None of these
catalogers expressed a preference for microfilm as a format over the
printed book, however.

Conclusion

While the results of this phase of the experiment are inconclusive, the consensus, based on the results of the two phases in which Cataloging Branch
participated, would be that microfilm would be a more acceptable substitute for the authority file than it would be for the book catalog and/or
supplements to the book catalog. It is open to question whether this conclusion might have been reached if the book catalog had achieved the same
bulk as the authority file. The authority file on microfilm as an acceptable
substitute would appear to be a more viable prospect than the book catalog at this time.

                                          /s/ *Allen J. Hogden*
                                          Allen J. Hogden
                                          Chief, Processing Division

REPORT ON MICROFILM CATALOG EXPERIMENT
(CLR Grant No. 516)

*Part III. **B.** Use of Microfilm as Substitute for Book Catalog
in Public Catalog Room*

The third part of the microfilm experiment was, as mentioned earlier, conducted both in the Processing Division and in the Public Catalog Room of The Research Libraries, under the administration of the General Research & Humanities Division. This part of the report deals with the latter location and with public response to microfilm as a substitute for the Research Libraries book catalog. The period covered extends from January 24 to March 31, 1972.

With the phasing out of the card catalog system as of December 31, 1971, the new book catalog of The Research Libraries came into use as the principal means of public access to titles with 1972 imprint dates. Accordingly, multiple copies of the January 1972 issue of the book catalog (representing books and book-like materials added to the collections since January 1, 1971) were placed in public service divisions of The Research Libraries, as well as in those areas of Preparation Services where consultation with the official catalog had been necessary.

As in Part I of the experiment, and in continuation of it, access to the holdings of The Research Libraries for this period was limited in the Public Catalog Room to microfilm in the case of the January cumulation and the February supplement of the new book catalog. Both were available in negative and positive copies for use on the two Memorex 1642 viewers retained from Part I of the experiment. The March supplement was used only in book form. In this way it was possible to obtain reader response to negative as opposed to positive microfilm, microfilm as opposed to the card catalog, and microfilm as opposed to the book catalog.

Throughout this period the assistants assigned to the project were asked to record comments by the public and to explain the nature of the experiment when this seemed appropriate. Comments recorded, as in Part I, covered a wide range of interest and opinion, but an attempt has been made to summarize tham as follows:

1. *Advantages of film and book over card catalogs:*

   a. Items easily missed in flipping cards rapidly. Items more visible in book catalog or on film.

   b. New material made known to reader faster. No delays in printing or filing cards.

   c. Search in a more limited area. Card catalog extends around a large room.

    d. Researcher from another institution can search file at a distance from New York if film or book catalog is generally available.

    e. Some readers find searching book catalog faster than card catalog.

2. *Advantages of card catalog over book and filmed catalogs:*

    a. All works by one author or on one subject filed together. Necessary to look in more than one place with book or filmed catalogs (both cumulation and supplement).

    b. If date of publication not known, search has to take place in both card catalog and book or filmed catalog.

    c. Tracings are present on cards, not in book or filmed catalog.

    d. Some readers find searching card catalog takes less time than either book or film. Reference librarians find card catalog helpful with telephone requests.

3. *Advantages of book over microfilm:*

    a. With book catalog, random access is possible. Open volumes where you wish. With microfilm, necessary to crank until you reach your destination.

    b. No problems with machines and maintenance.

    c. Some readers find film hard on the eyes.

4. *Technical problems:*

    a. Improved equipment would save time wasted during breakdowns (focusing chain found to slip off wheel too easily).

    b. The two machines were not found to operate with the same degree of ease on the part of the user.

    c. Focusing found to be a major problem, with constant manipulating necessary.

    d. Objections raised to time required for hand operated machines (automatic machines were not used in the Public Catalog Room).

    e. Plastic cassettes found to be easily breakable.

    f. Positive microfilm easily became dirty and scratched.

    g. No guides on film to indicate major alphabetical divisions. Large lettering suggested at intervals on file to indicate quickly how far reader has progressed in going to his desired item.

The foregoing represents in effect a distillation of over 200 pages of the journal which was kept by the assistants assigned to the project during this phase of the experiment. It should be noted that comments quoted reflect opinions both of the public and of the reference staff.

If it is possible to evaluate this phase of the experiment, it may be said that reader response was similar to that received in Part I of the experiment. One important difference, however, is the fact that the needed public information was in all instances legible on the film produced from the new book catalog; this was not the case in Part I, which involved microfilming of cards which were in themselves: illegible or damaged. The implication here is that, if the book catalog should not be available, the needs of the reader could be met, though perhaps imperfectly, by microfilm.

The New York Public Library
The Research Libraries Processing Division

Microfilm Project — Phase III

Staff of Processing Division who participated in Phase III of the Microfilm Project, the book catalog on microfilm, are requested to complete the following questionnaire. Many technical questions in the questionnaire for Phase II have been omitted. If you have altered your opinion on any of these questions, or didn't respond to some of the questions on Phase II, please comment on page 2 of this questionnaire.

1. Phase III used two Memorex readers and one Xerox reader. Please indicate your order of preference (1,2,3) for the three readers:

   (A) Xerox reader with two-part cassette _____

   (B) Memorex Reader, Model 1643 (automatic) _____

   (C) Memorex Reader, Model 1644 (automatic with manual override) _____

2. If you found any of the above readers unacceptable, please identify the reader, and list your objections:

3. In this phase of the experiment, the basic volume (January 1972) and the March cumulative supplement were reproduced on microfilm. At this stage of development of the book catalog, do you find any advantage in the use of microfilm over the printed volume?

   (A) Yes _____

   (B) No _____

4. Would you find microfilm an acceptable substitute for the printed book
   catalog once the latter has grown to considerable size, e.g., 20 volumes?

   (A) Yes _____

   (B) No _____

5. Would you find microfilm for the monthly cumulative supplement an
   acceptable substitute for the monthly printed volume, if the basic cumulation were made available in printed volumes?

   (A) Yes _____
   (B) No _____

6. If computer output microfilm (COM) were available, with upper and
   lower case characters similar to those used in the Authority File, would
   you find this

   (A) More acceptable than the photocomposed catalog with various
        type faces _____

   (B) Less acceptable   ”   ”   ”   ”   ”   ”
        type faces _____

   (C) No difference _____

7. At this stage of development of the new system of cataloging microfilm
   in a more acceptable substitute for

   (A) The Authority File _____

   (B) The Book Catalog, including supplements _____

8. *Additional comments:*

_____   _____   _____
     (Name)   (Unit)   (Date)

16MM MICROFILM AND
CARD CATALOG DUPLICATION

by Roger L. Christian and Claudia Jordan

The Washington County Library recently received an unusual loan from a local bank. They borrowed an idea—that of applying bank procedures in order to furnish a microfilm copy of the card catalog in the headquarters in Greenville to libraries throughout the county system.

Visiting the accounting department of a local bank, the Library Director observed a clerical employee using a Recordak 600K Rotary Camera to microfilm the bank's daily transactions. Upon inquiry, he learned that the film was returned to the bank completely processed within forty-eight hours and permanently stored for future use. The speed at which the equipment is able to photograph documents is 615 check-size targets per minute, and the camera can eject the targets in the same sequence in which they enter the machine. Thus, 3 x 5 library cards can be taken directly from the card trays, photographed, and then returned to the tray in the same order.

The project—providing a bibliographic record of the total library collection on 16mm microfilm in cartridges—was planned in three phases. The goal of Phase I was to determine the cost and time involved in duplicating the card catalog on microfilm. Phase II's objective is to determine patron-staff reaction during a period of twelve months. Phase III would be the actual purchase and installation of equipment on a permanent basis in the various libraries throughout the system.

Phase I

A sales representative of Southern Microfilm Corporation was contacted, and, for a monthly rental fee of $100, this firm agreed to supply the

Reprinted from *Mississippi Library News*, 37: 98-100 (June 1973) by permission of the publisher. Copyright © 1973 by the Mississippi Library Association.

library with a Recordak Rotary Camera with an automatic feed system and a 24X film unit.

The Recordak 600-K Microfilmer accommodates the special require-ments of a variety of systems. It is adjustable to operate at any of three speeds. Additional system adaptability is provided by the automatic feeder, which can be adjusted for variable spacing between images. The settings can be adjusted at any time to compensate for any change in sys-tem requirements. Targets can be microfilmed at a selection of reduction ratios available with Reliant 600-K interchangeable film units, which are extremely simple to load and interchange. Visual and audible alarm signals command operation attention when the film supply nears exhaus-tion or in the event of a film unit loading or threading error. A lamp-out signal glows and the machine stops when an exposure lamp needs replac-ing. The automatic exposure control accessory electronically reads the background density of the individual target and sets the correct exposure to provide high consistency of uniform image quality in microfilming tar-gets with varying background colors.

All controls and indicators are mounted on the front panel of the camera to provide the operator with complete finger-tip command of the microfilming operation. Target loading is a desk-top level and ejection at eye level.

The "Northstar Model 1," a Cartridge Reader was also provided at a rental fee of $25 a month. The "Northstar 1" is ideal for most industrial, commercial or institutional uses, combining ease of operation with main-tenance-free dependability and economy. Premium - price features, stand-ard on this model, include a 15" x 14" high-resolution, non-glare screen. It is easy to load, with a self-threading and automatic ejection system, and is ideal for patron use. It has a handy odometer for accurate indexing and the capacity of continuous 360 degrees optical image rotation. The total rental for equipment during Phase I of the project was $150. We used 19 rolls of 16mm x 100' microfilms at a cost of $100.70, and 19 3M Brand 16mm Microfilm Cartridges, which cost $38. Approximately 6700 catalog cards can be reproduced on one 200-foot reel of 16mm microfilm.

A clerk-typist, trained by the Southern Microfilm Corporation to oper-ate the rotary camera, was able to photograph 128,725 cards in four days. An additional day was used to label the processed film and to perform other administrative - maintenance operations. The labor cost for the five days was $83, making the total cost of Phase I come to $371.70.

Phase II

During the next twelve months, we will provide one cartridge microfilm reader to the library in Leland, and three times during this period we will supply a copy of the union catalog on nineteen rolls of microfilm loaded in cartridges for patron-staff use. This will enable us to obtain patron-staff reaction under actual working conditions, and it will provide an opportunity to test the equipment and software which would be used permanently with this system.

This phase of the project will require an expenditure of $600 for the rental of one rotary camera with automatic feed and one cartridge reader. The personnel cost during this period will be approximately $249. With software costing an additional $340, we will spend a total of $1,189.10 on Phase II.

Phase III

If the Library Board elects to enter Phase III, we will purchase five "North-star Model 1A Cartridge Readers" and one "3M Brand Microfilm Cartridge Loader," with an initial cost of $5,150. We project an annual operating cost of approximately $1,741.40, which would enable us to provide a catalog of holdings to each library (6) in our system.

The following advantages would be derived from the use of 16mm microfilm and equipment:

It provides uniformity between the catalog maintained at headquarters and the other libraries.

It provides access to the bibliographic information of all holdings in the library system to every member of the system.

It does not require highly skilled personnel, i.e., computer programmer, key punch operators, etc.

It does not require catalog maintenance at the smaller libraries.

The following disadvantages should be considered before a commitment to this system is made:

It is unable to provide information on the verso of the catalog cards at present. (This would affect only a small percentage of the cards.)

It requires a large initial investment for equipment and supplies, i.e., camera, readers, cartridge, loader, cartridges, etc.

It depends upon a supply of electricity.

The equipment will require maintenance, possibly on a contract basis.

Only one person can use the reader at any given time.

Although we feel that the advantages of this system outweigh the disadvantages, I do not think that this is the ultimate method of providing the bibliographic information of a library's holdings. This is only a stopgap until the computer's talents can be profitably used in manipulating large data files easily and efficiently in accomplishing library tasks, one of which would be a computer generator catalog for each branch library.

Until that time, it is our belief that this method is the most economical means of making the library holdings known, and therefore available, to all the people within a library system.

THE ILLINOIS STATE LIBRARY
MICROFILM AUTOMATED CATALOG (IMAC)

by Anthony W. Miele

Role of the Illinois State Library

The Illinois public library service consists of a network of eighteeen public library systems which include 97 percent of all local libraries and four research and reference centers (Chicago Public Library, Southern Illinois University, University of Illinois, and the state library). As one of the R&R centers, the state library has an obligation and responsibility to provide backup service for all other libraries in the state. To help perform this role, it has initiated a program to put its entire catalog of more than 1 million cards on microfilm.

The state library has a general book collection of more than 600,000 volumes (of which 280,000 are individual titles) and maintains a divided catalog of author/title and subject entries. The catalog lists the holdings of adult and juvenile fiction, nonfiction, and government documents.

The seventeen cooperative public library system headquarters (Chicago Public Library is both a system and R&R center), the other R&R centers, Sangamon State University, and Southern Illinois University (Edwardsville) have on deposit a copy of the Illinois Microfilm Automated Catalog (IMAC), making a total of twenty-two sets now deposited throughout the state. Eight additional sets are being held in reserve for other possible locations. Each set is mounted in cartridges.

Purpose of the Microfilm Catalog

Since the state library normally is the prime resource for material needed by the network of public library systems, the first step in an interlibrary loan request is to determine whether the state library owns the material. This initial probing involves long-distance telephone calls, inquiries via TWX, tedious transcription of bibliographic information, and the paperwork of interlibrary loan as well as call number determination. To eliminate

Reprinted from *Microform Review*, 2:1 (January 1973), pp. 27-31. Copyright © 1973 by Microform Review Inc.

this effort, the state library concluded that a microfilm catalog would vastly improve and expedite the interlibrary loan service. The New Jersey state library first developed the microfilm automated catalog.[1] We recognized the value and the workability of this project and proceeded to adapt it to our needs; the result was IMAC.

The saving in professional and clerical time has not yet been calculated, but it is significant that work loads have been increased and most of the work is now done on a clerical level. Microfilm facsimiles of the original catalog card enables the requesting library to know immediately if the state library owns a specific title. If it does not, then the requesting library can immediately refer its request to one of the other three R&R centers. This reduces the number of referrals as well.

Cost and Equipment Needed

Each system and R&R center provides its own reader-printer (approximately $1,900) which accepts cartridges and includes an odometer. Each also provides its own cartridge carousel (approximately $100) to hold the fifty-seven cartridges that represent the state library's retrospective collection (as of September 30, 1970) and current collection represented by the accumulated supplements. The current material (as of April 1, 1972) is contained in seven cartridges. The reader-printer with half-sheet and full-sheet capacity extends use to other 16mm micropublications available in cartridges, such as patients, the Illinois house and senate Bills, etc.

For our purposes, we did not figure in overhead costs. Adding 55 percent of labor costs to the figures given will give the approximate complete costs. For the state library, the total direct costs for this project amounted to $18,990.78 or $633.03 per set, and is broken down as follows:

I. State Library Labor
    A. Guide cards $4,956.40
        1. Preparation and filing
            Four catalogers, 3 1/2 hrs/day-30 days for total of 420 hrs
            @ 5.09/hr: $2,137.80
            One supervisor, 6 hrs/day-30 days for total of 180 hrs
            @ 6.73/hr: $1,211.40

        2. Typing
            Two clerk typists, 8 hrs/day-30 days for total of 480 hrs
            @ 3.14/hr: $1,507.20

    B. Transporting catalog cards to microfilm area   61.82
        One clerk, 1 hr/day-22 days for total of 22 hrs @ 2.81:
        $61.82

    C. Preparation of index   1,874.28
        1. Establishing odometer readings
            Two clerks, 7 hrs/day-15 days for total of 210 hrs @ 3.14/hr:
            $649.40

2. Editing
   One supervisor, 3 hrs/day-15 days for total of 45 hrs
   @ 6.73/hr: $302.85
3. Typing
   Two clerk typists, 7 hrs/day-10 days for total of 140 hrs
   @ 3.14/hr: $439.60
4. Laminating and cutting
   One clerk, 7 hrs/day-21 days for total of 147 hrs @ 3.08/hr:
   $452.76
5. Binding
   One clerk, 7 hrs @ 2.81/hr: $19.67

$6,792.50

II. Materials Purchased by State Library

A. Guide cards: 33,000 @ .015 .... $ 495.00

B. Paper and binders: 30 sets @ 1.75 .... 52.50

C. Cartridges: 1,770 @ 1.25 .... 2,212.50

D. Duplicating film: 500,000 ft @ $30,000/2,500 ft ... 6,000.00

TOTAL MATERIALS .... $ 8,760.00
TOTAL LIBRARY LABOR AND MATERIALS $15,522.50

III. Central Microfilm Section Labor Costs

A. Filming and inspection of master
   Two people, 7 1/2 hrs/day-29 days for total
   of 436 hrs @ 3.08/hr $1,324.88

B. Duplicating, processing, and loading of film into
   cartridges
   Six people, 7 1/2 hrs/day-18 days for total of
   630 hrs @ 3.08/hr $1,940.40

TOTAL CENTRAL MICROFILM LABOR $3,283.28

IV. Total Costs, Including Labor and Materials, for the IMAC
    Project

A. Library labor .... $ 6,792.50

B. Library materials 8,760.00

C. Central microfilm labor 3,283.28

D. Shipping and packaging 155.00

GRAND TOTAL $18,990.78

V. Cost per Set (30 sets of IMAC) ...... $ 633.03

Indexing a Cartridge

Before the catalog card file was filmed, it was planned that there would be one guide card for every thirty catalog cards. The number of guide cards varies from library to library. The state library catalog consists of 1,000 drawers. Each drawer contains 1,000 catalog cards and only seven guide cards per drawer. This meant that an additional twenty-six cards per drawer had to be prepared in order to have the one guide card per thirty catalog cards ratio. The old guide cards, however, did not lend themselves to filming with a rotary camera, so thirty-three guide cards had to be prepared for each drawer.

Catalog guide cards provide a natural index to the catalog. An index was made of each guide card and batched by cartridge number. Each cartridge was odometer-indexed for the 3-M "400 CT" reader-printer. For every guide card in a cartridge, there is an odometer reading that locates that guide card in about thirty seconds or less. The odometer index number for each guide card is posted to the index. Each cartridge is identified by cartridge number and by author/title or subject entry. The odometer puts the operator within a few frames of the desired catalog card. We have since discovered that a suitable index can be prepared without guide cards simply by using key words from an entry card heading. With a cartridge which is self-threading, the film is never touched by the operator, is always properly rewound, and is never put into a wrong box.

Updating of IMAC

Cumulative supplements, necessary to make IMAC effective, are done on a quarterly basis. To keep IMAC current, either a separate file for new cards had to be maintained or the public catalog had to be separated into a retrospective and current file. To avoid the duplication of cards for a separate file and the added costs that would result, it was decided to divide the public catalog with a retrospective (books cataloged prior to August 31, 1970) and current (books cataloged after September 1, 1970) file. At the end of each quarter, the new cards are filmed, loaded into cartridges, and sent to the locations possessing an IMAC. Since the supplements are cumulative, when a new supplement is received, the previous supplement is returned to the state library. This makes it possible to reuse the cartridges and helps to reduce future costs. At any one time there are never more than two places to search: the original holdings and the latest supplement.

How IMAC Operates

After locating the proper cartridge and mounting it on the reader-printer, the operator checks the printed guide index to find the odometer number, pushes the advance button, and locates the proper entry by advancing the film to the number. With simple adjustment of the lens, the cards are in a readable position. The reader-printer produces a printout in six seconds at a material cost of five cents per printout. This printout can be used as a request form. Thus, in a very few minutes, the user can: (1) snap on a cartridge and locate the desired card; (2) adjust the lens so that cards are in a readable position; (3) examine each individual catalog card within the guide card; (4) print out a number of the image desired; (5) rubber stamp *one* paper copy to show institution name, address, and any other essential information; (6) forward this copy to the state library as the interlibrary loan request; and (7) print out a second copy for his own internal records if so desired. The copy cost for a half-size copy is five cents per printout.

How IMAC Was Prepared

The microfilming, duplicating, loading, labeling of cartridges, and laminating of the printed index was done by the central microfilm operation of the office of the secretary of state (the state library is a division of this office). The preparation of guide cards and catalog for filming, the indexing of the microfilm, etc., was done by the state library staff.

The project utilized a new 2 1/2 mil, 16mm film, which is half the thickness of conventional film. One cartridge normally accommodates 100 feet of 5 mil film but holds 215 feet of thin film. One obvious advantage is that the number of cartridges is cut in half. Another advantage of this film is that being polyester, it is more resistant to tearing or breaking. This will help to eliminate the replacement of damaged film in the field. As of this date, there has been no replacement of film because of damage of any kind.

The filming was done with an automated-feed rotary camera which could process more than 400 cards per minute (this was the actual production rate) at a reduction ratio of 24x. With two operators working together on one camera, approximately 50,000 cards (two and a half reels) were filmed per working day. Each catalog card tray holds about 1,000 cards. One cartridge accommodates approximately 18,000 cards. The filming was completed in twenty-nine consecutive working days. Two rolls of 16mm film were filmed simultaneously: one for security and one for duplicating. Film processing was completed the following morning.

Following processing, the film was carefully inspected to observe the effects of varying print densities of light and dark type characters, type from different typewriters, and the various shades of white and off-white of the cards that were in the original file. This inspection also determined what retakes were necessary due to overlaps, distortion, image blurs, fog, or scratches that might impair the final results.

A 16mm 2 1/2 mil direct image duplicating film was used for printing distribution copies. One hundred eighteen rolls were duplicated and completely processed per day. To duplicate, inspect, and load 500,000 feet of film (thirty sets) into 1,770 cartridges took six people eighteen working days.

Methods of Requesting Interlibrary
Loans from the State Library

All requests for material should be checked against the public library system's holdings. If the material is owned and available, the system should fill the request directly. If not owned at the system level, the request can be processed by using IMAC. The identification label on the cartridge easily enables the operator to select the right cartridge for his catalog search.

With the advent of IMAC, there are now three methods to handle interlibrary loans by requesting libraries: the regular ALA form, the TWX, and the printout of IMAC.

Benefits of Using IMAC

The benefits in using IMAC are many. Specifically, IMAC: (1) allows for immediate access to the state library's holdings; (2) provides users with a valuable reference and bibliographic tool; (3) fills interlibrary loan requests in less time; (4) reduces the public library system interlibrary loan work load; (5) eliminates verification at the state level; (6) provides cataloging information; (7) provides data for bibliographies; (8) provides basis for a possible statewide bibliographic data bank; and (9) provides an archival copy of the state library's catalog for safekeeping and for additional copies if necessary.

From an interlibrary loan standpoint, IMAC means that the requesting library knows what the state library owns and, more important, what it does not own, within the limits of a three-months acquisition period. The library no longer needs to type out ALA interlibrary request forms or use TWX except for books too recent for the IMAC supplement. Being able to search the state library's catalog by subject provides for improved and faster reference service.

For the state library, IMAC means that the costly and time-consuming verification of bibliographic entry and catalog search of interlibrary loans have been eliminated for most requests. Since replies to interlibrary loans requests now take less time, more requests are filled without an increase in staff. In fact, the present staff can easily absorb a sizable increase in requests. Professional staff time for interlibrary loan has been reduced since most of the work is now clerical or semi-professional.

References

1. Oliver P. Gillock, Jr., and Roger H. McDonough, "Spreading State Library Riches for Peanuts," *Wilson Library Bulletin* (December 1970); 354-7.

SPECIFICATIONS FOR 16MM MICROFILMING OF LIBRARY CARD CATALOGS

Introduction

Because of the bibliographical importance of library card catalogs, the use of microphotography offers unique advantages both as a means of preserving this vulnerable asset and as a way to disseminate copies to other libraries and research and reference centers. For maximum usefulness, the film should be made to specifications which allow either automatic regeneration of full-size cards by means of a continuous-flow enlargement printer (such as a Copyflo machine) or the use of copies in standard microfilm reading equipment.

Two types of cameras may be used in the filming. The planetary camera photographs documents that are stationary and on a plane surface. In a rotary camera, during exposure both the film and the documents move, controlled by a transport mechanism so that there is no relative movement between them. The continuous movement of the rotary camera generally results in less control of image placement and a lower film definition and, therefore, generally lower quality hardcopy reproduction. The planetary camera produces film that is particularly adaptable to making full-size copies of the cards.

Since each use requires different film specifications, the microfilm technology outlined here includes separate specifications for production of the film on a planetary camera (allowing full-size regeneration) and on a rotary-type camera. Both specifications should produce an archival quality film. However, the advantages of high speed and low initial cost of the rotary camera as contrasted with the planetary must be weighed against the disadvantages of a microfilm of generally lower definition, less control of image placement, and consequently, a generally lower quality hardcopy reproduction should reconstitution of the hardcopy catalog ever be necessary.

This is a reprint of the Library of Congress pamphlet, *Specifications for 16mm Microfilming of Library Card Catalogs*. Washington: Library of Congress, 1974. Available from the Government Printing Office, stock no. 3000-00073, Supt. of Docs. no. LC 1.6/4:M58/3.

Description of Card Catalogs

The card catalogs of a library typically consist of cards measuring approximately 75mm x 125mm, in varying thickness. In addition to the catalog cards, each file contains a quantity of guide cards with tab and generally of heavier card stock than the card file. A shelflist or authority file may have relevant information, which also must be filmed, on the reverse of many or all cards. The size of the file to be filmed may be estimated by approximating the number of cards in each drawer and multiplying this figure by the number of drawers in each separate card catalog to be filmed.

Conditions of Filming

Library Responsibilities

The entire filming process must be under the general supervision of a responsible library staff member. To minimize the risk of losing or misfiling cards, the filming should be accomplished within the confines of the library. If space is not available, a limited and specified number of card drawers may be given to the microfilm producer for specified lengths of time, depending upon the amount of use the catalog receives. The library may furnish tables, chairs, and electrical power; all other equipment and supplies are the responsibility of the microfilm producer. The decision as to work schedule should be based on the use factor of the catalog being filmed.

Before filming the catalog, the contents of the file should be reviewed to ensure proper sequence of card trays. A reading of the entire file may also be advisable to correct misfilings, remove obsolete temporary entries, etc. The completed microfilm can be no more accurate than the file itself.

Since tab cards do not flow evenly through a rotary type camera, it may be desirable to retype the guide cards onto regular card weight stock measuring 75mm x 125mm. These would serve as targets, which would be particularly useful for films used as reference and research tools on a regular basis. To improve legibility of the guide information on the microfilm, a large type size is recommended.

Contractor Responsibilities

The filming of the contents of all catalogs should be in strict file order, with respect to both the sequential order of cards within each drawer and the numerical order of drawers in their cases. If necessary, the film should be rearranged and spliced, so that the filing sequence of the catalog and the order of drawers in the catalog is maintained on the delivered film.

Each card should be carefully placed or fed into position for filming and returned to its proper location in the file so that file integrity will be ensured. However, proper feeding of a rotary camera will not necessarily ensure file integrity, since the cards can get out of order at the camera exit.

It should be the responsibility of the microfilm production agency to ensure that the cards and catalog drawers are returned to their correct location.

The entire performance agreement (contract), including the delivery of processed, inspected, labeled, and packaged film, should be completed within a time period specified by the library. If partial deliveries of completed film rolls are required, shipments should be divided into lots and inspected as outlined in sections 7 and 11 below. After receipt of a shipment, the library should accept or reject the lots within a few working days at the rate of at least one lot per working day.

Except for testing purposes, the microfilm producer should not make, without permission, any films or copies besides those prepared according to the agreement.

Technical Specifications for Microfilming on a Planetary Camera

The microfilm to be provided through this process should conform to the following specifications. However, if any of these provisions should be found inconsistent with those published by the American National Standards Institute or other standards referred to, the specifications in this agreement should govern.

The Camera Negative Master

The master microrecord should be photographic camera negative images on unperforated 16mm microfilm. This microfilm should be a document-recording panchromatic silver halide emulsion of camera speed and very fine grain, applied to a suitable triacetate film base with an antihalation coating. The camera negative film must conform to the following American National Standards Institute specifications:

PH1.25-1965, or latest: *Safety Photographic Film*
PH1.28-1969, or latest: *Photographic Films for Permanent Records*
PH5.3-1967, or latest: *Specifications for 16mm and 35mm Silver Gelatin Microfilms for Reel Applications*

Format

Image Orientation

Images of the cards should be oriented and filmed in the 1A position so that the long edges of the card are perpendicular to the long edge of the film to within 45 minutes. The 1A position is described in ANSI PH.5.3-1967, or latest: *Specifications for 16mm and 35mm Silver Gelatin Microfilm for Reel Applications.*

Image Location

Each card image should be centered on both axes within the frame in both directions to within ± 0.005 inch (0.128mm).

Reduction Ratio

The ratio of the original card size to the recorded image must be $12\pm0.24{:}1$ or a comparable reduction ratio compatible with automatic enlargement equipment (e.g., Xerox Copyflo) and available microfilm reading devices.

Machine-Control Marks

There should be two machine-control marks associated with each image.

Image-Centering Mark

Each frame will contain an image-centering mark as described in the National Microfilm Association MS-8 *Industry Standard Document Mark (Blip) Used in Image Mark Retrieval Systems*, 1974. This will be a black mark on a transparent background at the left side of each card image (see figure 1 in appendix A). This mark is used in automatically retrieving card images on the roll film.

Card-Cutting Mark

A transparent card-cutting mark on a continuous black (i.e., an overlapping of frames) background must be provided which will enable automatic cutting of individual cards after regeneration by an enlargement printer, such as the Xerox Copyflo. A cutting machine using a photosensing device, such as an Alves Cutter, should be used. The exact size of this mark or position is determined by the microfilm producer so long as it does not interfere with the centering mark and so long as it can be used successfully with commercially available equipment and materials.

Resolution

Resolution should be measured by following *Instructions for the Use of the National Bureau of Standards Microcopy Resolution Test Chart.* All five lines of the eight-line-per-millimeter target of the NBS Microcopy Resolution Test Chart 1963A (1010) must be counted with reasonable confidence in both directions, as described in the instructions, when the film is exposed and processed so that the density of the 90-percent reflectance chart is 1.15 to 1.35 and the base-plus-fog density is 0.15 or less. This resolution must be maintained in both charts on beginning and ending test cards.

Density

Density should be measured in accordance with ANSI PH2.19-1959, or latest: *Diffuse Transmission Density.* The density difference in the microimage between the image areas of the card and the ink should be such that subsequent contact and reduction film copies and enlargement prints could be made without appreciable loss of information. When good cards of cream color and black ink are being recorded, the image density of the card (background) should usually be between 1.1 and 1.35 inclusive, with a base-plus-fog density of unexposed areas of 0.15 or less. For badly faded cards (ink or paper), the exposure must be adjusted to give a density difference between card and ink images which will produce the best contact or enlargement prints in a practical production system.

Film Processing and Handling

All silver halide film used for the archival recordings should be processed and handled carefully in accordance with the following ANSI specifications, or their most recent revisions:

PH1.28-1969: *Photographic Films for Permanent Records*
PH4.8-1971: *Method for Determining the Thiosulphate Content of Processed Black and White Photographic Films and Plates.*
PH5.4-1970: *Practice for Storage of Microfilm.*
PH5.6-1968: *Dimensions for 100-foot Reels for Processed 16mm and 35mm Microfilm.*

The recommendations made in National Bureau of Standards Technical Note 261, *Summary of Current Research on Archival Microfilm* (Washington, 1965), should also be followed.

Other Photographic Requirements

Leader and Trailer

All reels should have at least three feet of clear (unfogged) film or uncoated triacetate film base of the same base thickness for leader and three
feet of the same material for trailer.

Mechanical Defects

Microfilm produced in accordance with these specifications should have
no scratches, holes in the emulsion or base, tears, finger marks, chemical
residue, or any other defect that might adversely affect the quality and
legibility of the microimages. There should be no notches in the camera
negative.

Splicing

There should not be more than six splices in each 100 feet of film. When
splicing is required, a thermally welded joint should be used.

The Camera Test Card

The camera test card (see figure 2 in appendix A) is an assembly of the
center sections of two NBS Microcopy Resolution Test Charts (1963A
1010), three 30mm square gray scale reflectance patches, and a 76mm
scale, all mounted on a 75mm x 125mm card as illustrated in figure 2.
    The test card should be filmed at the beginning and end of each reel
with the original documents on the same camera, at the same time, and
under conditions which will yield the same density for the 90-percent
gray scale reflectance patches. To ensure that these conditions have been
met, there should be no splices between the test cards and the adjacent
10 frames.

Targets

Following the initial test cards and a blank frame, there should be a target
giving the name of the specific catalog and the date of filming. Images of
characters on this and all targets as they appear on the film must be at
least 2mm in height.
    An additional target showing the information on the drawer label, in-
cluding drawer number and roll number, should be recorded if a reel of
film corresponds to a drawer of cards; otherwise, the target should indicate the beginning and end of the sequence included on the reel.

Guide Cards

Guide cards should be recorded so that the caption appearing in the tab area is not cut off when cards are enlargement printed and automatically cut.

When filming guide cards, position the top edge of the tab as if it were the top edge of the card in order to ensure that the information on the tab is retained when cards are enlargement printed and automatically cut.

Packaging and Labeling

Film Packaging

Boxes

Film should be supplied by the contractor in standard 4- x 4- x 7/8-inch boxes which must be approved for use as archival storage containers. These boxes, as well as the reels, should be made of an inert material and be free from chemicals harmful to the film contained within them. Paper ties or string ties used should also be free from chemicals harmful to the film. No rubber bands or paper clips should touch the film at any time or be placed within the boxes.

Cartridges

Film designed for reference and research use may also be loaded in cartridges for quicker threading and access in reading equipment designed for this purpose. Since each guide card serves as an index point to the catalog on film, an external index could be generated by determining the appropriate control points (depending on the type of rapid-access reading equipment employed) for each guide card and posting this number plus the correct cartridge number to the external index.

Labels

On one end of each box there should be a label showing the name of the content of the enclosed roll, the date, and the roll number. Neither the paper of the label nor the adhesive should contain substances potentially harmful to the film.

Responsibility of Microfilm Producer

It is the responsibility of the microfilm producer to inspect the quality of all images within one calendar week after filming to ensure that the specifications herein stated are fully met. Should a subsequent inspection by the library reveal appreciable divergence from these specifications, the microfilm producer should be required to refilm whatever portion of the catalog is necessary, at no cost to the library. Library inspection procedure giving acceptable limits on divergence from specifications is covered below.

Inspection and Quality Control Procedure
for Planetary-Type Camera Microfilm

The filming specifications for microfilm require that all images conform to the quality requirement contained in section 4 above. The library should inspect samples of the completed film by following an accepted sampling procedure, such as the one outlined in MIL-STD *Sampling Procedures and Tables for Inspection by Attributes*. If the acceptance quality level (AQL) of the samples is not within the specifications for all requirements, the lot should be returned to the microfilm producer for correction and reinspection. All defects found should be corrected by the microfilm producer, even if the lot is accepted.

Format

Image Centering and Orientation: ±0.005" (0.128mm) with the long edges of the card perpendicular to the long edge of the film to within 45 minutes.
   Inspect 10 frames per roll from at least two rolls selected at random from each lot.
   AQL 0.65%

Reduction Ratio: 12±0.24:1
   Inspect 2 frames per rolls from each camera for every second lot. All frames must show proper reduction ratio.

Machine Code Marks (See figure 1 in appendix A)
   Inspect 10 frames per roll from each camera for every second lot.
   All code marks must have proper size and location.

Image Clarity
   RESOLUTION: 10 lines/mm pattern at proper density
   Inspect both microresolution test charts in two frames per roll from four rolls per lot.
   AQL 0.65%

   LEGIBILITY: Inspect 50 frames per roll from four rolls per lot.
   All frames must be legible (assuming the original cards are legible) and capable of producing legible reproductions from third-generation negatives.

Density
   GROSS FOG: 0.15 or less

Inspect four rolls per lot
AQL 0.65%

BACKGROUND AND MACHINE CONTROL MARK DENSITY: 1.15 through
1.35
Inspect 50 frames and code marks per roll from four rolls of each lot.
AQL 0.65%

CONTRAST: 1.00 through 1.20
Inspect 50 frames per roll from four rolls of each lot.
AQL 0.65%

Contrast limits take precedence over background density. Badly faded
ink or paper of original document must be considered when judging image
background density.

Hypo Content: microgram per sq cm or below
  Inspect one roll per three lots.
  Roll must conform to specifications.

Other Photographic Requirements

Leader & Trailer: 3 feet each, clear
  Inspect one roll per lot.
  All must have proper leaders and trailers.

Mechanical defects, such as
  (a) holes, scratches, tears, blemishes, notches, water marks etc., in
         base or emulsion which obliterate the image formation, and
  (b) fine scratches, dirt, fingerprints, etc., which do not obliterate
         information.
  Inspect with at least an 8X lens, 50 frames per roll, four rolls of each lot.
  (a) Major AQL 0.65%
  (b) Minor AQL 1.5%

Thermal-Weld Splices

  Inspect two rolls per lot.
  All splices must be strong, complete, and thermal welded, and should
not exceed six for each 100 feet of film.

Target and Guide Card Requirements

  Inspect four rolls per lot.
  All targets should contain proper identification information.
  All targets should contain a cut mark.
  AQL 0.25%

Reels: proper material and winding

Inspect two rolls per lot.
All must be of proper material and wound as specified.

Packaging and Labeling

Packages: Size and material of boxes

Inspect four boxes per lot.
AQL 0.65%

Box Labels: "Archival"

Inspect four labels per lot.
AQL 0.65%

Technical Specifications for Microfilming on a Rotary-Type Camera

The security film to be provided through this process should conform to
the following specifications. However, if any provision of the following
specifications should be found inconsistent with American National
Standards Institute and other specifications referred to, the specifications
in this agreement should govern.

Camera Negative Master

Each microrecord should be photographic camera negative images on unperforated 16mm microfilm. This microfilm should be a document-recording panchromatic silver halide emulsion of camera speed and very fine
grain, applied to a suitable triacetate film base with an antihalation coating.
The camera negative film must conform to the following American National Standards Institute specifications:

PH1.25-1965, or latest: *Safety Photographic Film*
PH1.28-1969, or latest: *Photographic Films for Permanent Records*
PH5.3-1967, or latest: *Specifications for 16mm and 35mm Silver Gelatin Microfilms
  for Reel Applications*

Format

Image Orientation

Images of the cards should be oriented and filmed in the 1A position so that the long edges of the card are perpendicular to the long edge of the film to within 2 degrees 15 minutes. The 1A position is described in ANSI PH5.3-1967, or latest: *Specifications for 16mm and 35mm Silver Gelatin Microfilms for Reel Applications.*

Reduction Ratio

The ratio of the original card size to the recorded image must not exceed 24±0.48:1 or a comparable reduction ratio compatible with automatic enlargement equipment (e.g. Xerox Copyflo) and available microfilm reading devices.

Resolution

Resolution should be measured by following *Instructions for the Use of the National Bureau of Standards Microcopy Resolution Test Chart.* All five lines of the four-line-per-millimeter target of the NBS Microcopy Resolution Test Chart 1963A (1010) must be counted with reasonable confidence in both directions, as described in the instructions, when the film is exposed and processed so that the density of the 90-percent reflectance chart is 1.15 to 1.35 and the base-plus-fog density is 0.15 or less. This resolution must be maintained in both charts on beginning and ending test cards.

Density

Density should be measured in accordance with ANSI PH2.19-1959, or latest: *Diffuse Transmission Density.* The density difference in the micro-image between the image areas of the card and the ink must be such that subsequent contact and reduction film copies and enlargement prints can be made without appreciable loss of information. Where possible, the density difference in the image between the images of the card and the ink shall be 1.0 to 1.2. When good cards of cream color and black ink are being recorded, the image density of the card (background) should usually be between 1.1 and 1.35 inclusive, with a base-plus-fog density of unexposed areas of 0.15 or less. Rotary camera equipment with built-in light control feature is recommended to ensure specified density.

Film Processing and Handling

All silver halide films used for the archival recordings should be processed and handled carefully in accordance with the following ANSI specifications, or their latest revisions:

PH1.28-1969: *Photographic Films for Permanent Records*
PH4.8-1971: *Method for Determining the Thiosulphate Content of Processed Black*

and White Photographic Films and Plates
PH5.4-1970: *Practice for Storage of Microfilm*
PH5.6-1968: *Dimensions for 100-foot Reels for Processed 16mm and 35mm Microfilm*

The recommendations made in National Bureau of Standards Technical Note 261, *Summary of Current Research on Archival Microfilm* (Washington, 1965), should also be followed.

Other Photographic Requirements

Leader and Trailer

All reels should have at least three feet of clear (unfogged) film or uncoated triacetate film base of the same base thickness for leader and three feet of the same material for trailer.

Mechanical Defects

Microfilm produced in accordance with these specifications should exhibit no scratches, holes in the emulsion or base, tears, finger marks, chemical residue, or any other defect that might adversely affect the quality and legibility of the microimages. There should be no notches in the camera negative.

Splicing

Splicing of corrected film for each group of approximately 12 or more consecutive cards should not exceed six for each 100 feet of film. When splicing is required, a thermally welded joint should be used. For remakes of fewer than 12 consecutive cards, film the cards on a single piece of film and splice at end of reel. Insert a target at beginning of reel as follows: Remakes of defective images made at initial filming, or of omitted cards, are spliced in a separate sequence at the end of this reel.

The Camera Test Card

The camera test card (see figure 2 in appendix A) is an assembly of the center sections of two NBS Microcopy Resolution Test Charts 1963A (1010), three 30mm square gray scale reflectance patches, and a 76mm scale, all mounted on a 75mm x 125mm card as illustrated in figure 2.

The test card should be filmed at the beginning and end of each reel with the original documents on the same camera, at the same time, and under conditions which will yield the same density for the 90-percent gray scale reflectance patches. To ensure that these conditions have been met, there should be no splices between the test card and the adjacent 10 frames.

Targets

Following the initial test cards and a blank frame, there should be a target giving the name of the specific catalog and the date of filming. Images of characters on this and all targets as they appear on the film must be at least 2mm in height.

An additional target showing the information on the drawer label, including drawer number and roll number, should be recorded if a reel of film corresponds to a drawer of cards; otherwise, the target should indicate the beginning and end of the sequence included on the reel.

Packaging and Labeling

Film Packaging

Boxes

Film should be supplied by the contractor in standard 4- x 4- x 7/8-inch boxes which must be approved for use as archival storage containers. These boxes, as well as the reels, should be made of an inert material and be free from chemicals harmful to the film contained within them. Paper ties or string ties, if used, should also be free from chemicals harmful to the film. No rubber bands or paper clips should touch the film at any time or be placed within the boxes.

Cartridges

Film designed for reference and research use may also be loaded in cartridges for quick threading and access when used in reading equipment designed for this purpose. Since each guide card serves as an index point to the catalog on film, an external index could be generated by determining the appropriate control points (depending on the type of rapid-access reading equipment employed) for each guide card and posting the number plus the correct cartridge number to the external index.

Labels

On one end of each box there should be a label showing the name of the catalog, beginning and ending point of the content of the enclosed roll, the date, and the roll number. Neither the paper of the label nor the adhesive should contain substances potentially harmful to the film.

Responsibility of the Microfilm Producer

It is the responsibility of the microfilm producer to inspect the quality of all images within one calendar week after filming to ensure that the specifications herein stated are fully met. Should a subsequent inspection by the library reveal appreciable divergence from these specifications, the microfilm producer should be required to refilm whatever portion of the catalog is necessary, at no cost to the library. Library inspection procedure giving acceptable limits on divergence from specifications is covered below.

Inspection and Quality Control Procedure for Rotary Camera Microfilm

The filming specifications for microfilm require that all images conform to the quality requirement contained in section 8 above. The library should inspect samples of the completed film by following an accepted sampling procedure, such as the one outlined in MIL-STD *Sampling Procedures and Tables for Inspection by Attributes*. If the acceptance quality level (AQL) of the samples is not within the specifications for all requirements, the lot should be returned to the microfilm producer for correction and reinspection. All defects found should be corrected by the microfilm producer, even if the lot is accepted.

Format

Image Orientation: long edges of the card perpendicular to the long edge of the film to within 2 degrees 15 minutes.
Inspect 10 frames per roll from at least two rolls selected at random from each lot.
AQL 0.65%

Reduction Ratio: 24±0.48:1 or comparable reduction ratio agreed upon by microfilm producer and library
Inspect 2 frames per roll from each camera for every second lot.
All frames must show proper reduction ratio.

Image Clarity
RESOLUTION: 4 lines/mm pattern at proper density
Inspect both microresolution test charts in two frames per roll from four rolls per lot.
AQL 0.65%

LEGIBILITY: Inspect 50 frames per roll from four rolls per lot.
All frames must be legible (assuming the original cards are legible) and capable of producing legible reproductions from third-generation negatives.

Density
GROSS FOG: 0.15 or less

Inspect four rolls per lot.
AQL 0.65%

BACKGROUND DENSITY 1.15 through 1.35
Inspect 50 frames per roll from four rolls of each lot.
AQL 0.65%

CONTRAST: 1.00 through 1.20
Inspect 50 frames per roll from four rolls of each lot.
AQL 0.65%

Contrast limits take precedence over background density. Badly faded ink or paper of original document must be considered when judging image background density.

Hypo Content: 0.8 microgram per sq cm or below

Inspect one roll per three lots.
Roll must conform to specifications.

Other Photographic Requirements

Leader and Trailer: 3 feet each, clear

Inspect one roll per lot.
All must have proper leaders and trailers.

Mechanical defects, such as
  (a) holes, scratches, tears, blemishes, notches, water marks, etc., in base or emulsion which obliterate the image formation, and
  (b) fine scratches, dirt, fingerprints, etc., which do not obliterate information.
Inspect with at least an 8X lens, 50 frames per roll, four rolls of each lot.
  (a) Major AQL 0.65%
  (b) Minor AQL 2.5%

Thermal-Weld Splices

Inspect two rolls per lot.
All splices must be complete, and thermal welded. No more than six splices should be made in a 100-foot roll. Remakes may appear in one sequence at end of reel. Consecutive runs of 12 or more remade cards should be spliced in correct sequence. See appendix A for suggested procedure for replacing occasional omitted or improperly filmed cards.

Target Requirements

Inspect four rolls per lot.

APPENDIX A FIGURES

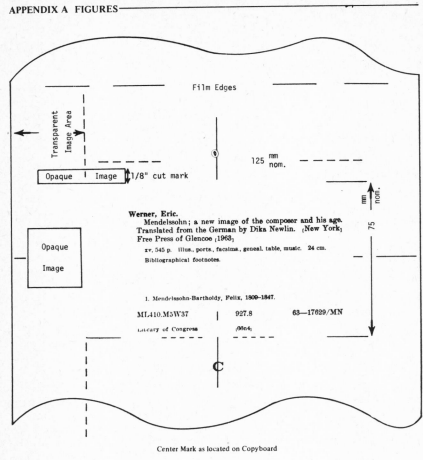

Center Mark as located on Copyboard

Figure 1

All targets should contain proper identification information.
AQL 0.25%

Reels: proper material and winding

Inspect two rolls per lot.
All must be of proper material and wound as specified.

Packaging and Labeling

Packages: Size and material of boxes

Inspect four boxes per lot.
AQL 0.65%

Box Labels: "Archival"

Inspect four labels per lot.
AQL 0.65%

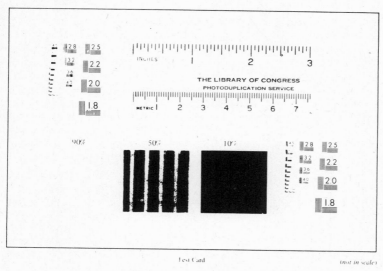

Test Card   (not in scale)

Figure 2

Appendix B Reference Materials

American National Standards Institute, 1430 Broadway, New York, N.Y. 10018, publishes and sells the ANSI standards cited in this specification. It is advisable to request their annual catalog of publication before placing an order.

Miele, Anthony W. "The Illinois State Library Microfilm Automated Catalog," *Illinois Libraries* 54, 1972, no. 3, pp. 199-202.

NMA Standard Glossary of Micrographics. Available from National Microfilm Association, 8728 Colesville Road, Silver Spring, Md. 20910. 5th ed. MA100-1971. Specify most recent edition when ordering.

U.S. Department of Defense. *Military Standard. Sampling Procedures and Tables for Inspection by Attributes*. Available from the Superintendent of Documents, Government Printing Office, Washington, D.C. 20402. MIL-STD-105-D. Request most recent edition when ordering.

REPRODUCTION OF CARD CATALOGS ON MICROFILM AND MICROFICHE

Additional Readings

"Australian Union Catalog on Microfilm," *UNESCO Bulletin for Libraries*, 29:108 (March 1975).

Carrol, C. E., "Microfilmed Catalogs: a More Efficient Way to Share Library Resources," *Microform Review*, 1:274-78 (October 1972).

Christian, R. and Steele, M., "Little Things Can Mean a Lot: Microfiche Catalog," *Library Scene*, 3:14-15 (December 1974).

Kennedy, John P., "The Georgia Tech Library's Microfiche Catalog," *Journal of Micrographics*, 6:120-30 (July 1973).

Microform Catalog Data Retrieval Systems. Chicago: American Library Association, 1975 (Library Technology Project, May 1975).

Miele, Anthony W., "The Illinois State Library Microfilm Automated Catalog (IMAC), *Illinois Libraries*, 54:199-202 (March 1972).

III □ COM (COMPUTER OUTPUT MICROFILM) AND LIBRARY CATALOGS

COM (COMPUTER OUTPUT MICROFILM): A BRIEF INTRODUCTION

by Albert Diaz

COM recorders print-out information processed by computers. Instead of printing on paper, the "print" on microfilm or microfiche. Printing computer-generated data on film rather than paper offers many advantages, foremost among which are: (1) speed; (2) less expensive; (3) compactness.

Data generated by computers was originally printed by what were essentially heavy duty typewriters activated by the computer. As the amount of data processed by computers increased, line printers were developed to do the print-outs. These are similar to typewriters in that the image is produced by the interaction of paper, ribbon, and characters embossed on metal; they are called line printers because they print one line at a time in contrast to the typewriter's one letter. They were considered high speed printers relative to what had been available before, but as computer speeds increased, line printers became bottlenecks—e.g. 1000 to 3000 characters per second printed by the line printer, 100,000 characters per second turned out by the computer.

A solution to this problem was found in COM devices, devices which convert electronic signals to characters on microfilm. A COM recorder films an electronic display of characters activated either on-line (the electronic signals come directly from the computer), or, more commonly, from magnetic tape which has been brought to the COM device (off-line).

The electronic display of characters most commonly used is similar to a television receiver. Other approaches include light-emitting diodes similar to those found in pocket calculators and laser beams which reproduce images directly on the film. All have speed as a characteristic with the latest recorders producing 10,000 to 50,000 lines of text per minute (line impact printers do 500 to 1500 lines per minute).

COM-produced film is usually 16mm microfilm or 105 x 148 (4"x 6") microfiche with images reproduced at 1/24th or 1/48th their original size.

The advantages offered by COM over other methods of computer print-out are: (1) speed; (2) cost savings; (3) greatly reduced weight and bulk, permitting duplicate copies to be made and distributed inexpensively—a 48X microfiche can contain up to 420 pages; (4) an almost unlimited number of characters (type faces and sizes, symbols, etc.); (5) an unlimited number of copies can be made inexpensively from the COM-generated master (e.g. 8¢ to 20¢ per fiche; $8.00 to $12.00 per 16mm reel); (6) pre-printed forms can be superimposed over textual information.

COM is attractive to libraries as it combines the computer's ability to alphabetize, sort, add, delete, and otherwise automatically manipulate data, with a process that allows that data to be printed and distributed inexpensively. Thus COM-produced catalogs can be updated quickly and cumulations issued with relative ease at minimal cost.

Nor is COM's use in libraries limited to catalogs. The Library of Congress recently announced the availability of two COM-produced microform publications: *Library of Congress Subject Headings in Microform* and the *Register of Additional Locations*. According to the *LC Information Bulletin*, "The combination of the microform and COM processes has made it possible for the Library to distribute these products in a more timely fashion as well as in a cumulation pattern heretofore impossible."[1] The article goes on to note, "LCSH in Microform is the direct result of a pilot project conducted by the Library to test the acceptance by outside users of microforms in a technical processing environment."[2]

In the case of the *Register of Additional Locations*, an experiment was not conducted but purchasers will be surveyed by the Library in order to determine the most desirable frequency of publication and whether the microform edition can supplant the printed edition. The *Register* is available on both fiche (98 frames, 24X, 150 fiche) and 16mm microfilm (24X 14,700 frames). A 48X reduction microfiche (270 frames per fiche) will be made available if there is sufficient interest. Elsewhere experiments have been conducted to evaluate the feasibility of issuing *Books in Print* on microfiche.[3]

References

1. *LC Information Bulletin*, July 30, 1976, pp. 433.
2. Ibid., p. 434.
3. Schleifer, Harold B., and Adams, Peggy A., "Books in Print on Microfiche, a Pilot Test,": *Microform Review*, 5: 10-24 (January 1976).

THE DISPLAY MEDIUM AND
THE PRICE OF THE MESSAGE

by S. Michael Malinconico

Microforms have always been an unpalatable option grudgingly relegated to those tasks for which more satisfying media prove impractical. Perhaps for this reason they have grown up as the servitor of the odd cause, and a maverick prodigal technology. Throughout their checkered career, microforms have been more successful at firing the creative, rather than the practical, imagination. Numerous stories of intrigue find seemingly innocuous punctuation in a Balkan newspaper revealing itself to be a "micro-dot" concealing surprising stores of information. These observations may help explain our ambivalent attitude toward microforms—a medium with fabulous properties, the mystery of the quasi-invisible, and primarily associated with marginal applications. The practitioners of the clandestine never found any problem with such a medium. They quickly perceived its unique properties, and applied them. In fact, it was the French military that made one of the first practical applications of microreproduction. During the Franco-Prussian war, dispatches to be delivered behind enemy lines were photographically reduced onto bits of film. They were, thus, made small and light enough to be entrusted to pigeons for delivery.

Librarians eventually began to experiment with microreduction. The initial impetus for this experimentation was the same then as it is now: the promise of lower text cost. Other properties of this medium were also analyzed. A major ancillary property was its compactness; it was expected that this would result in great storage economies. It was further noted that microforms are both impervious to deterioration, and infinitely reproducible—ideal attributes for conserving scarce or infrequently used library materials.

Reprinted from *Library Journal*, 101: 2144-2149 (October 15, 1976) by permission of the author.
Published by R. R. Bowker Co. (a Xerox company). Copyright © 1976 by Xerox Corporation.

   Librarians were also quick to note the serious defects inherent in this medium. The quality of the image, when magnified, was poor. Despite other technical advances, the image has remained so. As a result, microforms are extremely troublesome to read, especially if one must concentrate on the murky image for an extended period of time. The storage economy possible with a reduced image is only gained if many individual frames, or pages, are contained on a single microcard or microfilm. Since the contents are invisible to the unaided eye, they are difficult to access. Once a desired frame has been located, access to other parts of a microform proves extremely awkward.

   Microforms have been relegated to those tasks in which their superiority over other media is so marked that their shortcomings can be ignored by comparison. The ideal conditions which ensure their acceptability are offered by those applications where no viable alternative exists. Fremont Rider cogently stated this attitude by noting, "that practically all . . . users, if they are confronted with a free choice between a micro-reduced copy . . . and no copy of it at all, will prefer the micro-reduced copy" ("Microcards vs. The Cost of Book Storage," *American Documentation*, January 1951, Vol. 2 p. 41).

   Microforms have been more successful as a means for preserving facsimiles of materials whose demise is imminent due to deterioration; as an alternative to those collections one can't afford in their original form; as a surrogate for those items the owning institution is unwilling, or unable, to subject to interlibrary lending; and as a means for preserving those vast bodies of recorded information, which, with great likelihood, consist of unadulterated ephemera, but might just possible be the raw material of history, or the primeval embodiment of a profound idea.

   Microfilm still is used extensively for recording circulation transactions. This application is actually very similar to the most common commercial use of microforms: a photographic record of a transaction made for security purposes, e.g., facsimiles of checks processed by a bank. In these cases, the primary purpose of the microfilm is to provide an archival record to be used only under exceptional circumstances; it is expected that the film will only need to be accessed infrequently. This highlights the prevalent attitude toward microforms: something which one hopes he does *not* have to use.

   These applications almost completely describe the use of microforms by libraries in the four decades between 1930-1970. Public use of microforms was generally confined to the crepuscular shade of designated microfilm reading rooms. Perhaps this was more than just a result of utilitarian considerations; it might be indicative of the "fondness" librarians had for them. During the latter half of the 1960's, librarians earnestly began to seek the solid state salvation offered by computer technology. Almost contemporaneously in 1959, electronic data processing, the nubile technology of the era, and micrographics were coupled. The result was a new mutant, Computer Output Microfilm (COM). The synergistic combination of these technologies has created superb opportunities for confusion and innovation. The confusion might be traced to the esoteric disciplines underlying micro-graphic technology: data processing, photography, optics, and even elemen-tary projective geometry. The opportunities for innovation are provided by the power of computing machinery, and the extremely low cost of micro-forms themselves.

If the computer can be characterized as "an information engine," then libraries represent, at least, alluvial deposits of information. A computer has a unique ability to reconstitute information into a myriad of new forms. Given the rich raw material processed by libraries, the result can be a truly staggering use of ancillary resources, as information synthesized by a com-puter requires some medium for its display. If that medium is not reusable, prodigious quantities of it are required. The paper shortage of 1974 and the attendant increase in paper prices highlighted the inadequacy of wood pulp products as an optimum medium for computer output. These facts com-bined to make computer output microforms a much more attractive display medium than earlier microforms had ever been.

Description of COM

First, it's no secret that the data which a computer manipulates are *not* in a form intelligible to humans. In order to make any use of the results of a computer's ruminations, we normally instruct it to present the results in some written form. The most common technique of rendering such infor-mation is with a high-speed computer line-printer. This device behaves very much like an ultra high-speed typewriter. Since each character is only known to the computer as a series of unique electrical signals, a computer printer must be capable of recognizing such signals and striking the appro-priate character in response. In a sense, even a printer is a computer of limited ability. A more sophisticated device could be programmed to trans-duce the unique electrical impulses associated with a character into a draw-ing of its likeness on the face of a TV-like cathode ray tube (CRT). This is exactly the basis of the CRT displays with which we are now all familiar. The two major problems with a CRT display are: 1) that responses are gen-erally customized, hence such an expensive resource can serve only one user at a time; and 2) a CRT is eminently capable of "writing" much faster than we can read. A simple solution could be found if we were to enclose the CRT in a light-tight box, place a lens in front of the screen, and photo-graphic film behind the lens. We could then let the CRT operate as rapidly as it wishes, capture the data on film, duplicate the film into as many copies as we wish, and then read the filmed results at our leisure. If the lens re-duces the image many times, we could have direct generation of a micro-form by computer. This, in simplest terms, is the process by which COM is created. Even such a device is much too slow for a computer, so one nor-mally records a computer's output on magnetic tape, and then transfers it to a separate COM recorder. Although this results in a duplication of much of the electronics associated with a computer and its peripheral devices, the net result is still an efficient, economical use of the devices.

Since the process that transduces electrical signals into a display requires the intervention of a miniature "computer program" for each character, great graphic flexibility can be realized. One can, for example, create output with graphic quality similar to that produced by a human typesetter. One can also produce output of lesser quality, e.g., similar to that obtained from an ordinary CRT terminal, computer printer, or even a typewriter. The major differences are legibility and *cost*. The former is sometimes referred to as *Graphic Art* COM, and the latter as *Alphanumeric* COM. Both can be many times cheaper than printed copy.

Cost Comparisons

Since we rarely use a computer to create a printed report to serve only a single user, we shall deal with output produced in multiple copies. This fact will make costs somewhat difficult to discuss, as the price of most printed products is a function of two quite independent parameters: the cost of creating a master copy (first copy) and the cost of making additional copies. In order to avoid these complications, let us assume 50 copies of a 500-page publication as a basis for comparison. Such a publication is too large to produce directly on a computer printer. In fact, we could show that the costs involved would gainsay such an approach, even if multi-ply paper were used. A fairly commonly employed technique would involve the creation of a single copy on a computer printer, with additional copies electrostatically produced (i.e., by Xerox machines). Produced in this way, our hypothetical publication would cost approximately $955, exclusive of the cost of computer time. The next most popular method would employ offset printing to make additional copies. Print plates would be photographically created from a single, clean, computer produced copy. This would cost about $985 (almost the same price as Xerox copies). (For more than 50 copies, offset printing becomes increasingly cheaper than making Xerox copies.) The same publication produced in 42X microfiche by COM would only cost approximately $35 (2 cents per page for a master copy, and one-tenth of a cent per page for additional copies). This is only a theoretical cost, as most COM vendors would actually probably invoice us $42. The reason is that a 42X microfiche contains 207 frames, hence, we would require three fiche. It matters little to the vendor in his processing that half of the third fiche would be blank. We can, nonetheless, use the former figure to arrive at comparisons without fear of introducing any significant bias. We can note from this that a COM publication can be approximately 1/27th the cost of an

Prices cited in this paper are only intended to be representative of what is currently being quoted by commercial vendors. Geography, volume, and a myriad of other factors can dramatically affect what will be charged in any particular instance. The ultimate and only reliable source for such information will be a salesman for the vendor selected.

equivalent printed publication! (This ratio is extremely dependent on the number of copies produced. See figure 1 for the behavior of cost as a function of the number of copies.)

In what follows we shall be discussing micrographic applications which are radically different from those heretofore commonly employed in libraries. Whereas traditional uses of microforms might be characterized as micorepublication for preservation or dissemination, COM is more akin to micropublishing of newly synthesized information. Since COM products are invariably created from an evolving machine readable data base, they are, by virtue of this fact, ephemeral. We shall be considering the display of *any* given machine readable file; however, in order to reify the ideas presented, we shall use a computer maintained catalog as an example.

COM is considerably more than just an output product of computer processing. In a very real sense, it can provide a means whereby the potential of computer processing can be more fully realized. Although computers are very adept at maintaining, and reorganizing, machine readable files, this does no one any good unless the results of this activity are displayed. If activity against a machine readable file is frequent, the problem is all the more acute. On-line systems solve this problem very directly. All activity against on-lines files immediately manifest themselves to an observer on demand. Unfortunately, *totally* on-line systems, certainly on-line catalogs, are still beyond the reach of most libraries which can, nonetheless, benefit from computer assisted processing.

A "Waste Margin"

On-line systems employing CRT display terminals have as one of their major advantages the ability to produce a customized response. Such responses are created on a reusable writing surface—the CRT screen. Conversely, the re-usability of the writing surface, in part, permits the system to address its response to a single individual making a discrete inquiry. When we cannot afford such customized service, we attempt to supply the information in a pre-coordinated form such that it will provide responses to as many queries as we can reasonably anticipate. Such solutions can never be totally satisfactory. In general, a query for information will be such that it has never been made before, nor will it, with high likelihood, ever be made again. As a logical corollary, any system that attempts to pre-satisfy queries must of necessity provide responses to queries that will never be made. The result is a *waste margin*.

A waste margin is an inescapable requirement in any information system. The term is not meant to evoke any pejorative connotation, but is merely intended to describe those products and services provided in anticipation of demand, but which are never, or infrequently, utilized. The inescapable nature of this phenomenon is invariably brought out in all studies of the use of library collections, which show that only a very small fraction of the

collection is ever consulted in any finite period of time. Does this imply
that the remainder of the collection is of no value? The answer, of course, is
no; at any given instant of time each volume has the same *a priori* proba-
bility of being consulted as any other. Lacking the simple quality of omni-
science, we can only ensure that an unknown request will be satisfied by
maintaining a comprehensive collection. In fact, there is a very definite cor-
relation between the depth of a research library's collection and its value to
a scholar. The user of a library is quite indifferent to the millions of volumes which he does not consult. He is concerned, however, that he be
assured that the material or information he is seeking will, with high likelihood, be found in the library he chooses to use. It is only upon *a posteriori*
reflection that some fraction of a collection can be characterized as of
marginal value. Thus, a waste margin is only a waste margin *after, not before*, the fact.

A waste margin necessarily occurs in most aspects of library related operations. OCLC, for example, has no choice but to maintain on-line nearly
one-half of all the MARC records distributed by the Library of Congress
without any of its 600 member libraries using them. A similar inexorable
law is operative whenever we create a bibliographic display. There is pre-
cious little we can do about unaccessed items in a collection, or unused
MARC records. We can, however, by appropriately choosing the display
medium, exercise great control over the price exacted by the waste margin
in a bibliographic display. We have already noted that a COM display can
cost 1/27 as much as the same display in conventional printed form. If 10
percent of this list is assumed to be of marginal value to most users, but
nonetheless still provides a useful additional service, if we seek to increase
service by proving more information of such a nature, and if we are not
simultaneously seeking to lower costs, then we would be free to increase the
amount of this additional information to where it would comprise 97 percent of the list! We could, if we did not wish to increase the waste margin,
simply pocket a 96 percent saving (see appendix).

Let us consider a hypothetical example: assume that a printed bibliographic list contains an average of four entries per title—a main entry and
three added entries, and that a majority of users employ only the main
entry as an access point. The three added entries are then provided only for
that minority of users who do not know the main entry. The added entries
may be considered a waste margin. If the list is produced in COM, at 1/27
the cost of print, then with no increase in cost we would provide an average
of 107 added entries! This might be a bit excessive, but we could exercise a
whole spectrum of options; e.g., we could double the number of added entries and still realize a 94 percent saving.

One often avoids making too many added entries in a card catalog simply
because of the cost of creating and filing the additional cards. There are,
however, a great number of bibliographic lists produced by computer in
which multiple access can be generated completely, or in part, by programming logic, but the cost of the resultant list prevents us from exercising this

option. For example, the Hennepin County Library in 1971 produced a 2500-page list of materials on-order, through an automated acquisitions system. The list was originally produced only in author sequence. By converting to COM from printed output, they could include both author and title access, at 10 percent the cost of the original list. As an added bonus, copies of the list, which formerly took up to a week to produce, could be ready for distribution in 24 hours. The simplest type of added access, which may be completely generated by computer, is provided by a key word index. Even when such an index is possible, we often avoid creating it solely because of the increased size, and the cost of the resulting list.

One of the major advantages of an interactive system is that it can respond to queries through post-coordinated access to information. That is, within limits, it can respond to customized queries. On the other hand, a static system can only respond through a set of pre-coordinated access points (those "added entries" provided at the time the static display was created). A library catalog in book or card form is a static system. Although static systems can never hope to equal the efficacy of interactive systems, they can be made to approach them by increasing the number of pre-coordinated access points. We have already noted how this, or any other approach must be considered within the constraints of available resources.

An Evolving Machine Readable File

Another major advantage of on-line systems is the timeliness of the information presented. A static display, created from an evolving machine readable data base, can only present us with a snapshot of the file—a still photograph of that frozen moment in the evolution of the file when the display was created. Static displays are by their very nature anachronisms practically at the moment they are created. A book form catalog can never be "up-to-date" and large, manual, card catalogs are rarely current, as filing backlogs are an inescapable fact of life.

The problems of timeliness of the catalog when the bibliographic data are maintained in machine readable form are subtly, but significantly, different from those posed by a manual catalog. As already noted, a computer is very adept at maintaining and reorganizing a file of bibliographic data. If we attempt to maintain a parallel manifestation of that file, say in card form, then we must expend manual effort to integrate activity taken by the computer against the machine readable file into its manual analog. This is not meant to gainsay the savings that a computer can effect, but we are left with an intuitive suspicion that the computer is not being used to full advantage; we are in effect asking humans to duplicate some aspects of work already performed by a computer.

If we are to use a computer to maintain, and control, a file effectively, we must cede to it control over display of that file. The extent to which we delegate this control is proportional to the degree of efficiency we can effect in the entire operation. Ceding total responsibility for display to a computer implies either an on-line display, or a static display created in its entirety by computer. Frequently recreating a large publication in order to incorporate the results of new activity can be an extremely expensive proposition. Several not altogether satisfying solutions have been found which help improve timeliness within the constraints of finite resources. They permit frequent publication of less than the entire file. The most popular technique involves the publication of a complete cumulation of the contents of a file at some infrequent interval, and augments this at a greater frequency, with supplements containing the results of all activity since the time of the last cumulation.

Cumulation/supplement patterns can be conceived of in an almost unlimited variety, but we shall only deal with the two most common. A *cumulative supplement* is one in which each issue contains a complete record of all activity since a previous cumulation (each supplement supersedes, and replaces the last). A *chronological supplement* contains only a record of activity since the issuance of the previous supplement (a complete history can only be discovered by consulting all supplements). Librarians are already aware of the satisfying nature of such a publication pattern. For example, a search in the *National Union Catalog* can require the examination of 1) the most recent quinquennial; 2) up to four of the most recent annuals; 3) up to three of the most recent quarterly issues; and 4) up to two of the most recent monthly issues.

It is easy to see that the major service difference between the two techniques of supplementation is the difference in the number of alphabets that must be consulted—a maximum of two in the first case, and a maximum of ten in the second case. The reasons for choosing the latter, over the former, are simply economic, not the result of creative sadism. It should be obvious that if we were to publish a cumulation augmented by chronological supplements, the total cost of providing supplements is equal to the cost of the first supplement multiplied by the number of each supplement. On the other hand, the total cost of cumulative supplements is nearly proportional to the cost of producing the first, times the square of the number produced. If we were to consider supplements produced in each of the 11 months, following an annual cumulation, then cumulative supplements would cost us *six times* as much as chronological supplements. Librarians, unlike employees of the Department of Defense, would shudder violently at such a 500 percent increase. If the cost of the display medium could negate or help ameliorate this difference, then one might feel free to choose the alternative which provides better service. COM can potentially provide a 27-fold decrease in the cost of publication: this is more than enough to offset a 6-fold increase required by cumulative supplementation.

The ideal situation would result if we could eliminate supplements altogether, and produce a complete cumulation each time. Users would then have only one alphabet to search. In some cases this has proven practicable by converting to a COM catalog. Fairfax County Park Library in Virginia and Clark County Public Library in Nevada, among others, now produce their book catalogs in COM. They are able to dispense with supplements completely and provide complete cumulations every two to three months. Even with the low cost of COM, this is still not practical in all cases. Each case is so complicated by considerations of format and file size that no simple generalizations can be made.

Regardless of the publication pattern chosen, COM invariably provides greater timeliness. A COM publication in multiple copies can be produced in a matter of days. This is in contrast to the several weeks necessary to produce a similar publication by offset printing. Because of the speed of production and the extremely low cost of COM, it is actually possible to create a COM version of a printed catalog to serve during the period between computer creation of the data and delivery of the printed books. The Dance Collection of the New York Public Library has actually done this while waiting for delivery of its first, 7000-page, 10-volume catalog. Incidentally, the COM version of this catalog was contained on only 86 microfiche.

Character Sets & Typography

Up until this point we have been discussing the cheapest form of COM. Alphanumeric COM, which only has a simple upper/lower case character set. More sophisticated forms also exist at higher prices. When recording bibliographic data, there is often a need for special characters and diacritics not normally encountered in commercial applications. A character set has been developed by the Library of Congress and endorsed by ALA. This ALA character set has been judged adequate for the transcription of cataloging data in languages employing a roman script, and in those languages which can be romanized. This character set is quite large, containing 175 discrete graphics. COM can be obtained with this character set; however the number of COM vendors who possess this capability is very limited. Probably due to the uniqueness of this service at this time, prices quoted by vendors vary significantly, from 1.4 to 9.3 cents/frame. For purposes of comparison with other forms of output, we can use an average of 5 cents/frame.

This apparent 150 percent increase in price is somewhat deceptive. It represents only the increased price of the master copy. Additional copies still cost only about one tenth of a cent per frame. To illustrate this point, let us once again consider our 500-page publication. Recall that 50 copies of this publication would have cost $35. If produced with a full ALA character set, its cost would be $50—albeit a 43 percent increase in price, but not as menacing a prospect as the increase augured by the cost of the master copy. The reason is quite simple: the fixed cost of 50 copies tends to mask the effect of an increase in the price of the master. Even with such a relatively extraordinary increase in price, the cost is still only about 1/19 that of printed copy.

The relative price increase may be great, but as we see from this example, the absolute increase paid for such an enhancement can be quite tolerable. In many cases an extended character set is essential for the representation of bibliographic data; this is especially so if we are attempting to record romanized forms of data originally in a non-roman script. Consider the ambiguities that a simple macron helps resolve in the following romanizations of the Japanese words: *OTO*, a sound; *OTO*, to throw up; and *OTO*, the Royalists. Similar examples can be found in cyrillic languages. Even Western European languages can present ambiguities of meaning that are only resolved by diacritical marks.

There is yet a more sophisticated form of COM, Graphic Art COM. With this, we can create output of the same quality as that produced by a typographer setting type. In fact, we can employ a range of typefonts not normally available to a human printer. Devices capable of this type of output are more commonly used to produce full size copy than COM. This is easily accomplished by exchanging the 16, 35, or 105mm film, in the COM recorder, for 10-inch photographic paper, and adjusting the lens to project a full-size image. The result is known as phototypesetting. Full-size copy is then used in another photographic process to make offset printing plates. The book catalog of the NYPL Research Libraries is an example of the end result of this process. This catalog contains text employing the full ALA character set as well as the Hebrew alphabet, both in normal and bold face type in various sizes.

Photocomposed output can cost approximately $1/page if produced on photographic paper, and 35 cents/page if produced on film. Again, the costs can be deceptive. In addition to the added copy phenomenon discussed earlier, another effect comes into play. In typeset copy each character is accorded "proportional spacing," e.g., an *i* requires less space than an *M*. Alphanumeric COM, computer printer, or even typewriter copy all employ fixed spacing for each character. The result is that typeset output can be over 30 percent more compact than equivalent monospace copy. Our 500-page publication would therefore be reduced to 350 pages; 50 copies would then cost $140. This is about four times the price of ordinary Alphanumeric COM, but still about seven times cheaper than duplicating line printer copy. Preparation of data for photocomposition does require more computer time and sophisticated software than simple Alphanumeric COM, but the additional computer time only adds about $11 to the cost of the publication under consideration. Since we are only concerned here with the costs for display media, we shall ignore these added complications.

An equivalent phototypeset, printed publication would cost only slightly ($85) more than one derived from computer copy (raising the price to $1040) This is so despite the relatively high price, $1/page, for photocomposed copy. The offsetting effect is provided by a reduction in the size of each volume. In the course of producing 50 copies, we recover most of the high initial investment made in each page with a 30 percent reduction in the number of pages. In fact, reference to Figure 1 will show that beyond 150 copies photocomposition becomes more economical than duplicating line printer copy.

We should note the qualitative advantages of Graphic COM and related products. The advantages are not simply aesthetic. Typeset copy is much easier to read than a typewriter-like display, as typographic characters are more distinctive. In addition, a typeset line contains a greater number of characters within a fixed extent. More text is presented to a single scan of the eye; reading is more rapid. Finally, variations in type style and size can be used to convey information. For example: Highlighting the principal filing element of each entry with bold type can greatly facilitate scanning a page or frame for an entry; setting detailed information in small type makes it easier to ignore when one is reading rapidly to locate likely entries; italic type can be used to call attention to important elements in an entry, such as a call number; etc.

Self-Refreshing Catalogs

The frequent republication of the contents of a machine readable data base in order to ensure the timeliness of that publication is only one aspect of a more general consideration. Periodically, republishing a catalog in its entirety permits us to create a self-refreshing catalog. We have already seen the advantage such a catalog can offer when we reorganize its contents—reorganization becomes manifest without manual intervention after we have instructed the computer to effect the alterations. One additional advantage is provided by such a technique. We can permit provisional or volatile data temporarily to exist in the catalog, as we can fully expect that it will be replaced automatically, by permanent data. A trivial example might include the use of CIP data derived from LC/MARC. A library could accept a CIP record with the knowledge that it will be replaced in subsequent publications of the catalog by a complete, authoritative record when it is issued by LC. If the library rigorously adheres to LC practices, replacement can be effected automatically without human intervention.

A less trivial example may be provided by a new MARC service scheduled for implementation in the near future—distribution of LC's Automated Process Information File (APIF) records. The APIF contains preliminary descriptive cataloging for all materials received by the LC processing department. These records are created at the very beginning of the processing cycle, hence, represent the earliest bibliographic control records for materials processed by LC. The records, although of high quality, are created by para-professionals and are later revised and upgraded by professional catalogers. Generally the preliminary record is enriched with notes, added entries, subject headings, and classification numbers. If one could make use of these records, they could provide at least main entry and title access in a catalog until the full, authoritative record is issued. The full record would then provide full access and bibliographic data. (The lack of call numbers poses a serious problem in this scheme. Nonetheless, libraries which do not rely on classed shelving of materials, and which can assign a temporary call number, or which are able to assign a call number without the assistance of LC's subject analysis can probably make this scheme work.) The temporary record can be replaced automatically by computer. If one can solve the call number problem, then the self-refreshing nature of the catalog permits one to provide very timely, albeit limited, access to materials covered by APIF records. The efficacy of such schemes are directly dependent on the degree of conformity with LC practice, and the frequency with which a catalog or its supplements are issued. The latter considerations are directly dependent on the cost of publication. We have seen that costs associated with COM publication are so low that they impose no very serious constraints.

Perhaps the most dramatic effect of the self-refreshing catalog can be a solution to the classical problems posed by anachronistic or derogatory headings (see M. Freedman, "Processing for the People," *LJ*, January 1, 1976). The main reason that these headings present a problem is that attempting to do anything about them can require massive maintenance of an existing catalog. With terribly little bother, computers can in general effect the necessary changes. If the catalog is maintained by a computer, produced in book form, and replaced periodically, the effort required to make these changes is substantially reduced and one can feel free to make them when appropriate. Sanford Berman, one of the most incisive critics of the quality of LC subject headings, is able to put his recommendations into practice fairly easily at the Hennepin County Library, since he has access to a highly sophisticated automated cataloging system, and Hennepin's catalog appears in book form. Changes are fairly easy to effect, and appear as soon as the next issue of the catalog is published.

Here then is the real advantage of an inexpensive display medium. It permits a librarian to devote his creative energies to developing innovative tools for enhancing service rather than seeking mundane economies that can be effected without too adversely affecting service. COM prices are so low that enormous latitude is permitted when seeking such enhancements. The latitude is generally so great that one can hope to reduce costs, improve service, and make more effective use of the expensive computer resources available to a library.

Appendix

Here we shall attempt to derive the amount of additional marginal information permitted in a list produced on a less inexpensive medium. Let E represent that part of a list, which contains essential information. Then the cost of this list including a 10 per-cent margin for inessential, but useful additional information is given by:

$$[E + 0.1E] \times C$$

Where C is a constant proportional to the cost on which the medium is produced.

If this same list is produced on a less expensive medium, for which the constant C is represented by C', and we now assume that a quantity of marginal material represented by M is some fraction f of the total list than we have:

$$f = \frac{M}{E + M}$$

since the total list will now contain E & M data. Simple algebra will show that:

$$M = \frac{f}{1 - f} \cdot E$$

And C' is obviously equal to C/27.

If we now assume that the price of the lists is to be equal we get

$$[E + 0.1E] \times C = [E + M] \times C'$$

$$[E + 0.1E] \times C = \left[E + \frac{f}{1 - f} E \right] \times \frac{C}{27}$$

Solving for f we find:

$$f = 1 - \frac{1}{1.1 \times 27} = .966.$$

or 97 percent.

If we did not add any marginal material to the original list, then the price is simply reduced to 1/27, or 3.7 percent of the original price, hence a 96.3 percent saving.

COMPUTER-PRODUCED MICROFILM LIBRARY CATALOG

by William A. Kozumplik and R. T. Lange

Production of the library catalog depends on the correct blend of the following ingredients: capability, cost, and user acceptance. This axiom was tested in the nineteenth century when the card catalog displaced catalogs in book form.

With the advent of computer technology, the book catalog has come full circle within a century. To be sure, the first catalogs produced by computers were in card form, which was a natural evolutionary advance when passing from manual to automated systems. Irrespective of format, the point to be stressed is that each of these computer-produced catalog systems, whether card or book, was required to stand the test of capability, cost, and user acceptance. And it is precisely this test that the third catalog system passed convincingly.

This third system is the computer-produced library catalog in microfilm form. It is a product of off-the-shelf hardware and of programming excellence. Administrators of large specialized libraries as well as directors of research will be particularly interested in the microform system because it is the least costly and the most advanced, effectively user-oriented catalog system in operation today.[1]

Such a system was installed in the Technical Information Center (TIC) of Lockheed Missiles & Space Company (LMSC) and became fully operational in July 1966. The capabilities of this new system far outshine its predecessors and will be discussed in detail here. Besides achieving these advanced capabilities, the present system actually returns a moderate savings in comparison to its forerunners. Having passed the capability and costs tests, the system was presented to the public—the operational as well

Reprinted from *American Documentation*, 18: 67-80 (April 1967) by permission of the publisher. Copyright © 1967 by the American Society for Information Sciences, 1155 16th St., N.W., Washington, D.C. 20036.

as the administrative user, that is, the scientist on the one hand and the librarian on the other—with favorable results. The user found that look-up time was greatly reduced and that the system was easy to operate.

Lockheed's experience has affirmed user acceptance to be broadly based and has brought requests to TIC management to install a microfilm catalog in R&D oriented buildings. This can be done at no extra computer costs and is beneficial whenever high-priced scientists and engineers are located at a considerable distance from the library. Obviously convenience of look-up on the premises of his own building will revolutionize the researcher's work and should improve the quality of his product and prevent unwanted duplication; this, after all, is the *raison d'être* of the special library. The point to be emphasized is that a catalog that is located a few feet from the researcher's work station dynamically improves his accessibility to the company's cataloged literature resources.[2]

The computerized catalog system installed and operating at LMSC delivers the following products in accordance with design requirements:

1. An updated library catalog in microfilm form
2. A listing of new publications added, using the keyword-in-title (KWIT) format
3. An updated report of open-entry items contained in the library
4. A source authority list, with appropriate cross-references
5. A subject authority list, with "see" and "see also" references appropriate

These products are processed quarterly with the exception of the KWIT, which is issued semi-monthly. Basic to all products is the system-derived and magnetic-tape stored master file on all publications contained in the library together with the ability to delete, add, or change records on the master file as determined by the controlling organization, namely, the library management.

It is worthy of note that these products listed can be delivered for several separate libraries within the same computer-processing cycle. At LMSC for instance, these products are currently separately generated for two collections while two additional collections are in the process of converting to this low-cost retrieval system.

The system originates with source documents being keypunched and forwarded to the computer (Fig. 1). These records are of various types, the most predominant being catalog additions and deletions. The cards are generated onto magnetic tape and sorted. The input transactions are subjected to certain editing requirements, reformatted, and exploded into various multiple records. This explosion is based upon the number of tracings in each document. During this phase of the operation, the documents that pertain to new publications are also generated on a separate tape that produces the keyword-in-title listing.

The next step in the system operation is to sort the edited-exploded transactions into the same sequence as the master file. These sorted transactions are processed against the master file to produce the updated catalog and an updated master file. Also during this pass, a tape is generated that produces the source and the subject authority listings.

The user-related visible components of the computer-produced microfilm library catalog system are microfilm cartridges and a microfilm reader together with the semi-monthly KWIT entitled *New Reports & Books*.

The catalog's 1,051,060 look-up points or entries are organized in six sections: source, title, author(s), contract number, subjects, and report numbers/call number (Figs. 2, 3, 4, 5, 6, 7, 8). Both reports and books which heretofore had been cataloged and shelf-ordered according to separate systems, resulting in separate catalogs, are now for the first time integrated into a single catalog. The 16mm microfilm compressing these million-plus retrieval points are loaded into 40 cartridges; each cartridge contains 100 ft. of film on which are exposed 1,800 two-column pages of computerized catalog text processed by the SC 4020. Each page contains approximately 14 entries. Altogether, this is a significant compression of text and space since the million-plus records when in card form had previously occupied 720 standard library catalog drawers. The cartridges are housed in an 80-compartment rack that stands next to the reader on a 60 x 30 in. work table. Each cartridge is labeled as to contents. The labels are colored differently to provide visual ease in distinguishing the six separate sections of the catalog.

Any on-shelf automatic microfilm reader and associated cartridges may be used to display the microfilmed text. For the installation at LMSC the Bell & Howell Microfilm Reader, Model 531, was selected because it provides not only visual reading comfort with its zoom lens and its three intensities of lamp brightness but also speed. The latter is derived from the use of the Bell & Howell patented automatic no-rewind cartridge. The user simply removes the cartridge after his look-up; the next user of that cartridge does not have to rewind the film but merely commences his search to the left or right as the case may be. The zoom lens enlarges text size up to 100%.

A complete, cumulated, and corrected microfilm catalog is produced quarterly: Computer processing time together with duplicate microfilm processing label generation, cartridge loading; and distribution to the operating location takes ten work days. The decision to schedule production on a quarterly basis rather than bi-monthly or even monthly was founded on production costs and computer availability. For instance, the bi-monthly production cycle would cost $3,000 more annually.

Between periodic microfilm catalog production runs, users are kept informed of titles added to the collections by the semi-monthly computer product in KWIT format, *New Reports & Books*. This is a variant of Bell Telephone Laboratory's BEPIP program and is structured in two parts, Title, and Bibliography. It is not a retrospective retrieval tool of any great effectivity but serves basically to announce works newly added during the period reported to the inventory of literature resources that are available to qualified users. For the user whose approach is by subject, author, or contract number, the three-month gap in currency of the catalog denies him access to the latest information in the inventory. But when the user's approach is by source, report number, or title, the KWIT is moderately helpful; consequently, this type of user will be but mildly adversely affected in his exploitation of the most recent resources.

Queuing problems caused by multiple simultaneous catalog utilization are forestalled by installing multiple readers and catalogs at a ratio of two to one for the library's clientele and one to one for library technical services staff. The cost of these added equipmetns and components is more than offset by savings in compression paid for the four catalogs and eight readers installed on library premises for use of scientist/engineers and for the five catalogs and five readers for use of library staff. In addition, the microfilm system operates at a net saving of $13,000 annually because (1) card filing costs are avoided; (2) there are no catalog cases to purchase; and (3) there is a 200% saving in space to house the microfilm installation.

The computer-produced microfilm catalog provides bonuses that are immediately attractive to librarians. Perhaps the chief bonus is a separate catalog with reader for the library's technical services staff. This point is the more important at LMSC because its TIC has separate staffs for reports and for book acquisitions and cataloging. Having the complete catalog in their own work stations obviously permits the technical services librarians to function more efficiently.

Similar bonuses that have equal beneficial effects on efficiency of library operations are the separate catalog/reader installations for the literature search corps and the reports and books circulation desks at one of the TIC's two libraries; namely, the one that serves approximately 11,051 scientists, engineers, and administrative support personnel. The needs of literature search are self-evident, and the volume of loan requests handled by these two service desks, as well as their distance from the public catalog installation, made it operationally and economically feasible to install these catalogs.

Additional bonuses generated by this computer-produced microfilm library catalog system are: (1) authority list of sources; (2) authority list of subject headings; and (3) list of open-entry items. While these lists are products of the system's specifications, they can be identified as bonuses in relation to their nonexistence under the displaced system. There is no need to stress the operational importance of the first two lists, especially since they are automatically updated to reflect professional decisions of deletion and addition as well as of augmentation by integrative cross-referencing. Operational utility is enhanced by printing sufficient copies to supply a set to each cataloger and a set for the literature search corps. The third list identifies the TIC's holdings of cataloged "serial" titles. Included in this concept are reports generated on a specific contract, project, task,

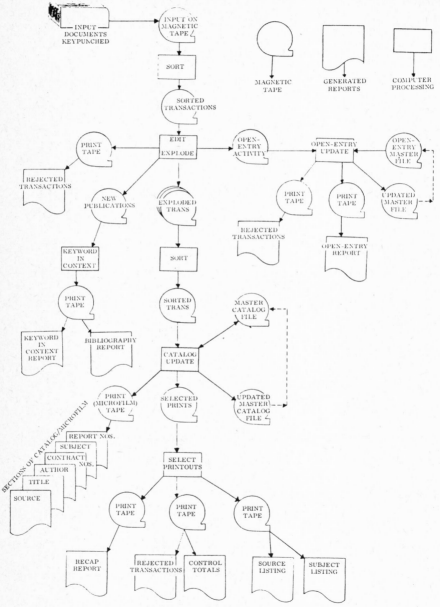

FIG. 1. LMSC Library Catalog, Data system flow

```
TDR 32-401                          PA + SV   LIBRARY    06-07-66                        PAGE 1054
    NONE                                          HYDROGEN PEROXIDE PROPELLED TORPEDO.  SEMI-
    MUSEUM OF SCIENCE AND INDUSTRY, CHICAGO, ILL.     YEARLY REPORT ON PROJECT I-14-MWP-N-58.
    JULY 59      13P          C-SV                    PERIOD - 1 JULY 1961 - 31 DEC 1961.
                                                      NONE
INSTITUTE FOR TECHNICAL MECHANICS (GERMANY)           31 DEC 61  1P              SV
ABD-TDR-63-513                            UM
    INVESTIGATION OF THE DISTRIBUTION OF TENSILE   INSTITUTE OF CHEMISTRY FOR EXPLOSIVES(ITALY)
    AND BENDING STRESSES IN NOTCHED FLAT BARS.     ICE-60-SYR-(1)                              S
    NEUBER, I.M.                                       HIGH SPEED ANTISHIP TORPEDO.  SEMI-YEARLY
    MUNICH, GERMANY                                    REPORT ON PROJECT I-23-MWP-N60.  PERIOD -
    JULY 63      59P          C-1-P                    1 JULY - 31 DEC 1961.
                                                      NONE
INSTITUTE FOR TELECOMMUNICATION SC...             MARIPERMAN LAB.
    SEE                                               31 DEC 61  2P          C-SV
        NATIONAL BUREAU OF STANDARDS
                                                  INSTITUTE OF ELECTRICAL + ELECTRONICS ENG.
INSTITUTE OF ANDEAN BIOLOGY(PERU)                 806  159                       563
AIRU-SAM-TDR-62-87                        UM          ARTIFICIAL INTELLIGENCE--A COMBINED PREPRINT
    THE INFLUENCE OF HIGH ALTITUDES ON THE            OF PAPERS PRESENTED AT...WINTER GENERAL
    ELECTRICAL ACTIVITY OF THE HEART.                 MEETING, N.Y., 27 JAN - 1 FEB 1963.
    ELECTROCARDIOGRAPHIC AND VECTORCARDIOGRAPHIC      (S-142).
    OBSERVATIONS IN ADOLESCENCE AND ADULTHOOD.        NONE
    PENALOZA, D. + ET AL                              NEW YORK
    FACULTY OF MEDICINE, LIMA, PERU                   1963        168P BIBS.              PA
    AUG 62     22P          C-1-P
                                                  INSTITUTE OF ELECTRICAL AND ELECTRONICS ENGS.
INSTITUTE OF ANDEAN BIOLOGY(PERU)                 519.9  159   1963              764
AIRU-SAM-TDR-62-89                        UM          RELIABILITY OF SPACE VEHICLES - 4TH ANNUAL
    MYOGLOBIN CONTENT AND ANZYMATIC ACTIVITY          SEMINAR, LOS ANGELES, 6 DEC 1963.
    OF HUMAN SKELETAL MUSCLE - THEIR RELATION WITH    NONE
    THE PROCESS OF ADAPTATION TO HIGH ALTITUDE.       N. HOLLYWOOD, CALIF.
    REYNAFARJE, B.                                    1963        1 VOL.       PA    SV
    DEPARTMENT OF PATHOLOGICAL PHYSIOLOGY, LIMA,
    PERU                                          INSTITUTE OF ELECTROCHEMISTRY
    NOV 62     8P          C-1-P                  541.37  161                   565
                                                      ELECTROCHEMISTRY OF MOLTEN AND SOLID
INSTITUTE OF ANDEAN BIOLOGY(PERU)                     ELECTROLYTES.  AUTHORIZED TRANSLATION FROM THE
AIRU-SAM-TDR-62-88                        UM          RUSSIAN.  INSTITUTE OF ELECTROCHEMISTRY.
    PYRIDINE NUCLEOTIDE OXIDASES AND                  TRANSACTIONS.
    TRANSHYDROGENASE IN ACCLIMATIZATION TO HIGH       INSTITUTE OF ELECTROCHEMISTRY
    ALTITUDE.                                         N.Y., CONSULTANTS BUREAU
    REYNAFARJE, B.                                    1961-      2 VOLS     C-P(V.1+2) C-SV(V.1)
    DEPARTMENT OF PATHOLOGICAL PHYSIOLOGY, LIMA,
    PERU                                          INSTITUTE OF ENGINEERING RESEARCH
    NOV 62     6P          C-1-P                      SEE
                                                          CALIFORNIA, UNIVERSITY OF
INSTITUTE OF AVIATION MEDIC.(NORWAY)
    SEE                                           INSTITUTE OF ENVIRONMENTAL SCIENCES
        ROYAL NORWEGIAN AIR FORCE                 616.98  159                   665
                                                      ENVIRONMENTAL ENGINEERING LECTURE NOTES,
INSTITUTE OF AVIATION MEDICINE (NORWAY)               PRESENTED BY NORTHERN CALIF. CHAPTER,
RNAF-FMI-63-3                             UM          INSTITUTE OF ENVIRONMENTAL SCIENCES AND
    COMBINED EFFECT OF COLD AND ALCOHOL ON HEAT       ENGINEERING AND SCIENCE EXTENSION, UNIV. OF
    BALANCE IN MAN.                                   CALIFORNIA, BERKELEY, FALL, 1961.  ED. BY
    LANGE, K. + ET AL                                 JOHN D. CAMPBELL AND OTHERS.
    OSLO, NORWAY                                      INSTITUTE OF ENVIRONMENTAL SCIENCES + ET AL
    DEC 63      VAR. PAGING PA                         N.D.     VOL.      C-P         C-SV

INSTITUTE OF CHEMISTRY FOR EXPLOSIVES (ITALY)     INSTITUTE OF INTER-AMERICAN AFFAIRS
ICE-50-SYR-(1)                           C        338.98  USA                     665
```

Fig. 2. Sources

TDR 32-402   PA + SV   LIBRARY   08-07-66   PAGE 8493

    SEPT 62   4P   C-1-2-P 2C-SV C-VN   NATIONAL BUREAU OF STANDARDS
                                                          NBS-4943   UN
THERMODYNAMIC PROPERTIES OF OXYGEN   THERMODYNAMIC PROPERTIES OF SOME BORON
    GEORGIA INST. OF TECHNOLOGY   COMPOUNDS.
    GIT-A-593-TR-2   UN   EVANS, W.H. + ET AL
    THE THERMODYNAMIC PROPERTIES OF OXYGEN   31 AUG 56 VAR. PAGING C-1-P
    FROM 20 DEGREES TO 100 DEGREES K. TECHNICAL
    REPORT NO. 2.   THERMODYNAMIC PROPERTIES OF STEAM,
    MULLINS, J.C. + ET AL   NONE
    ENGINEERING EXPERIMENT STATION, ATLANTA, GA.   536.42 K25T   565
    1 MAR 62   VAR. PAGING C-SV   THERMODYNAMIC PROPERTIES OF STEAM,
                                                      INCLUDING DATA FOR THE LIQUID AND SOLID
THERMODYNAMIC PROPERTIES OF PARAHYDROGEN   PHASES.
    GEORGIA INST. OF TECHNOLOGY   KEENAN, JOSEPH HENRY + KEYES, FREDERICK G.
    GIT-K-593-TR-1   UN   NEW YORK, J. WILEY AND SONS, INC.
    THE THERMODYNAMIC PROPERTIES OF PARAHYDROGEN   1936   89P   C-SV
    FROM 1 DEGREE TO 22 DEGREES K. TECHNICAL
    REPORT NO. 1.   THERMODYNAMIC PROPERTIES OF SUPERHEATED
    MULLINS, J.C. + ET AL   AMERICAN DOCUMENTATION INST.
    ENGINEERING EXPERIMENT STATION, ATLANTA, GA.   ADI-5824   UN
    1 NOV 61   68P   C-SV   THERMODYNAMIC PROPERTIES OF SUPERHEATED
                                                      ACETYLENE.
THERMODYNAMIC PROPERTIES OF SALINE WATER.   NONE
    MONSANTO RESEARCH CORP.   N.D.   9P   C-1-P
    OSW-PR-194   UN
    THERMODYNAMIC PROPERTIES OF SALINE WATER.   THERMODYNAMIC PROPERTIES OF TECHNETIUM AND
    FOWER, W.H. + FABUSS, B.M.   PURDUE UNIVERSITY
    BOSTON LABS., EVERETT, MASS.   AFOSR-TN-59-968   UN
    JULY 64   79P   C-SV   THERMODYNAMIC PROPERTIES OF TECHNETIUM AND
                                                      RHENIUM COMPOUNDS. (VII). HEATS OF FORMATION
THERMODYNAMIC PROPERTIES OF SALINE WATER.   OF RHENIUM TRICHLORIDE AND RHENIUM TRIBROMIDE.
    OFFICE OF SALINE WATER   FREE ENERGIES AND ENTROPIES.
    628.16 F11   466   KING, J.P. + COBBLE, J.W.
    THERMODYNAMIC PROPERTIES OF SALINE WATER.   LAFAYETTE, IND.
    RESEARCH AND DEVELOPMENT PROGRESS REPORT   OCT 59   19P   C-1-P
    NO. 136.
    FABUSS, B.M.   THERMODYNAMIC PROPERTIES OF THE ATMOSPHERE
    GPO   RAND CORP.
    1965   63P   SV   RAND-RM-2292   UN
                                                      THERMODYNAMIC PROPERTIES OF THE ATMOSPHERE
THERMODYNAMIC PROPERTIES OF SEVEN METALS AT   OF VENUS.
    LOS ALAMOS SCIENTIFIC LAB.   RAYMOND, J.L.
    LAMS-2640   UN   SANTA MONICA, CALIF.
    THERMODYNAMIC PROPERTIES OF SEVEN METALS AT   26 NOV 58 51P   C-1-2-P   3C-SV
    ZERO PRESSURE.
    CARTER, W.J.   THERMODYNAMIC PROPERTIES OF URANIUM
    LOS ALAMOS SCIENTIFIC LAB., LOS ALAMOS, N.MEX.   PRATT AND WHITNEY AIRCRAFT
    9 MAY 62   62P   C-1-P   PWAC-478   UN
                                                      THERMODYNAMIC PROPERTIES OF URANIUM
THERMODYNAMIC PROPERTIES OF SOME ABLATION   MONOCARBIDE.
    GENERAL ELECTRIC   C   VOZZELLA, P.A. + DECRESCENTE, M.A.
    GE-64SD954   MIDDLETOWN, CONN.
    THERMODYNAMIC PROPERTIES OF SOME ABLATION   SEPT 65   24P   C-1-P   C-SV
    PRODUCTS FROM PLASTIC HEAT SHIELDS IN AIR.
    (U)   THERMODYNAMIC PROPERTIES OF URANIUM
    BROWNE, W.G.   PRATT AND WHITNEY AIRCRAFT
    RE-ENTRY SYSTEMS DEPT., PHILADELPHIA, PA.   PWAC-479   UN
    24 AUG 64 174P   C-SV   THERMODYNAMIC PROPERTIES OF URANIUM
                                                      MONONITRIDE.
THERMODYNAMIC PROPERTIES OF SOME BORON   NONE

FIG. 3. Titles

```
TDR 32-403                                   PA + SV   LIBRARY   08-07-66                 PAGE 4147

NEAL, J.T.
    AIR FORCE CAMBRIDGE RESEARCH LABS.
    AFCRL-65-575                                      UN
  GIANT DESICCATION POLYGONS OF GREAT BASIN
  PLAYAS.  ENVIRONMENTAL RESEARCH PAPERS,
  NO. 123.
  NEAL, J.T.
  BEDFORD, MASS.
  AUG 65      30P            C-1-P

NEAL, J.T., ED.
    AIR FORCE CAMBRIDGE RESEARCH LABS.
    AFCRL-65-266                                      UN
  GEOLOGY, MINERALOGY, AND HYDROLOGY OF U.S.
  PLAYAS.  ENVIRONMENTAL RESEARCH PAPERS,
  NO. 96.
  NEAL, J.T., ED.
  BEDFORD, MASS.
  APR 65      176P           C-1-P      2C-SV

NEAL, L.
    NATIONAL AERONAUTICS AND SPACE ADMIN.
    NASA-TN-X-816                                     C
  AN EXPLORATORY INVESTIGATION AT A MACH
  NUMBER OF 6.9 INTO THE USE OF AERODYNAMIC
  CONTROLS FOR MODULATING THE LIFT-DRAG RATIO
  OF AN APOLLO TYPE CONFIGURATION. (U)
  NEAL, L.
  LANGLEY RES. CTR., LANGLEY STATION,
    HAMPTON, VA.
  MAY 63      18P            C-1-2-P    4C-SV

NEAL, L.G.
    ARGONNE NATIONAL LAB.
    ANL-6625                                          UN
  LOCAL PARAMETERS IN COCURRENT MERCURY-
  NITROGEN FLOW.
  NEAK, L.G.
  ARGONNE, ILL.
  JAN 63      73P            C-SV

NEALE, D.M.
    NONE
    621.384  N25                                466
  COLD CATHODE TUBE CIRCUIT DESIGN.
  NEALE, D.M.
  PRINCETON, N.J., D. VAN NOSTRAND INC.
  1965        259P           SV

NEALE, L.C.
    WORCESTER POLYTECHNIC INST.
    WPL-ANL-49                                        UN
  REPORT ON EXPERIMENTAL INVESTIGATION OF
  CAVITATION ON BEHIND AN ACCELERATED DISC.
  NEALE, L.C. + STEVES, H.K.
  ALDEN HYDRAULIC LAB., WORCHESTER, MASS.
  FEB 68      13P            C-1-P

NEAVES, A.
    FRANKLIN INST.
    ASD-TDR-62-375                                    UN
  RESEARCH ON SPONTANEOUS MAGNETIZATION IN
  SOLID BODIES.
  NEAVES, A.
  PHILADELPHIA, PA.
  APR 62      31P            PA

NEBIKER, F.R.
    GOODYEAR AEROSPACE CORP.
    FDL-TR-65-27                                      UN
  AERODYNAMIC DEPLOYABLE DECELERATOR
  PERFORMANCE-EVALUATION PROGRAM.
  NEBIKER, F.R.
  AKRON, OHIO
  AUG 65      305P           C-1-P

NEBLETTE, C.B.
    NONE
    771.35  N271                                366
  PHOTOGRAPHIC LENSES.
  NEBLETTE, C.B. + MURRAY, A.E.
  HASTINGS-ON-HUDSON, N.Y., MORGAN AND MORGAN
  1965        152P           SV

NECHAYEV, Y.N.
    FOREIGN TECHNOLOGY DIV.
    FTD-MT-64-301                                     UN
  AIR INTAKE DEVICES OF SUPERSONIC AIRCRAFT.
  NECHAYEV, Y.N.
  24 AUG 64  130P            C-SV

NECHELES, R.M.
    LOCKHEED-CALIFORNIA CO.
    LAC-LR-18759                                      UN(P)
  FULL LENGTH STRESS STRAIN CURVES AND UNIFORM
  ELONGATION MEASUREMENTS ON SELECTED TITANIUM
  ALLOYS - SST.
  NECHELES, R.M. + ET AL
  BURBANK, CALIF.
  5 APR 65   22P             C-SV

NECHELES, R.M.
    LOCKHEED-CALIFORNIA CO.
    LAC-LTN-50461                                     UN
  METALLURGICAL ANALYSIS OF FAILED BEARING
  TRUNNION NUT-MODEL 188.
  NECHELES, R.M.
  ENGINEERING RES. LAB., BURBANK, CALIF.
  19 AUG 63  VAR. PAGING  C-1-P

NECHELES, R.M.
    LOCKHEED-CALIFORNIA CO.
    LAC-LTN-50878                                     UN
  METALLURGICAL ANALYSIS OF SERVICE FAILED
  STABILIZER HOT LEADING EDGE - MODEL P-3A.
  NECHELES, R.M.
  ENGINEERING RES. LAB.
  2 MAR 64   VAR. PAGING  C-1-P

NECHELES, R.M.
```

Fig. 4. Authors

PA + BY   LIBRARY   06-07-66   PAGE 852

15 APR 64   VAR. PAGING   C-1-P(27)

AF-33 (657)-11144
   STANFORD UNIVERSITY
   AFSC-AL-TDR-64-198
AN INSTANTANEOUS MICROWAVE POLARIMETER   C
RECEIVER (U). TECHNICAL REPORT NO. 1821-2.
CRANE, M.
STANFORD ELECTRONICS LAB., STANFORD, CALIF.
MAY 64   80P   MICRO

AF-33 (657)-11144
   STANFORD UNIVERSITY
   AFSC-AL-TDR-64-227   UN
TUNING OF CW LASERS OVER ANGSTROM
BANDWIDTHS - SOME POSSIBLE APPROACHES.
MORRIS, R.J.
AUG 64   40P   C-SV

AF-33 (657)-11154
   SYRACUSE UNIVERSITY
   AFSC-ML-TDR-64-144   UN
A STUDY OF THE EFFECT OF SUPERIMPOSED
STRESS CONCENTRATIONS.
WEISS, V. + ET AL
SYRACUSE, N.Y.
APR 64   34P   C-1-P

AF-33 (657)-11183
   AEROJET-GENERAL NUCLEONICS
   APL-TDR-64-124-VOL. 1   UN
RESEARCH IN HIGH TEMPERATURE PLASMAS FOR
SPACE APPLICATIONS. VOL. 1 - PHYSICS.
NONE
SAN RAMON, CALIF.
OCT 64   180P   C-1-P

AF-33 (657)-11184
   MINNESOTA, UNIVERSITY OF
   FDL-TDR-64-156   UN
A SECOND ORDER SOLUTION FOR THE VELOCITY
DISTRIBUTION IN A TURBULENT WAKE.
HEINRICH, H.G. + RUST, L.W.
MINNEAPOLIS, MINN.
APR 65   42P   C-1-P

AF-33 (657)-11200
   AEROJET-GENERAL CORP.
   AFSC-ML-TDR-64-260   UN
NON-EVACUATED CRYOGENIC THERMAL INSULATION
STUDIES.
JOHNSON, C.L. + HOLLWEGER, D.J.
AZUSA, CALIF.
SEPT 64   81P   C-1-P   C-SV

AF-33 (657)-11217
   AERONUTRONIC
   ASI-8-2577   S
APPLICATION OF MATERIALS TO ADVANCED
ROCKET NOZZLE AND HOT GAS CONTROL SYSTEMS.
(U) THIRD QUARTERLY PROGRESS REPORT.
BLAES, H.M. + ET AL

AF-33 (657)-11223
   GENERAL ELECTRIC
   GE-11223-QPR-3   UN
THE STRUCTURAL STABILITY OF WELDS IN
COLUMBIUM ALLOYS. PERIOD - NOV 1, 1963 -
FEB 1, 1964.
YOUNT, R.E. + KELLER, D.L.
MATERIALS DEV. LAB. OPERATION, CINCINNATI,
OHIO
10 FEB 64 25P+   C-SV

AF-33 (657)-11233
   FRANKLIN INST.
   FRAN-I-B2122-1   UN
DISTILLATION OF BERYLLIUM BY SUBLIMATION
AND EVAPORATION. INTERIM REPORT. PERIOD -
AUGUST 15 TO NOVEMBER 30, 1963.
LONDON, G. + HERMAN, M.
LABORATORIES FOR RES. AND DEV., PHILADELPHIA
PA.
N.D.   11P+   C-SV

AF-33 (657)-11253
   UNION CARBIDE CORP.
   AFSC-ML-TDR-64-175-PT. 3   UN
HIGH TEMPERATURE PROTECTIVE COATINGS FOR
GRAPHITE. PART -III.
CRISCIONE, J.M. + ET AL
PARMA, OHIO
OCT 65   199P   C-1-P

AF-33 (657)-11316
   HONEYWELL, INC.
   FDL-TDR-64-89   UN
TRAINABLE FLIGHT CONTROL SYSTEM
INVESTIGATION.
SMITH, F.B. + ET AL
ST. PAUL, MINN.
AUG 64   175P   C-1-P

AF-33 (657)-11326
   ELECTRO-OPTICAL SYSTEMS, INC.
   EOS1-3390-Q-1   UN
OPTICALLY PUMPED IMAGE LIGHT AMPLIFICATION.
QUARTERLY REPORT NO. 1. PERIOD - 10 MAY -
10 AUG 1963.
BERNSTEIN, H. + ET AL
PASADENA, CALIF.
AUG 63   53P   C-SV

AF-33 (657)-11331
   SANTA RITA TECHNOLOGY, INC.
   NRL-TDR-63-60   UN
AN ELECTRONIC ANALOG OF THE EAR.
GLAESSER, E. + ET AL
BIOACOUSTICS LAB. DIV., MENLO PARK, CALIF.
JUNE 63   66P   C-1-P

FIG. 5. Contract numbers

PA + BY   LIBRARY   06-07-66   PAGE 17096

WEDGES--SUPERSONIC CHARACTERISTICS
    NATIONAL AERONAUTICS AND SPACE ADMIN.
    NASA-TN-D-2634   UN
A MODIFIED METHOD OF INTEGRAL RELATIONS FOR
SUPERSONIC NONEQUILIBRIUM FLOW OVER A WEDGE.
NEWMAN,   \.
LANGLEY RLG. CTR., LANGLEY STATION, HAMPTON,
VA.
FEB 65   39P   C-1-2-P   4C-SV

WEDGES--SUPERSONIC CHARACTERISTICS
    PRINCETON UNIVERSITY
    AFOSR-65-0002   UN
HYPERSONIC FLOW OVER A WEDGE WITH UPSTREAM
NON-UNIFORMITIES AND VARIABLE WEDGE ANGLE.
GEORGE, A.R.
GAS DYNAMICS LAB., PRINCETON, N.J.
DEC 64   95P+   C-1-P

WEDGES--SUPERSONIC CHARACTERISTICS
    SOUTHERN CALIFORNIA, UNIV. OF
    AFOSR-TN-58-344   C
A METHOD OF ALLEVIATING THE EFFECTS OF THE
BOUNDARY LAYER SHOCK-WAVE INTERACTION AT A
COMPRESSION CORNER.
WILLIAMS, J.C.
ENG. CTR., LOS ANGELES, CALIF.
31 MAY 58   46P   C-1-P

WEDGES--TRANSONIC CHARACTERISTICS
    VIRGINIA POLYTECHNIC INST.
    AFOSR-TR-55-14   UN
INVESTIGATION OF WEDGES IN TRANSONIC FLOW.
FINAL REPORT.
TRUITT, R.W.
VA. ENG. EXPERIMENT STATION, BLACKSBURG, VA.
MAY 55   52P+   C-1-P

WEDGES--WAKE
    AVCO CORP.
    AFBSD-TDR-64-150   UN
THE NEAR WAKE OF A WEDGE.
WEISS, R.
AVCO EVERETT RES. LAB., EVERETT, MASS.
DEC 64   42P   C-1-P   C-SV

WEDGES--WAKE
    AVCO CORP.
    AVCO-RAD-TM-63-19   UN
TWO-DIMENSIONAL WAKE MEASUREMENT - PART 1,
WAKE DEVELOPMENT.
TODISCO, A. + SANDBORN, V.A.
9 APR 63   25P   C-SV

WEDGES--WAKE
    LOCKHEED MISSILES AND SPACE CO.
    LMSC-801 624   UN
THE EFFECT OF A LONGITUDINAL GRAVITY FIELD
ON THE RE-ENTRANT JET IN A STEADY SYMMETRIC
'AVITY FLOW.

CUTHBERT, J.W.
N.D.   19P   ARC-C-1-P

WEDGES--WATER ENTRY
    COLUMBIA UNIVERSITY
    CU-1-64-ONR-266(86)   UN
IMPACT OF AN ELASTIC WEDGE ON A COMPRESSIBLE
FLOW.
FEIT, D. + ET AL
DEPT. OF CIVIL ENGINEERING AND ENGINEERING
    MECHANICS
NOV 64   56P   C-SV

WEIBULL DISTRIBUTION
    AIR UNIVERSITY
    AIRU-GRE-MATH-64-12   UN
RELIABILITY ANALYSIS OF NON-ELECTRONIC
COMPONENTS USING WEIBULL, GAMMA, AND LOG
NORMAL DISTRIBUTIONS. THESIS.
STOY, D.G.
AIR FORCE INST. OF TECHNOLOGY,
    WRIGHT-PATTERSON AFB, OHIO
AUG 64   73P   C-SV

WEIBULL DISTRIBUTION
    GENERAL ELECTRIC
    GE-61SD55   UN
RELIABILITY MEASUREMENT FOR LONG LIFE
SYSTEMS.
FRITZ, E.L.
MISSILE AND SPACE VEHICLE DEPT.
28 MAR 61   22P   C-SV

WEIBULL DISTRIBUTION
    MOTOROLA, INC.
    MOT-(1)   UN
USE OF THE WEIBULL DISTRIBUTION FUNCTION
IN THE ANALYSIS OF MULTIVARIATE LIFE TEST
RESULTS.
PROCASSINI, A.A. + ROMANO, A.
SEMICONDUCTOR PRODUCTS DIV., PHOENIX, ARIZ.
N.D.   NO PAGING   C-SV

WEIGHING-MACHINES
    NONE
    389.16   J45   765
THE EXAMINATION OF WEIGHING EQUIPMENT.
A MANUAL FOR STATE AND LOCAL WEIGHTS AND
MEASURES AGENCIES. ISSUED MAR 1, 1965.
JENSEN, MALCOLM W. + SMITH, RALPH W.
GPO
1965   279P   C-SV

WEIGHING-MACHINES
    NONE
    389.1   M21T   565
TESTING OF WEIGHING EQUIPMENT. NATIONAL
BUREAU OF STANDARDS HANDBOOK H37.
SMITH, RALPH WEIR
GOVERNMENT PRINT. OFF.

Fig. 6. Subjects

```
TBB 32-496                     PA + SV  L.GRAR:   CR-C7-66              PAGE 4776

K-1589                    G50593        UNION CARBIDE CORP.
    UNION CARBIDE CORP.                     NASA-CR-54255                    C
    K-1589                         UN  PHASE 1 - SUMMARY REPORT, FABRICATION OF
A FIXED FILTER PAPER ALPHA AIR MONITOR.     TUNGSTEN-URANIUM DIOXIDE HONEYCOMB
SEABORN, G.B.                               STRUCTURE".
NUCLEAR DIV., OAK RIDGE, TENN.              WHITE, D.E. + FOLEY, E.M.
23 MAR 64  18P       C-1-P                  NUCLEAR DIV., OAK RIDGE, TENN.
1A.T. 2A.ALPHA SPECTROMETERS 2B.ALPHA       19 MAR 65  61P       C-1-P
PARTICLES--DETECTION AND MEASUREMENT 3A.
SEABORN, G.B. 4A.K-1589 5A.W-7405-ENG-26  K-1632-PT. 1              068783
                                               UNION CARBIDE CORP.
K-1590                    049786               K-1632-PT. 1                UN
    UNION CARBIDE CORP.                    A GRAVIMETRIC GAS FLOW STANDARD - PART 1
    K-1590                         UN  DESIGN AND CONSTRUCTION.
INSTRUMENTATION FOR MEASURING FREEZING      COLLINS, W.T. + SELBY, T.W.
POINTS OF URANIUM HEXAFLUORIDE-HYDROGEN     18 MAY 65  7GP       C-1-P
FLUORIDE SAMPLES.                           1A.T. 2A.GRAVIMETRIC ANALYSIS 2B.GAS FLOW--
BARTKUS, M.J.                               MEASUREMENT 3A.COLLINS, W.T. 4A.K-1632-
NUCLEAR DIV., OAK RIDGE, TENN.              PT. 1
12 MAR 64  14P       C-1-P
1A.T. 2A.INSTRUMENTATION 2B.URANIUM     K-1636                    067783
FLUORIDES--TEMPERATURE FACTORS 2C.HYDROFLUORIC  UNION CARBIDE CORP.
ACID--TEMPERATURE FACTORS 3A.BARTKUS, M.J.      NASA-CR-54376                  CRD
4A.K-1590 5A.W-7405-ENG-26             FABRICATION OF TUNGSTEN-URANIUM DIOXIDE
                                            HONEYCOMB STRUCTURES.  (U) PHASE -II -
K-1621(REV.)              064289        QUARTERLY REPORT, FOR PERIOD ENDING MAR 15,
    UNION CARBIDE CORP.                    1965.
    NASA-CR-54275                  CRD  FOLEY, E.M. + ET AL
DETERMINATION OF IMPURITIES IN TUNGSTEN-    NUCLEAR DIV., OAK RIDGE, TENN.
URANIUM DIOXIDE MIXTURES.  FINAL REPORT.    21 MAY 65  77P       C-SV
WEBER, C.W., ED. + KWASNOSKI, T., ED.
NUCLEAR DIV.                           K-1637                    067784
14 SEPT 64 76P       C-SV                   UNION CARBIDE CORP.
19 FEB 65  (REV.)                           NASA-CR-54377                  CRD
                                        PROGRESS REPORT FOR THE PERIOD - 1 JULY
K-1624                    062795        1964 - 15 MAR 1965.  PART 1 - PREPARATION OF
    UNION CARBIDE CORP.                    HIGH PURITY URANIUM OXIDE POWDERS.  PART 2 -
    K-1624                         UN  CLADDING AND JOINING OF TUNGSTEN CERMETS BY
ANALYSIS OF THE USE OF SOLUBLE NEUTRON      PLASMA SPRAYING.  PART 3 - TUNGSTEN COATING
ABSORBERS IN DIFFUSION PLANT EQUIPMENT.     OF URANIUM DIOXIDE PARTICLES.  (U)
BAILEY, J.C. + ET AL                        COCHRAN, W.L. + ET AL
NUCLEAR DIV.                               NUCLEAR DIV., OAK RIDGE, TENN.
16 DEC 64  25P       C-1-P                  29 MAR 65  74P       C-SV
1A.T. 2A.NEUTRON ABSORPTION ANALYSIS 2B.
CRITICALITY STUDIES 3A.BAILEY, J.C. 4A.  K-1643                    076793
K-1624 5A.W-7405-ENG-26                    UNION CARBIDE CORP.
                                            K-1643                         UN
K-1629                    066281        ASYMPTOTIC COVARIANCES FOR THE MAXIMUM
    UNION CARBIDE CORP.                    LIKELIHOOD ESTIMATORS OF THE PARAMETERS OF A
    K-1629                         UN  NEGATIVE BINOMIAL DISTRIBUTION.
MINIMUM CRITICAL CYLINDER DIAMETERS OF      BOWMAN, K.O. + SHENTON, L.R.
HYDROGEN MODERATED U(4.9) SYSTEMS.          NUCLEAR DIV.
NEWLON, C.E.                                1 JULY 65  150P      C-1-P
NUCLEAR DIV., OAK RIDGE, TENN.              1A.T. 2A.BINOMIALS 2B.PROBABILITY 2C.
15 MAR 65  15P       C-1-P                  ASYMPTOTIC EXPANSION 2D.SERIES 3A.BOWMAN,
1A.T. 2A.CRITICALITY STUDIES 2B.HYDROGEN    K.O. 4A.K-1643 5A.W-7405-ENG-26
MODERATED REACTORS 2C.URANIUM SYSTEMS 3A.
NEWLON, C.E. 4A.K-1629 5A.W-7405-ENG-26  K-1647                    076190
                                           UNION CARBIDE CORP.
K-1630                    065288            NASA-CR-54462                  CRD
```

FIG. 7. Report numbers

```
TBP 32-496                                      PA + SV   LIBRARY    08-07-68                            PAGE 11917

510.78  A73P                              810128
   ARMOUR RESEARCH FOUNDATION, CHICAGO
   510.78  A73P                                   565
  PROCEEDINGS OF THE ANNUAL COMPUTER
  APPLICATIONS SYMPOSIUM.
  ARMOUR RESEARCH FOUNDATION, CHICAGO
  CHICAGO
  FOR HOLDINGS SEE LIBRARIAN.***
  1A.T. 2A.ELECTRONIC CALCULATING-MACHINES--
  CONGRESSES 2B.ELECTRONIC DATA PROCESSING--
  CONGRESSES 2C.COMPUTER APPLICATIONS SYMPOSIUM
  4A.510.78  A73P

510.78  A83  1961                         810129
   ASSOCIATION FOR COMPUTING MACHINERY
   510.78  A83  1961                              565
  PREPRINTS OF SUMMARIES OF PAPERS PRESENTED
  AT THE 16TH NATIONAL MEETING, SEPT 5 - 8,
  1961.
  ASSOCIATION FOR COMPUTING MACHINERY
  NEW YORK
  N.D.       1VOL.        C-SV
  1A.T. 2A.ELECTRONIC CALCULATING-MACHINES--
  CONG. 2B.PROGRAMMING(ELECTRONIC COMPUTERS)
  2C.ELECTRONIC DATA PROCESSING 2D.NUMERICAL
  CALCULATIONS 4A.510.78  A83  1961

510.78  A96                               807005
   NONE
   510.78  A96                          565
  BUSINESS DATA PROCESSING.
  AWAD, E.M.
  ENGLEWOOD CLIFFS, N.J., PRENTICE-HALL
  1965       310P          SV
  1A.T. 2A.ELECTRONIC CALCULATING-MACHINES
  2B.ELECTRONIC DATA PROCESSING 2C.PUNCHED CARD
  SYSTEMS 3A.AWAD, E.M. 4A.510.78  A96

510.78  B11                               810130
   NONE
   510.78  B11                                    565
  CHARLES BABBAGE AND HIS CALCULATING
  ENGINES.
  BABBAGE, CHARLES + ET AL
  NEW YORK, DOVER
  1961       400P.BIB.     C-P
  1A.T. 2A.CALCULATING-MACHINES 2B.CALCULATING
  ENGINES 3A.MORRISON, PHILIP, ED. 4A.510.78
  B11

510.78  B23                               810131
   NONE
   510.78  B23                                    565
  EXPERIMENTAL CORRELOGRAMS AND FOURIER
  TRANSFORMS.  INTERNATIONAL TRACTS IN COMPUTER
  SCIENCE AND TECHNOLOGY AND THEIR APPLICATIONS,
  V. 5.
  BARBER, N.F.
  NEW YORK, PERGAMON
  1961       136P          C-P          C-SV

   1A.T. 2A.ELECTRONIC ANALOG COMPUTERS 2B.
   CORRELOGRAMS 2C.FOURIER TRANSFORMS 2D.
   INTERNATIONAL TRACTS IN COMPUTER SCIENCE AND
   TECHNOLOGY AND THEIR APPLICATIONS, V. 5 4A.
   510.78  B23

510.78  B26                                    803202
   AIR FORCE, ROME AIR DEVELOPMENT CENTER
   510.78  B26                                   1163
  COMPUTER ORGANIZATION, PROCEEDINGS OF THE
  1962 WORKSHOP SPON. BY AIR FORCE, ROME
  AIR DEVEL. CENTER AND WESTINGHOUSE ELECTRIC
  CORP, AIR ARM DIV.
  BARNUM, A.A. + KNAPP, M.A.
  WASHINGTON, D.C., SPARTAN BOOKS
  1963       242P          PA
  1A.T. 2A.COMPUTER ORGANIZATION
  2B.SOLOMON(COMPUTER PROGRAM LANGUAGE)
  2C.ELECTRONIC DIGITAL COMPUTERS
  3A.BARNUM, A.A. 3B.KNAPP, M.A.
  3C.WESTINGHOUSE ELECTRIC CORP.
  4A.510.78  B26

510.78  B261                                   820919
   NONE
   510.78  B261                                        166
  COMPUTER TYPESETTING - EXPERIMENTS AND
  PROSPECTS.
  BARNETT, MICHAEL P.
  CAMBRIDGE, M.I.T. PRESS
  1965       245P
  1A.T. 2A.ELECTRONIC DIGITAL COMPUTERS 2B.
  TYPE-SETTING 2C.PROGRAMMING(ELECTRONIC
  COMPUTERS) 4A.510.78  B261

510.78  B28                                    810132
   NONE
   510.78  B28                                         565
  DIGITAL COMPUTER FUNDAMENTALS.
  BARTEE, THOMAS C.
  NEW YORK, MCGRAW-HILL
  1960       342P          2C-P  C-SV  C-MO
                           2C-VAFB
  1A.T. 2A.ELECTRONIC DIGITAL COMPUTERS 4A.
  510.78  B28

510.78  B281                                   810133
   NONE
   510.78  B281                                        565
  THEORY AND DESIGN OF DIGITAL MACHINES.
  BARTEE, THOMAS C. + ET AL
  NEW YORK, MCGRAW-HILL
  1962       324P.BIB.     2C-P  C-SV  C-MO
  1A.T. 2A.ELECTRONIC DIGITAL COMPUTERS 2B.
  SWITCHING THEORY 3A.LEBOW, IRWIN L. 3B.REED,
  IRVING S. 4A.510.78  B281

510.78  B34                                    804202
   NONE
   510.78  B34                                         564
```

FIG. 8. Book call numbers

or other effort which are uniquely identifiable by the same report number in extension, e.g., LMSC 1481-2, LMSC 1481-3, etc. Such report titles are listed but once in the official microfilm catalog and then with the notation: "See librarian for holdings." The librarian consults her open-entry list and satisfies the requestor as to holdings.

The most far-reaching spin-off of the computer-produced microfilm library catalog system, however, is its power to deliver a printed book catalog at exceptionally low costs. The savings reside chiefly in the absence of photographic expenses and of press set-up costs. The library administrator, whose clientele would object to using a microfilm catalog, could use the computer-produced microfilm system as the printing base for his book catalog since it cuts printing costs by two-thirds (Table 1).

Table 1. Comparative printing costs of library book catalog processed, A, from microfilm master (using Copyflo process) and, B, from computer print-out (using ITEK process)—based on 1,800 pages printed head-to-head, simple binding, each volume 300 pages.

Operation	A Copyflo		B Multilith Printing	
	20 Copies	1 Copy	20 Copies	1 Copy
Plates	$136.80	—	$ 642.60	$ 642.60
Press Set Up	—	—	$ 343.80	343.80
Bond Paper	—	$73.80	——	——
Press Run	216.00	—	—	—
Impressions	—	—	180.00	9.00
Collation	36.00	3.60	36.00	3.60
Binding	20.80	4.16	20.80	2.08
Total	$409.60	$81.56	$1223.20	$1001.08

TDR 32-408	SUNNYVALE	SOURCE HEADINGS 06-12-66		PAGE 64	
HEADINGS	**COUNTS**		**HEADINGS**		**COUNTS**
WESTON INSTRUMENTS, INC.	1		WRIGHT AIR DEVELOPMENT DIV.		
WHEELER LABORATORIES	1		WRIGHT AIR DEVELOPMENT DEV.		1
WHEELER LABS., INC.	1		WRIGHT AIR DEVELOPMENT DIV.		119
WHIRLPOOL CORP.	6		SEE ALSO		
WHITE ELECTROMAGNETICS, INC.	1		WRIGHT AIR DEVELOPMENT CENTER		
WHITE SANDS MISSILE RANGE	7		WRIGHT AIR DEVLOPMENT CENTER		1
WHITE SANDS PROVING GROUND	12		WRIGHT DEVELOPMENT CENTER		1
WHITE-RODGERS CO.	1		WRIGHT DEVELOPMNT DIV.		1
WHITTAKER CONTROLS	2		WRIGLEY, WALTER		1
WHITTAKER CORP.	8		WYANDOTTE CHEMICAL CORP.		1
WICHITA, UNIV. OF	1		WYANDOTTE CHEMICALS CORP.		26
WICHITA, UNIVERSITY OF	6		WYETH LABS.		1
WILEY ELECTRONICS CO.	1		WYLE LABS.		5
WILKES COLLEGE	1		WYMAN-GORDON CO.		1
WILLIAM MARSH RICE UNIVERSITY	1		WYOMING, UNIVERSITY OF		2
SEE			XEROX		1
RICE UNIVERSITY			XEROX CORP.		5
WILLIAMS, (CLYDE) AND CO.	1		YALE UNIV.		4
WILLIAMS(CLYDE) AND CO.	1		YALE UNIVERSITY		22
WILLIAMSON DEVELOPMENT CO., INC.	1		SEE ALSO		
WILMOT CASTLE CO.	1		YALE UNIVERSITY OBSERVATORY		
WILMOTTE, RAYMOND M., INC.	1		YALE UNIVERSITY OBSERVATORY		8
WILSON, NUTTALL, RAIMOND ENGINEERS, INC.	1		SEE ALSO		
WINDSCALE LABS.	1		YALE UNIVERSITY		
WINIFRED MASTERSON BURKE RELIEF FOUNDATION	1		YALE UNIVERSITY OF		7
WISCONSIN UNIVERSITY UF	1		YARDNEY ELECTRIC CORP.		1
WISCONSIN, UNIV. OF	92		YARSLEY RESEARCH LABS., LTD.		1
WISCONSIN, UNIVERSITY	1		YERKES LABS. OF PRIMATE BIOLOGY, INC.		1
WISCONSIN, UNIVERSITY OF	73		YERKES OBSERVATORY		1
WOLF RESEARCH AND DEVELOPMENT CORP.	2		YOUNG DEV. LABS., INC.		1
WOODS HOLE OCEANOGRAPHIC INST.	9		YOUNG DEVELOPMENT LAB., INC.		1
WOODS HOLE OCEANOGRAPHIC INSTITUTION	62		YOUNG DEVELOPMENT LABS., INC.		3
WOODS HOLE OCEANOGRAPHIC INSTITUTION	1		YUBA CONSOLIDATED INDUSTRIES, INC.		1
WORCESTER FOUNDATION FOR EXPERIMENTAL BIOLOGY	2		YUMA PROVING GROUND		1
WORCESTER POLYTECHNIC INST.	1		ZAHORSKI ENGINEERING, INC.		1
WORK PROJECTS ADMIN. NEW YORK CITY	1		ZATOR CO.		7
WORK PROJECTS ADMINISTRATION, NEW YORK CITY	1		ZATOR COMPANY		2
WORK PROJECTS ADMINISTRATION, N.Y., CITY	1		ZENITH PLASTICS CO.		1
WORK PROJECTS ADMINISTRATION, NEW YORK CITY	2		ZENITH RADIO CORP.		1
WORLD DATA CENTER A	1		6595TH AEROSPACE TEST WING		3
WORLD FEDERATION FOR MENTAL HEALTH	1				
WORLD MEDICAL ASSOCIATION	1				
WORLD METEOROLOGICAL ORGANIZATION	1				
WORTHINGTON CORP.	1				
WRIGHT AERONAUTICAL CORP.	1				
WRIGHT AIR DEV. CTR.	121				
WRIGHT AIR DEV. DIV.	7				
WRIGHT AIR DEVELOPEMNT CENTER	1				
WRIGHT AIR DEVELOPMENT CENTER	224				
SEE ALSO					

*** END OF REPORT ***

Fig. 10. Source authority list

TDR 32-409	SUNNYVALE	SUBJECT HEADINGS 06-12-66		PAGE 241	
HEADINGS	**COUNTS**		**HEADINGS**		**COUNTS**
ELELECTROSTATICS	1		ELEVONS--MOMENTS		1
ELEMENTARY PARTICLE PHYSICS	1		ELF		1
ELEMENTARY PARTICLES	8		SEE		
SEE ALSO			EXTREMELY LOW FREQUENCY		
BOSONS			ELF PROJECT		1
NUCLEAR PARTICLES			ELF(EXTREMELY LOW FREQUENCY)		2
PARTICLES			ELGILOY		1
ELEMENTARY PARTICLES--ENERGY	1		SEE		
ELEMENTARY PARTICLES--MASS SPECTRA	1		CHROMIUM-COBALT-MOLYBDENUM (CONT)		
ELEMENTARY PARTICLES--MATHEMATICAL ANALYSIS	1		NICKEL ALLOYS		
ELEMENTARY PARTICLES--MOMENTUM	2		ELIMINATION		1
ELEMENTARY PARTICLES--THEORY	2		ELINT		16
ELEMENTS	1		ELINT SYSTEM		2
SEE ALSO			ELIP(ELECTROSTATIC LATENT IMAGE PHOTOGRAPHY)		1
ALKALI METALS			ELK RIVER POWER REACTOR		1
ALKALINE EARTH METALS			ELLIPSOIDS		5
CHEMICAL ELEMENTS			SEE ALSO		
DELAY ELEMENTS			BODIES OF REVOLUTION		
DENSITY SENSITIVE ELEMENTS			ELLIPSOIDS--AERODYNAMIC CHARACTERISTICS		4
HALOGENS			ELLIPSOIDS--BUCKLING		2
HEATING ELEMENTS			ELLIPSOIDS--CAVITATION		2
HUMIDITY SENSITIVE ELEMENTS			ELLIPSOIDS--COATINGS		1
RARE GASES			ELLIPSOIDS--HEAT TRANSFER		1
TEMPERATURE SENSITIVE ELEMENTS			ELLIPSOIDS--HYDRODYNAMIC CHARACTERISTICS		1
TRANSITION METALS			ELLIPSOIDS--MAGNETIC PROPERTIES		2
TRANSPLUTONIC ELEMENTS			ELLIPSOIDS--MATHEMATICAL ANALYSIS		2
TRANSURANIC ELEMENTS			ELLIPSOIDS--PRESSURE DISTRIBUTION		1
ELEMENTS--ABSORPTIVE PROPERTIES	1		ELLIPSOIDS--PRESSURE EFFECTS		1
ELEMENTS--PURIFICATION	1		ELLIPSOIDS--STRESSES		1
ELEMENTS--RADIATION EFFECTS	1		ELLIPSOIDS--SUPERSONIC CHARACTERISTICS		1
ELEMENTS--SYNTHESIS	1		ELLIPSOIDS--WATER IMPINGEMENT		6
ELEMENTS--THERMODYNAMIC PROPERTIES	1		ELLIPTIC DIFFERENTIAL EQUATIONS		4
ELEMENTS--WAVE TRANSMISSION	1		SEE ALSO		
ELETROMAGNETIC PUMPS			PARTIAL DIFFERENTIAL EQUATIONS		
ELEVATORS(AERIAL)	1		ELLIPTIC EQUATIONS		1
SEE ALSO			ELLIPTIC FUNCTIONS		2
CONTROL SURFACES			ELLIPTIC MAPPING		1
ELEVONS			SEE		
ELEVATORS(AERIAL)--ANALYSIS	1		COMPLEX VARIABLES		
ELEVATORS(AERIAL)--DEFLECTION	1		ELLIPTIC SPACE		1
ELEVATORS(AERIAL)--FAILURE	1		ELLIPTIC SYSTEMS		1
ELEVATORS(AERIAL)--FLUTTER	1		SEE		
ELEVATORS(AERIAL)--MOMENTS	2		PARTIAL DIFFERENTIAL EQUATIONS		
ELEVONS	1		ELLIPTICAL ORBITAL TRAJECTORIES--TABLES		1
SEE ALSO			ELLIPTOCYTOSIS		1
AILERONS			SEE		
CONTROL SURFACES			POLYCYTHEMIA		
ELEVATORS(AERIAL)			ELLOPSOIDS		1
ELEVONS--DEFLECTION	3		ELS(EARLY LUNAR SHELTER)PROGRAM		1
ELEVONS--EFFECTIVENESS	1		ELSEVIER MONOGRAPHS, CHEMISTRY SECTION: 4		1

Fig. 11. Subject authority list

```
TDR 32-410            OPEN ENTRY REPORT      07-03-66                      PAGE  15

LOC   REPORT  NUMBER      ACCESS  CODE  H O L D I N G    I N F O R M A T I O N

1     LMSD-378 210-       038273  0105  TITLE VARIES. SERIES CONTINUES UNDER A
                                  0110  DIFFERENT TITLE.

1     LMSD-380 111-       038274  0115  -9    25 FEB 61-3 MAR 61       NCN
                                  0120  -10   (NOT ISSUED)
                                  0125  -11   11 MAR 61-17 MAR 61      NCN
                                  0130  -12   (NOT ISSUED)
                                  0135  -13   (NOT RECEIVED)
                                  0140  -14   1 APR 61-7 APR 61        NCN
                                  0145  -15   8 APR 61-14 APR 61       NCN
                                  0150  -16   (NOT RECEIVED)
                                  0155  -17   (NOT RECEIVED)
                                  0160  -18   29 APR 61-5 MAY 61       NCN
                                  0165  -19   6 MAY 61-12 MAY 61       NCN
                                  0170  -20   13 MAY 61-19 MAY 61      NCN
                                  0175  -21   20 MAY 61-26 MAY 61      NCN
                                  0180  -22   27 MAY 61-2 JUNE 61      NCN
                                  0185  -23   3 JUNE 61-9 JUNE 61      NCN
                                  0190  -24   10 JUNE 61-16 JUNE 61    NCN
                                  0195  -25   (NOT RECEIVED)
                                  0200  -26   24 JUNE 61-30 JUNE 61    NCN
                                  0205  -27   1 JULY 61-7 JULY 61      NCN
                                  0210  -28   8 JULY 61-14 JULY 61     NCN
                                  0215  -29   15 JULY 61-21 JULY 61    NCN
                                  0220  -30   22 JULY 61-28 JULY 61    NCN
                                  0225  -31   29 JULY 61-4 AUG 61      NCN
                                  0230  -32   5 AUG 61-11 AUG 61       NCN
                                  0235  -33   12 AUG 61-18 AUG 61      NCN

1     LMSD-380 111-       039279  0000  -1    31 DEC 60-6 JAN 61       NCN
                                  0005  -2    7 JAN 61-13 JAN 61       NCN
                                  0010  -3    (NOT ISSUED)
                                  0015  -4    (NOT ISSUED)
                                  0020  -5    2d JAN 61-3 FEB 61       NCN
                                  0025  -6    4 FEB 61-10 FEB 61       NCN
                                  0030  -7    (NOT ISSUED)
                                  0035  -8    (NOT ISSUED)
                                  0040  TITLE VARIES.  SERIES CONTINUES UNDER A
                                  0045  DIFFERENT TITLE.

1     LMSD-423 000-       038827  0000  -1    24 APR 59               C-E-49
                                  0005  -2    17 JUNE 59 (SUPERSEDES LMSD-423 000-1)
                                  0010                                C-F-501
                                  0015  -3    24 SEPT 59 (SUPERSEDES LMSD-423 000-2)
                                  0020                                C-E-99

1     LMSD-436 000-       037959  0000  -6    (SEE LMSD 429 253)
                                  0005  -7    (SEE LMSD 445 213)
                                  0010  -8    (SEE LMSD 445 242)
```

Fig. 12. Open-entry list

References

1. On-line real time dialog library catalog systems, admittedly more powerful are still excessively costly.

2. The increased volume of use and reuse of cataloged information, of course, inevitably introduces the problem of logistics; that is, the need to acquire or generate multiple copies to satisfy simultaneous multiple user needs.

COMPUTER-OUTPUT MICROFILM

by Doris Bolef

As machine readable data files become almost commonplace in special libraries, the potential of COM (Computer-Output Microfilm) for increasing services while decreasing costs is an option that librarians might well consider. Some advantages and disadvantages of COM are reviewed as they relate to libraries and where and how COM can be used to best advantage are suggested.

The computer has provided librarians with the means for handling the information avalanche because of its capacity to store and rearrange vast amounts of information and then print it out faster than the most expert typist. Until recently, these capabilities sufficed, but a bottleneck began to develop beyond the computer in the shape of the perforated, fan-folded sheets. These printouts require massive amounts of storage space, high reproduction costs and costly distribution charges. We have here an example of an advanced form of technology producing the printed page essentially unchanged since the printing of the Gutenberg Bible in 1456.

One solution is the on-line cathode ray tube screen or reactive typewriter giving us the exact information required, thus eliminating the need to examine pages and pages of printout. But on-line systems have the disadvantages of being expensive, depending upon the conditions at a given moment of the host computer, telephone lines, and the output terminal, and the requirement of an increasingly large computer storage unit on call for considerable periods of time.

Another solution, miniaturization, in batch mode, increases certain options available to the user. In miniaturization, the common printout reductions range from 20 times to 200 times. Since such reductions cannot be read with the naked eye, highpowered magnifying equipment must be used. The miniaturized output is on microfilm, and the process Computer Output Microfilm has become known by its acronym COM.

What is COM?

COM is a process that transforms computer data onto microfilm. It uses specially designed pieces of equipment to achieve this. Some of these pieces are extensions of the computers themselves; others are specialized minicomputers with cathode ray tube screens and photographic equipment designed for this purpose. It is with this latter group that many special libraries have had experience.

No attempt will be made in this paper to discuss the various kinds of equipment. This is outside its purview. Avedon, in his book, *Computer Output Microfilm (1)*, describes three different types and then takes 121 pages of text to list the different kinds and specifications by manufacturer.

Industry, commerce, and government have found many uses for COM. With consolidations of companies into corporations and then into conglomerates, with the proliferation of city, state, and federal agencies, the need for up-to-date specifications, directives, registration lists, pricing, and manuals of organization and procedures can be quickly and inexpensively met for distribution in many copies. To date, the greatest successes of COM have been found where multiple copies of large computer files are printed and mailed to other locations. As three examples, the state of Illinois has reduced its automobile registration list from 17 printed volumes to 100 microfiche at a 50% cost savings. The state of Maryland produces its interstate vehicle tax records on COM roll film and claims to have paid for the cost of development and production in collected revenue. Sears Roebuck placed all its spare parts lists on microfiche for the Sears catalog stores. The journal, *COM*, abounds with examples of such successful applications. It must be remembered that the users of COM in many of these applications are not library patrons but paid employees who have the choice of either using microfilm or seeking other employment.

Use in Libraries

Somewhat belatedly, libraries using computers have begun to take a serious look at COM. The use most frequently made of microfiche is in the production of large quantities of bibliographic information from the computer tape for use at many locations.

The first reported large scale use of COM in the library environment was in 1966 when the Technical Information Center of Lockheed Missiles and

Space Company reported a 16mm COM cartridge catalog system (2, 3).
This first successful application was followed by several other applications
notably at Los Angeles County Public, Los Angeles City Public, Yale University, and the University of Cambridge libraries (4).

A recent announcement in *College and Research Libraries News* (June
1973) concerns one ambitious application of COM. The Louisiana Library
Association has produced a new computer output microfiche union catalog containing locations for over one million volumes in 21 Louisiana libraries—19 academic, one public, and the state library. The catalog, called
"Louisiana Numerical Register" (LNR), is regarded as a breakthrough in
terms of rapid listings of massive holdings. Thanks to a lot of thoughtful
negotiations and advance planning, one of the first effects of LNR was the
reduction of ILL requests to the large libraries, spreading them among all
the participants, an effect that libraries in other states may well ponder
(5).

It will be interesting to follow LNR developments, to see what happens
when it becomes time to update the catalog and what effects it has on
library services, resources, and costs. As in most cooperative projects at
this time, the technological problems present less of a challenge than the
negotiating and communications problems. As described in this announcement, the Louisiana librarians have been singularly successful in this respect so that no library loses; every library gains something.

Before describing the experiences of one library, an analysis of its advantages and disadvantages deserves our attention.

Disadvantages

The necessity for additional equipment, the microfilm or microfiche
reader, to read COM has already been mentioned. This equipment increases the costs. There is, however, an additional disadvantage; namely,
the resistance of users to the use of microforms because of their inconvenience. Patrons will sometimes choose not to read a publication when
told it is available in some sort of microform only. It is assumed that librarians are not quite as reluctant, but it would be a mistake not to take
this reluctance into consideration. This resistance by both librarians and
patrons is stronger than is usually reported by COM manufacturers and
service bureaus.

In conjunction with an SDI program at WU School of Medicine Library,
we produced a computer based index to the literature of health care research. Considerable interest in this index was evinced, and we decided to
reproduce it. Because the cost of printing proved to be quite high, we included, in a brochure describing the index, the possible output formats
with the following prices and asked in what form our patrons wanted the
index (see Table 1).

Table 1.

A Microfiche copy @ $8.00
A Computer printout @ $10.00 (either first or second/third copy)
A Multilith printing @ $28.00
A Photoduplication
    on one side only of paper @ $18.00
    on both sides @ $33.00

Of the first 30 responses, only one person wanted microfiche even though the Medical Library and other departments in the Medical Center possess not only microfiche readers but also reader/printers capable of enlarging a frame to readable page-size and then printing it out.

Another disadvantage is the lack of standardization and the wide variation in reduction from original size. The disadvantage is not in the variation itself but in the need for different reading machines with different magnifications, an added expense which limits, therefore, the microfiche/microfilm that libraries can use. Our budgets are not limitless. Some microfilm/microfiche readers are equipped to handle several reductions but none for the complete range from 20X to 200X now in use. This lack of standardization renders some COM unusable to some libraries. Perhaps concerted action for standardization (or at least a decision on our part to produce COM at one specified reduction) is worth pursuing.

Summing up the disadvantages of COM, it is fair to say that the most serious limiting factor to the potential use of COM is the acceptance of the medium of output by the library user.

Advantages

The savings in cost and in time, particularly for special libraries, are considerable. It is often the case that the time of the patron is valuable, and the information in which the library specializes is not easily acquired and must be kept up-to-date. Provided, of course, the information is already on computer tape or stored in a computer, COM can produce and update multiple copies of catalogs, indexes, or lists inexpensively, which the patron can consult wherever he wishes without making the physical journey to the library.

Further, the spacious and ornate buildings of some public libraries have no counterpart in special libraries and space requirements must often be carefully accounted for. In addition, office and laboratory space allocations are just as carefully accounted for, and the saving of storage space in a 4"x 6" card over sixty to several hundred pages of bulky printout should not be overlooked.

Let me point out still another advantage to COM. With the increasing interest in cooperation between libraries, the exchange of bibliographic holdings records and catalogs takes on an added importance. A cheap, portable record that can be updated, that presents few storage problems and can be inexpensively distributed should not be overlooked. Union lists—merged bibliographic holdings which tend to become voluminous with revised editions and increasingly expensive to reproduce—can be assured a continued existence, thanks to COM.

The Equipment

The history of companies with COM facilities is like the history of other forms of technology. When the equipment became commercially feasible in the 1960s, there was a rush into the market by both computer hardware manufacturers and special COM service bureaus. Avedon, in his book (1), listed 50 COM companies and a directory of 100 COM bureaus located in this country and in Canada. Many companies hoped to become the COM equivalent of IBM. There were more COM service bureaus established—both independent companies and departments of larger ones—than the market required. At the same time, more COM filmers were manufactured than the market could absorb, and the first ones left something to be desired.

Arthur Teplitz, in the *Annual Review of Information Science and Technology*, v. 5, reviews COM technical developments as reported in the literature (6). The developments are rapid and startling. The message is clear; we can expect to tailor COM to our specialized needs in newer and more sophisticated ways with less effort on our part, more quickly and at lower costs as time goes on.

There are several factors to be considered in selecting a COM service bureau. First, the company itself has to be investigated to ascertain that it has the resources to do the job and will not go out of business before the job is completed. No matter how euphoric the salesman, the company should be checked with the Better Business Bureau and with several customers. Payment should bot be made until satisfactory microfilm/fiche is in hand and the computer tape returned.

Second, the data on the magnetic tape has to be reformatted in preparation for COM. Mini-computers or processors designed to reformat automatically are available in some COM service bureaus. If a service bureau does not possess such equipment, a special computer program will have to be written, and then the data on magnetic tape will have to be rerun, constituting an additional cost. Unless one has available the service of a computer and programmer support, preference might well be given to the COM service bureau that possesses this added facility.

Third, the company has to be willing and able to give you what you want. If, for example, you want 24 times reduction fiche with frames ordered from top to bottom, left to right, and the first word of each entry in "caps," don't believe the company that says it can't be done. All of your requirements, including the format of the data, the "headers," or the labels, and your deadlines, should be carefully spelled out before the work begins.

Fourth, samples of the company's work should be examined for quality control. The quality level acceptable to the library should be agreed upon before work begins. Since quality standards are difficult and time consuming to quantify, several acceptable samples could be the basis for a general agreement.

Costs

A comparison between COM and its two chief competitors, computer printout and printing, has to take into consideration a number of variables, such as the number of pages and number of copies to be reproduced, local rates for computer line printing, postal rates, distance material is to be sent, and rates for regular printing. The values for these variables presented on the next page are based on the experiences of a medical school library in a midwestern city which is attached to a university with its own computer on campus.

If a single copy of a computer printout is desired, COM is not cost competitive. A single page of computer printout at the facility used costs $0.003. On the other hand, a single frame, which is a roughly equivalent page, in microform costs us $0.167 for the first and $0.006 for each subsequent one. It should be borne in mind, however, that computer center directors do not welcome long printouts of hundreds of pages because it ties up the printer for long periods of time. In fact, very few computer center directors will permit the use of the printer for printouts much in excess of 1,000 pages except at special times and by special arrangement.

It is when multiple copies are required that COM begins to have a clear cost advantage over computer printout. Depending on line charges at your computer center and rates at the local COM service bureau, COM output becomes less expensive than computer printout in the ranges from 10 to 40 copies. The first copy of COM from the Medical Library costs about $10.00 per fiche. (This figure ranges considerably from institution to institution, from locality to locality.) Reproductions of this fiche cost about $0.30 each. Thus:

1 fiche (the master) costs	$10.00
next 9 copies cost	$ 2.70
10 copies cost	$12.70 or $1.27 per fiche
next 30 copies cost	$ 9.00
40 copies cost	$21.70 or $0.54 per fiche

If the master microfiche copy is saved, future reproduction costs of the fiche will be minimal—a boon when the number of copies required is not immediately apparent. If the exact number of copies of a computer print-out required is not immediately apparent, the data must either be stored in the computer or placed on tapes or discs until such time as a decision is needed.

The 1970-1972 cumulation of the Washington University School of Medicine Library *Catalog of Books* is on 25 microfiche. Forty copies were reproduced. The weight is 1½ ounces per set. That same catalog of books produced on the computer would have been 1500 pages per copy and each fanfolded copy would have weighed 32 pounds. To drop and scatter 1,000 pages of fanfold is a nightmare. Thus, the addition of binders, ranging in price from $1.30 to $8.00, becomes a necessity. It should be pointed out that the printing of 40 copies of the catalog on the computer printer, if the computer center director would have allowed it, would have produced 60,000 pages or 1,280 pounds of paper, and that is "paper pollution." An analysis of other forms of reproduction for 40 copies would show they are not cost feasible in such small numbers.

The time element and the manhours also deserve to be considered. Let us suppose 15 copies of a 50 page index to technical reports is run off on the computer printer. Typically, the data would be printed 5 times on 3-ply paper. The printout would then be sent to a processing room where the carbon paper would be removed and the printout divided into 15 separate copies of the index. Someone would have to wrap and ship them either by U.S. mail or by commercial shipper. From 2 to 5 days later, depending on the way it is shipped, the printout is received. If it is to be used even occasionally, the printout would have to be enclosed in a binder and storage space set aside to house it.

Let us suppose this same index is produced on microfiche. The computer tape would be delivered to the COM service bureau. The bureau would then produce the master microfilm copy, make 15 copies and deliver them back to the library. There they would be inserted into 6"x 9" envelopes, addressed and mailed first class to 15 installations by the clerical staff. The difference in mailing or shipping costs is also considerable.

The Future

Additional technological developments in the next decade may change the picture of COM. Already we see a pattern of mergers developing between computer and printing firms so that the entire operation can be completed at one installation. Equipment with the capability of producing a photographic plate from a frame of microfiche/microfilm has been perfected, increasing our options.

In 1969-1970, the Washington University School of Medicine Library had the unfortunate experience of being among the first to try this new technology. In that year we produced our last printed *Catalog of Books*. In investigating the cost of normal printing, we found, to our horror, it had grown far beyond our budget. Printing from microfilm by a local COM service bureau, willing to explore the new technology, seemed to offer an economically viable alternative to traditional printing methods. The quality of the printing, however, turned out to be clearly unsatisfactory. There were a limited number of fonts available, and they were not sharp and clear. Since that time, significant advances in technology have been made. The quality is greatly improved in only 3 years. This micropublisher claims to be able to produce up to 500 copies of 250 pages at less than the costs of traditional printing. It appears that the library with something to publish now has another alternative to consider.

What, then, can we see as the place of COM in the library's future? As microfilm comes into common use—the federal government's massive micropublishing program almost assumes this—and as the technology of COM stablizes and increases its options, we can expect it to show an increasing advantage over computer printout and conventional printing in both speed and cost. On the other hand, COM will show increasing competition from on-line access to machine readable data bases via console printers and cathode ray tube screens.

Categories of information that we can expect will be candidates for COM are as follows.

■ Library information, produced for the staff itself with numerous branch locations, that has to be reasonably current, such as newly acquired publications not yet cataloged, lists of missing items, materials ready for binding, prohibited borrowers and other forms of specialized information. These would be by-products of data bases.

■ Library information produced for library patrons at remote locations. These include the now familiar catalogs of monographs, lists of serials, and we can expect to produce just sections or just updates of these catalogs and lists tailored to specialized requirements.

■ Library information produced for more than one library for cooperative and networking activities. These include union lists of serials and their holdings, union and shared catalogs of monographs or distribution of multiple copies of catalogs among a number of libraries, union lists of technical reports or distribution of multiple copies.

Most of these uses have in common one or more of the following characteristics.

1. The importance of the data is such that it does not justify on-line computer access costs.
2. Multiple copies are needed.
3. There is a large quantity of data.
4. Library staff rather than patrons are primary users.
5. Patrons at remote locations rather than those in close physical

proximity to the library are primary users.

6. The data has to be reasonably up-to-date but less than 100% current.

7. There are cooperative arrangements with other libraries, such as shared technical services and resources.

In the past, we have been content to handle our information on an individualistic basis. In the future, libraries and patrons will find computers linked to each other, as well as to those who supply them with information. Instead of the information avalanche constituting a threat to the future and viability of our libraries, COM is the medium that welcomes the use of information.

Literature Cited

1. Avedon, Don M. *Computer Output Microfilm*. 2d ed. Silver Spring, Md., National Microfilm Association, 1971.

2. Kozumplik, W. A. Computerized Microfilm Catalog. *Special Libraries* 57 (no. 7): 524 (September 1966).

3. Kozumplik, W. A. and R. T. Lange. Computer-produced microfilm library catalog. *American Documentation* 18: 67-80 (April 1967).

4. *Advanced Technology Libraries* 1 (no. 2) (September 1971).

5. *College and Research Libraries News* 34: 136 (June 1973).

6. Teplitz, Arthur. Microfilm and Reprography. *Annual Review of Information Science and Technology*. v. 5. Chicago, Encyclopaedia Britannica for ASIS, 1970. p. 87-111.

Received for review September 7, 1973. Manuscript accepted for publication November 15, 1973. Presented June 13, 1973, as a Contributed Paper, during SLA's 64th Annual Conference in Pittsburgh.

APPLICATIONS AND FINDINGS

by Basil Stuart-Stubbs

Westminister City Libraries[1]

The Westminister City Libraries introduced a computer-based acquisitions-cataloguing system in April 1970, and converted to COM catalogues a year later, when the expense of hard copy cumulations became prohibitive. At the time that the new system was introduced, the existing card catalogue was closed, and it is intended to convert this old catalogue to machine-readable form, although work on this has not begun.

Approximately fifty thousand titles are now included in the new system, and the descriptive entries and location records for these titles fit within the limits of two film cassettes, one devoted to author entries, the other to a classed catalogue. Through the use of a form overlay, locations of copies in all branches are clearly shown, making complete information about the resources of the entire library system available in the main library and all twelve branches (Illus. 1). Using the present layout and input format, a maximum of sixty thousand titles can be accommodated on the three thousand frames of a cassette, using 24.1 reduction and thin polyester film or Kalvar.

In creating the data base, nineteen characters are allowed for the classifications, seventy for the author, and a hundred and forty for the rest of the entry. This does not permit the use of full AACR descriptive cataloguing, but enough information is provided to satisfy the needs of users. The only difficulties encountered in using this shorter entry were in the cases of some government bodies and collections of plays where analytics were desired.

Reprinted by permission of the author and publisher from "Section II: Applications" and "Section III: Implications" of Basil Stuart-Stubbs, *Developments in Library and Union Catalogues and the Use of Microform in British Libraries; report of an inquiry conducted on behalf of The Canadian Union Catalogue Task Group*, pp. 15-46. Ottawa: National Library, March, 1973. Copyright © 1973 by the National Library of Canada.

Illustration No. 1

FOR STAFF USE

CLASS No.	AUTHOR AND TITLE	CENTRAL REF	OR. NCH ST	MARYLEBONE	G. CHARING WOOD	OPENING PARK	ROCHESTER	MAIDA VALE	PIMLICO	PORTLAND	CHARING CROSS	G. SMITH ST	AUDLEY SQ.	B F Road
F 755.43PCCLOCK	ROSE, BERNICE. JACKSON POLLOCK: WORKS ON PAPER. MUS. OF MOD. ART, 1969	X53C3C213												
370.968	ROSE, BRIAN. EDUCATION IN SOUTHERN AFRICA. COLLIER MAC., 1970	C2973C703												1
301	ROSE, CAROLINE DAER. SOCIOLOGY: THE STUDY OF MAN IN SOCIETY. VERRILL, 1965	X53002243X												1
500	ROSE, HILARY, AND ROSE, STEVEN. SCIENCE AND SOCIETY. A. LANE, 1969	713991241						1						
613.2	ROSE, IAN F. FAITH, LOVE AND SEAWEED. PRENTICE, 1963	13901064 CN CREEP												
301.243	ROSE, JOHN. TECHNOLOGICAL INJURY. GORDON, 1969	A77136404 CN CREEP												
823.FORSTER 7	ROSE, JOHN (B. 1917). TECHNOLOGICAL INJURY: EFFECT OF TECHNOLOGICAL ADVANCES ON ENVIRONMENT. GORDON, 1969	Y50C0C557	1 R						1					1
738.0942	ROSE, MARTIAL. E.M. FORSTER. EVANS., 1970	23735143X				?		1						1
323.2	ROSE, MURIEL. ARTIST POTTERS IN ENGLAND. 2ND ED. FABER, 1970	571C46851											1	1
320	ROSS, PAUL. MANCHESTER MARTYRS: THE STORY OF A FENIAN TRAGEDY. LAWRENCE, 1970	853152098												1
630.1	ROSE, RICHARD. PEOPLE IN POLITICS: OBSERVATIONS ACROSS THE ATLANTIC. FABER, 1970	571C89247						1						
327	ROSE, WALTER. GOOD NEIGHBOURS. C.U.P., 1942	52106I2H8 CN CREEP												
755.C402 REN	ROSENAU, JAMES N. INTERNATIONAL POLITICS AND FOREIGN POLICY: A READER. REV. LITERATURE F., 1969	X50002757												
550.78	ROSENBERG, JAKOB. REMBRANDT: LIFE AND WORK. PHAIDON, 1964	X5CC1C402	1R						1	1			1	
	ROSENBERG, JERRY M. COMPUTER PROPHETS. COLLIER, 1969	X50C33C5												
	ROSENBERG, MORRIS. LOGIC OF SURVEY ANALYSIS. BASIC BKS., 1968	46504205B CN CREEP												1
375.8	ROSENBLATT, LOUISE M. LITERATURE AS EXPLORATION. HEINEMANN, 1970	~351-7759												
629.8312	ROSENBROCK, HOWARD HARRY. STATE-SPACE AND MULTIVARIABLE THEORY. NELSON, 1970	17781C025			X									1
362.11073	ROSEGREN, WILLIAM R. AND LEFTON, MARK. HOSPITALS AND PATIENTS. ATHERTON, 1969	X52C1468			X R				1					1
956.9405	ROSENSAFT, M.ZACHEV Z. NOT BACKWARD TO BELLIGERENCY... THE SIX-DAY WAR. YOSELOFF, 1965	468074552			R				1 R					1
968.T	ROSENTHAL, ERIC. ENCYCLOPAEDIA OF SOUTHERN AFRICA. 5TH ED. WARNE, 1970	723212600			1				1					1
811.POUND 7	ROSENTHAL, HAROLD. PRIMER OF EZRA POUND. GROSSET & D., 1966	X50C253.5							1					1
	ROSENTHAL, NORMAN. MISFORTUNATE MARGRAVINE. SEE- WILHELMINA, MARGRAVINE OF BAYREUTH	X705C2709												

Illustration No. 2

The use of abbreviated cataloguing was found to be the practice wherever computer-based catalogues were in operation. However, the decision to use abbreviated cataloguing seemed to have been taken not only because it reduces the costs of data handling and record production, but also because of a general conviction that users do not need and may even be confused by the display of full records.

Since the use of the shorter form of entry permits the present data file to be recorded on a single cassette of film, a completely revised COM catalogue is provided throughout the library system every month. Decisions on cumulation patterns are influenced not only by the costs of COM production, but also by the costs of revising the data base. When the file becomes larger, it is probable that complete monthly revision will no longer be possible, and a monthly cumulating supplement to the author file might be provided, with total file revision once or twice a year.

At the present time, each catalogue information point consists of two readers, one committed to the author file, the other to the classed file. Users are therefore not required to change cassettes, the only actions required of them being the switching on of the light and the twirling of a handle.

Users have responded favourably to the COM catalogue, to which they have adjusted with virtually no instruction. Some have complimented the library on becoming "modern." Despite initial concern over eyestrain, the library staff is pleased with the new catalogue, which generally requires less waste motion to consult. Its major limitation is that the reader cannot be moved to the shelves for the purpose of inventory, but this can be overcome by the creation of hard copy records whenever an inventory is taken.

Hand operated film readers are in use in all public areas; they are less expensive and probably less prone to breakdown than motorized readers. Since it takes less then fifteen seconds to go from one end of the film to the other with a manual reader, the advantage of a motorized viewer seems negligible. There have been occasional breakdowns of an inconsequential sort, but unfortunately these have been magnified by inadequate service from the manufacturer.

Shropshire County Library[2]

The Shropshire County Library, consisting of an administrative centre in Shrewsbury and seven area libraries throughout the county, also operates a computer based acquisitions-cataloguing system. Unlike other such systems inspected, it uses COM fiche on Kalvar for its catalogue, rather than cassette film. The reduction ratio used is 42.1, which permits the equivalent of two hundred and eight pages of printout to be stored on a single fiche. At an average of three lines per catalogue entry, over two thousand title records can be included on each fiche; information provided is author, title, classification, pagination, place, publisher, date, locations, price and ISBN number. Approximately thirty-seven thousand titles are now entered in the COM catalogue, but when the work of converting the old catalogue is completed, a quarter of a million titles will be included.

The catalogue is totally cumulated every six months; a weekly cumulating supplement for author records is provided, and a monthly cumulating supplement for the classed catalogue. Thus in the case of both author and classed catalogues, there is never more than two fiche to consult, for any given item.

At present a fiche reader and a box of fiche are made available to users in all branches. Consideration is being given to the use of folders with fiche pockets, hung on racks; this may be preferable for larger files. No difficulty has been experienced in keeping the fiche in order, and there has been only once instance of theft of a fiche, which was easily replaced for a few cents. The reader is mechanically reliable, simple to use, and bulbs are lasting longer than their stated life of one hundred and fifty hours. Portable hand viewers are improving, and the Library is anticipating the day when users may want their own copies of the catalogue, or portions of it.

Cheshire County Library[3]

About a year ago the Cheshire County Library, consisting of a headquarters, thirty full time branch libraries and about the same number of part-time branches and bookmobiles, put into successful operation an on-line acquisitions-cataloguing system. The production of the card catalogue has been stopped, and the system produces only a COM catalogue; since the Library does not catalogue fiction or children's books, the catalogue record is limited to adult non-fiction.

The catalogue consists of an author and classified sections, which are completely revised annually, and kept current by a monthly cumulating supplement. Cassette film at 24.1 is used, and manually operated viewers are available in all full-time branch libraries. Although the data base is BNB-MARC compatible, and although the system can work from the BNB tapes, delays in receiving tapes have caused the Library to carry on with its own cataloguing. Nevertheless, the cataloguing staff has been reduced from two to one; forty thousand new titles are added annually, and there is no backlog. Obviously, manual filing has been eliminated.

Two terminals are connected to the County Council's computer, and are operational from 9 a.m. to 5 p.m. Monday to Friday. All library records are retained on a disc file; the response time is 1.7 seconds on the average.

The data files are organized by book numbers. This system is greatly assisted by the fact that the majority of its purchases are of British books, most of which carry an ISBN. Where an ISBN is unavailable, the BNB number is used, and where this is lacking, the computer generates and assigns a number for the item. A cross-index to numbers is created, by author and by title. This computer-generated cross-index consists of three keyword entries: 1) the first six characters of the first significant word of the author entry, and the first four characters of the first significant word of the title; 2) the first six characters of the first significant word of the title, and the first four characters of the second significant word of the title; 3) the first six characters of the second significant word of the title and the first four words of the third significant word of the title.

Orders are initiated by the branch librarians, who are required to submit on a standard form the author, title, publisher, date, price, ISBN or BNB number, number of copies desired and a branch code number. The standard form provides up to ninety-six characters for the author entry, and up to three hundred for the title and other information.

Completed orders are delivered to the terminal operator, after vendor information is added, who keys in the ISBN or BNB number where it is given. The computer carries out a check digit verification process on ISBN's, notifying the operator if there is an error. If the number is correct, the computer checks to see whether the title is already in the system, which is the case for about 60 percent of all orders. If the number is located, the catalogue information is displayed so that the operator can confirm that the title is identical, or appears to be the same as the information on the order form. If it is, order information is added.

If the title is not held, the computer displays a data entry form, and the operator copies the information from the order form.

Where neither the ISBN or BNB number is available, the operator keys in the author and title. The computer analyzes the information, using the keyword approach mentioned above, searches the file, and displays any and all entries that approximate the information provided.

Each night an order list is printed out, and verified by library staff the next day; errors are corrected at the terminal.

Every Wednesday night, the computer pulls new orders from the file, and prints these out on multiple forms which are sent to the vendors.

Separate hard copy reports are produced for the library, giving in summary the status of orders placed with the numerous vendors. This acts as a report card on vendor performance, and expedites claiming.

Upon receipt of the book, catalogue information is revised in those cases where the title is new, and locations are added for titles already in the system.

Every four weeks, new accessions are read off on a stock tape, which is used to produce the latest edition of the COM catalogue supplement. At yearly intervals this tape is merged with the master stock tape, for the production on COM of a complete new edition of the catalogue.

Catalogue information is displayed in two columns, and resembles a card format; it is felt that this layout is easier to scan, and is more familiar to users.

This system has made it possible to place a complete union catalogue in every branch of the Library, has reduced processing times, and eliminated filing everywhere.

In the next phase of development, old catalogue records will be entered, and an on-line circulation system will be added.

Birmingham University Library

The first step toward the complete elimination of card catalogues has been taken at Birmingham University Library this year. The existing card catalogue, consisting of an author and classed catalogue, has been copied on 16mm film, eight cards to a frame at 27.1 reduction, and the film has been loaded in cassettes; there are eighty-two cassettes for the author catalogue, which held about 1,150,000 entries at the time of filming, and thirty cassettes for the classed catalogue. Sets of the catalogue and film readers are dispersed throughout the library system. The cassettes are held at present in modified steel shelving, and labelled with dymo tape; however, a special catalogue consulting unit is being designed, there being no such equipment commercially available (Illus. 2). The reader uses a 25× lens; the resulting image is slightly smaller than the size of the original card, a higher reduction ratio having been used to fit eight cards in each frame. To aid the user in locating the right part of the film, the second letter of the author's name for the first of the eight cards always appears to the left of the frame; for example, if the first of the eight cards in the frame has as a main entry the name SMITH, the letter at the left of the frame would be M.

The second step in the conversion process will be to supplement the filmed catalogue with a COM catalogue for books acquired after January 1972. Until final work on the system is completed, a separate card catalogue of recent accessions is being maintained. The COM catalogue will be revised completely every six months, and kept current by monthly cumulating supplements. Since there will be twenty entries per page in the COM catalogue, fewer cassettes will be needed for more titles. It is esimated that a year's accessions, about 100,000 titles, will require two cassettes. The Periodicals Catalogue will also be issued in COM.

Birmingham University Library decided to abandon card catalogues only after an intensive study of all alternatives. David Buckle and Thomas French summarized their conclusions as follows:

> Although the card catalogue is potentially the most up-to-date catalogue, it is extremely labour intensive and would require constant manual attention. . . . As the data base of the catalogue is within the machine, the machine version clearly can be reorganised and edited at will, but the cost of reproducing it in card form would be prohibitive; similarly so the costs of producing multiple copies of the card cata-

logue. Access to the catalogue data contained in a card catalogue is also restrictive, firstly because of the nature of a unit record system, which only allows one entry to be seen at a time, and secondly because of the size constraints upon the amount of data that can be entered onto the card. However, the breakdown of the catalogue into drawers of cards can offer greater access to users in reducing queuing problems. Although there are access and up-to-dateness advantages, the card catalogue is an expensive and inflexible medium.

. . . As a consequence of costing the production of a book form catalogue on a computer line printer to the specifications and quantities we require, it became apparent that alternative methods of output and reproduction must be evaluated. . . . Both card and book form catalogues produced on a computer line printer suffer from character set restrictions. The costs of production and reproduction move upward quite dramatically the greater the character set availability on the print chain of the line printer.

There is a severe cost/speed relationship in using a computer which is reflected in the use of the central processing unit and the peripherals; the more you can maximise the use of fast peripherals, the less cost incurred. . . . The line printer is a slow peripheral. . . . Magnetic tape is a fast peripheral medium; if this can be associated with an output medium of similar speeds, significant savings should be achieved. This search for such a medium directed us to Computer Output on Microform. . . .

The cost/benefits of COM imply that the flexibility of a computer held catalogue can be taken advantage of at a reasonable cost. Multiple copies of complete catalogues, or parts of catalogues, can be produced, cheaply offering standard catalogue entries in multiple locations.[4]

Whatever the practicability of COM is in relationship to a computer-based catalogue program, the ultimate question remains: will library patrons accept a catalogue on film? At Birmingham University, it appears that they do. The original card catalogue is still available to the public and is in use; but the same catalogue is available on film in several reading rooms, where it can also be seen in regular use. Perhaps the new generation of library users is so film-oriented that they fail to understand the concern librarians feel at the thought of bidding farewell to the card catalogue. Birmingham is dealing with two of the three major disadvantages of the microfilm catalogue in the following way: as a substitute for the multiple access provided by a bank of card cabinets, they are providing a sufficient number of copies of the catalogue and film readers in several places in the library, in effect placing the catalogue closer to the users. As for currency, monthly updates are believed to be adequate. In fact, although card catalogues have the capacity of being kept current, it is questionable that many are, there being filing backlogs in almost every library the author has visited, including his own. In the Westminister City Libraries system, order information is also added to the public catalogue, and this has the effect of keeping the catalogue more current; it at least reduced the number of times users ask about a book which is not listed. The third disadvantage of the COM catalogues described in this paper is that all catalogues are presently in three parts, the retrospective catalogue not having yet been converted and amalgamated with the machine file in any case. The difference

in the Birmingham system is that the old catalogue has been filmed and is
in the same format and accessible in the same way as the COM catalogue,
but it still means that the user has three files in which to look if he is uncertain about publication dates: the original catalogue, the COM catalogue,
and the COM catalogue supplement. How the patrons will adapt to this
remains to be seen.

London and South East Library Region (LASER)[5]

In 1969, representatives of eighty-two separate library authorities established a single organization for interlibrary cooperation, known as the
London and South East Library Region, or LASER. It embraces Greater
London and nine counties of the south east, and serves a population exceeding fifteen million. Basically, this was accomplished by the merging of
two existing organizations, the London Union Catalogue and the South
Eastern Regional Library System.

The London Union Catalogue was begun in 1946, and by 1969 held in a
common collection over half a million titles, many of which had been
transferred to the central stock from libraries in metropolitan London.
The South Eastern Regional Library System, formed in 1959, held a stock
of about another quarter of a million volumes. Both organizations maintained union catalogues of holdings for their participating libraries and
central collections. The London Union Catalogue was an author card catalogue, the SERLS catalogue a looseleaf catalogue, partly in British National Bibliography serial number order, and partly in author order for
foreign books and for English books published before the beginning of
BNB.

At the time of the merger, there was a backlog of over half a million
locations to be entered in the union catalogues, and another sizeable backlog of withdrawals. The annual additions of adult non-fiction titles in the
combined system was known to be in excess of six hundred thousand. It
was also known that some libraries were not reporting accessions.

It was determined that a single union catalogue system had to be developed which would have the capacity of recording locations from all libraries, which would simplify the reporting and recording of locations, and
which would eliminate the backlog.

This has been achieved, primarily through the abandonment of all catalogue records with the exception of the ISBN or BNB number. This was
an extension of the SERLS concept of a union catalogue arranged by BNB
number, carried on to the point of dropping the bibliographical description.

It was decided in 1969 to:

1)   set up and continuously update by computer a master file of ISBNs for all British and American books published from January 1, 1970, and to post locations to this file.

2)   convert and add to the master file earlier publications with ISBNs and BNB numbers, and already held in the LASER libraries.

Since August 1970, LASER libraries have been reporting on printed input sheets ISBNs for 1970-plus titles received (Illus. 3). Information on these sheets is keypunched and used to update the master file. Thus all sorting and filing has been eliminated for both the reporting libraries and the union catalogue staff, the entries being reported and keypunched in random order, sorting and filing of numbers being accomplished by machine. As a second file, the BNB number catalogue was converted, and libraries report by BNB numbers where no ISBN exists.

The ISBN file is completely revised every two months, the BNB file every six, and the files are printed out on COM in 16mm cassettes. Libraries receive the six ISBN and the two BNB updates for the equivalent of about $30 per year. This enables them to search for locations without reference to the central union catalogue, expediting the process of interlibrary lending on the one hand, and further decreasing the workload of the union catalogue on the other.

The fact that publications not bearing ISBNs or BNB numbers are excluded from this system is not particularly significant in the LASER situation, because over 90 percent of interlibrary loan requests are for works in English which are published in either the United Kingdom or the United States, where the ISBN is in regular use by publishers.

In the COM printout (Illus. 4) only twenty locations are shown for any number, this quantity being sufficient for the level of loan traffic; but the twenty locations shown are changed by the computer on a rotating basis with every update, space having been provided on the master tape for up to three hundred locations for each number. In this way, no library carries an unusual load.

A further extension of the file will be possible as the British National Bibliography proceeds with its programme of full conversion of its data back to 1950. When this project is completed, locations from the old union card catalogue could be posted to the BNB number file, reducing the contents of the catalogue to pre-1950 British publications and foreign books. It is questionable whether the number of requests for locations from this file would justify its conversion to any system.

There are two other future possibilities for further conversion, however.

LASER is considering the addition of author and title information to its numbered files, not entirely in order to provide further information for borrowing and lending libraries, but to make it possible for libraries in the system to create machine-readable catalogue files for their own collections by working back from their locations codes. The individual libraries could add their own classification numbers and any other desired information, and create COM or hard copy catalogues. By inputting BNB/MARC tapes prior to the posting of locations, LASER could offer further support for the creation of catalogue records, or for the setting up of acquisition/cataloguing systems similar to that at Cheshire. However, the LASER records would not be in full MARC format, but would be restricted to one hundred and twenty characters.

Beginning in January 1973, the East Midland and Northern regional systems have adopted the LASER approach to compiling their union catalogues, and it is expected that other library systems will follow their example. This points the way toward an eventual merging of all files, for a single union catalogue of the holdings of all public libraries, maintained by computer and disseminated on COM.

The British Library

In January 1971, the British Government published a white paper (Cmnd 4572) in which it was proposed to bring together as The British Library the following existing libraries and services: The British Museum Library; the National Central Library; the National Lending Library for Science and Technology; the National Reference Library of Science and Invention; and the British National Bibliography. Enabling legislation was passed during last summer, and The British Library is in the process of being organized at the present time, following upon two years of work and investigation by an Organizing Committee set up by the Paymaster General.

During 1973 the National Central Library will move from London to Boston Spa, there to join the National Lending Library for Science and Technology, and to become a single organization: The British Library Lending Services. Thus an enormous resource for library borrowing will have been created, to which libraries inside and outside of existing regional systems may turn. Because of the existence of this central collection, The British Library can adopt a different attitude towards the recording of locations in the union catalogues it maintains. For example, because the BLLS has as its object the acquisition of all worthwhile current English language monographs, wherever published, and since these will be available to British libraries through an efficient lending service, there seems little necessity to note other locations of such items.

The National Central Library does have a union catalogue, which was created by the merging of several separate union catalogues in 1962. This catalogue contains the holdings of the NCL collection, and the holdings information for about three hundred and twenty libraries which report on a regular basis, chiefly academic. The basic author file contains about a million and a half entries for non-fiction monographs published since 1801 in languages which use the Roman alphabet. A separate catalogue is maintained for titles in Slavonic languages, and another for English books published prior to 1801; the latter will be maintained in the future by the British Museum Library. To simplify filing and searching routines, entries in the main catalogue are filed under the author's surname, and then by the first significant word in the title. It is planned to close off this catalogue.

Libraries within regional systems, such as LASER, do not report directly to the NCL's union catalogue. Generally, a library in a regional system will search within the system before querying NCL, but with the broadening of collection policies and services under the BLLS scheme, it is felt that there will be increased collective use of the NCL collection.

The pattern of national union catalogues now being envisaged is as follows:

1) A catalogue of English books held by BLLS, to which might be added locations for titles not held by BLLs but held by the regional library systems.

2) A regional systems catalogue, as an extension of LASER, maintained by computer and based on ISBN and BNB numbers.

3) A catalogue of foreign books.

Conversion of the old union catalogue would depend on such considerations as the conversion of the British Museum Library catalogue, or the retrospective extension of the LASER catalogue, with the addition of authors and titles.

IMPLICATIONS

Findings

The principal lessons to be learned from current British experience are the following:

1) *Microform is a satisfactory medium for the display and use of library catalogues, from the point of view of both library staff and library patrons.*

Librarians responsible for the systems surveyed in this report were asked about the acceptability of microform catalogues to the users. Although some isolated complaints were admitted to, the librarians were unanimous in claiming a high level of acceptability, bordering in some cases on enthusiasm. The author witnessed both members of the public and staff using catalogues, and no overwhelming difficulties can be reported. However, the practical experience of British libraries does not

coincide with the findings of the New York Public Library, which conducted an experiment with a filmed portion of its catalogue. In a report
to the Council on Library Resources[6], which funded the study, the in-
vestigators stated that problems were encountered in the areas of searching and browsing. In the experiment, cassette film was used in association with a manually operated reader, and users encountered difficulty
in locating desired entries with ease, having little experience with estimating the effects of turning a crank in relationship to length of film
covered. But in the Birmingham application, the addition of large index
letters in each frame assisted readers in locating desired entries; this
feature was not available on the NYPL film, nor were the existing guide
cards photographed. The NYPL surveyor concluded:

> It appears as though most of the technical problems connected with film can be
> answered, but there are two—the searching and browsing problems—which can-
> not be overcome using the machines tested in the experiment. If other micro-
> film machines are developed which cut down searching and browsing time with-
> out too large an increase in cost, then the most important technical problem
> connected with microfilm will be reduced. However, motorized machines and
> machines with index numbers and special call-up devices may have their own
> problems.[7]

Thus the NYPL surveyor tends to look for improvement in the equipment, but does not give much consideration to the addition of finding
aids on the film itself.

2)   *Computer Output on Microform is an effective and economical
way of creating, displaying and deploying catalogue records which exist
in machine-readable form.*
   In a major report for The British Library, a research team summarized its findings:

> The advantages of microform library catalogues are cost and compactness.
> Microform is cheap to print, to duplicate and to store. If the catalogue is
> maintained by computer microform copies will normally be produced by
> computer output microform (COM). The cost of this is typically 1/2p. per
> frame containing 10 to 25 catalogue records, making it one of the cheapest
> forms of computer output. Duplication costs are low. Compactness is im-
> portant; a microform catalogue of 5 million entries can be placed within reach
> of a person sitting at a table.[8]

The leading member of this research team expressed the opinion to
the author that COM was the only sensible alternative for catalogue

production and maintenance for at least the next decade, or until on-line catalogues become feasible.

3)   *Bibliographical records can be greatly abbreviated without signifi-cantly affecting the usefulness of library catalogues to either staff or patrons.*

On the evidence of successful practice in British libraries, the con-tinued display of quantities of non-essential bibliographic detail in cata-logues must be seriously questioned, particularly when this detail is bring created and supplied many times over by individual libraries as well as by commonly held bibliographical works of reference. In study-ing this problem, The British Library research team concluded that the minimum data required by any item could be fitted into ninety-six characters, for practical purposes of catalogue use. At Bath University Library, an experiment in the use of shortened records containing up to 123 characters in a machine-based system is under way:

> The principle of the Bath Mini-Catalogue from the beginning was that of 'minimal data, maximal access'—it is better to have few details, and be able to get at all of them, than to have fuller details, as in a conventional card catalogue, and to be able to approach them only by author and class number.[9]

4)   *Reliance on a numbering system, to the exclusion of bibliographic information, simplifies the reporting, recording and searching of union catalogue locations.*

Simple in concept, efficient in operation, the LASER approach to its union catalogue is a thoroughgoing success. Its national adoption by the regional public library systems of Britain seems assured. Further, it is being adopted internationally: The State Library of South Africa at Pretoria has begun to publish on microfiche the union catalogue of 1972 plus imprints reported by one hundred and fifty participating South African libraries. Under the title South African Unicat, it is pub-lished quarterly and is cumulative with each issue. The gradual adop-tion of ISBNs by publishers around the world bodes well for the future of union catalogues maintained by number.

5)   *Total conversion of existing manual union catalogue files while desirable in principle may not be necessary in practice, if the end in view is to provide an efficient location service and not a complete bib-liographic record.*

Wherever a card or book form union catalogue exists in Britain, the approach of librarians seems to be first to analyze the use of the various elements within the catalogue and second to relate conversion of these elements to the level of use, and only then in connection with some national plan.

In relating these finds to the Canadian situation, two aspects of the present Canadian National Union Catalogue can be considered separately: 1) the existing card file. 2) incoming accessions.

Illustration No. 3

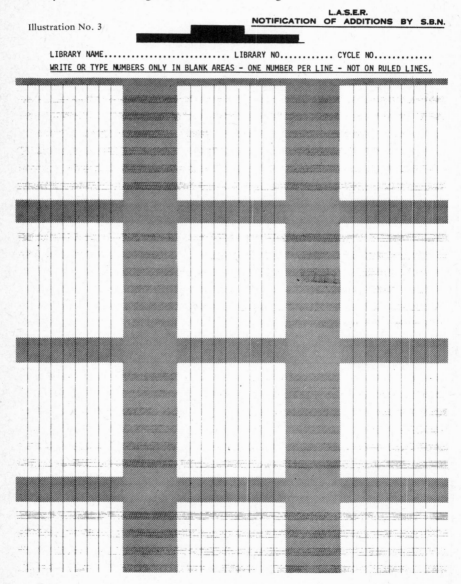

L.A.S.E.R.
NOTIFICATION OF ADDITIONS BY S.B.N.

LIBRARY NAME............................ LIBRARY NO............ CYCLE NO............
WRITE OR TYPE NUMBERS ONLY IN BLANK AREAS - ONE NUMBER PER LINE - NOT ON RULED LINES.

Illustration No. 4

R.B.LOCATION LIST - REGION P   0287

```
563-092-785   43
563-092-793   43
563-092-807   43
563-092-815   4    5    6    9   10   14   15   17   18   19   20   21   25   27   29   30   32   33   34   37
563-092-823   4   10   17   20   30   34   56   61   65   67   94   95  111  115  118
563-092-866  13   19   20   21   22   31   34   37   38   39   40   45   51   53   61   67   70   79   82   94
563-093-102  31   62   82  129
563-093-617  10   20   25   33   34   40   58   61   73   76   94  115
563-093-641   4   10   13   17   19   22   30   32   33   34   38   39   40   41   44   47   48   56   61   62
563-093-668  20   30   56   65   76   94  110
563-093-676   4   11   25   29   34   37   39   40   56   58   60   76   94  111
563-093-692  16   21   25   31   33   45   56   61   62   81   87  110    4
563-093-706  20   28   33   34   38   39   41   43   56   60   61   69   70   73   76   79   82   94  116  125
563-093-730  27   30   34   37   39   40   43   44   48   60   61   69   73   76   79   82   86   87   92   94
563-093-749  33   36   39   40   43   61   20   25
563-093-978  62   70   82   92   25   31
563-094-001  62   91   31
563-094-819  62   10   31
563-094-580  40   43   47
563-096-810  25
563-101-458  81   91   92   93   94   95  109  110  111  113  115  116  117  125  126  128  129    4    9   10
563-101-474  91   31   56   62
563-101-490 113  115  117    5   10   17   25   27   28   29   33   34   36   37   39   40   41   58   60   61
563-101-504 113  115  116  117    5    9   10   14   17   18   20   25   27   28   29   33   34   37   39   40
563-101-512 116   39   40   68   76  110  111
563-101-520 129    6    9   14   18   20   21   25   27   31   34   36   37   39   41   47   52   58   60   73
563-101-539  20   31   39   40   61   69   94  113  115
563-101-547  12   20   25   34   40   56   61   95  111  118
563-101-555   4    6    9   10   12   19   21   22   25   27   29   30   32   34   36   37   38   39   40   41
563-101-563  10   12   25   34   39   58   61   92   94  125  128  129
563-101-571  10   22   25   34   39   41   48   58   60   61   81   92   94  112  118  125  126  129
563-101-601  21   25   40   58   62   70   92  115  126
563-101-628   4    6   10   21   27   31   32   34   36   37   39   40   41   43   44   47   49   51   55   56
563-101-652  41   61
563-101-679  10   29   34   39   41   58   60   61   68   69   70   82  115  116  118  128
563-101-989  31   62  115
563-102-063  21   29   56   70   92   94  128
563-102-071   6   10   12   18   19   21   27   29   31   33   34   37   39   40   41   44   45   47   48   89
563-102-098  10   31   70   76  112
563-102-233  19   27   39   70  113  115  128
563-102-241  39   40
563-102-276  25   34   37   39   58   60   61   70   94  111
563-102-349  21   27   29   39   69   87   91  112
563-102-616  25   58   68   94   95
563-102-845  34   52   25
563-103-051  14
563-103-264  70   94   95   25
563-103-272  94   25
563-103-310  94   25   58
563-103-337  85  120   25   39   51   53   67   70
```

References

1. Larkworthy, Graham and Brown, Cyril G. Library catalogues on microfilm. *Library Association Record*, vol. 73, no. 12, December 1971, p. 231-232.

2. Hammond, Hilary I. The Computer catalogue system at Shropshire County Library. Program, vol. 6, no. 1, January 1972, p. 74-86.

3. Cheshire County Council. Libraries and Museum Services Department. Book ordering and cataloguing system description. (Chester, 1972) 33 p.

4. Buckle, D.G.R. and French, Thomas. The application of microform to manual and machine-readable catalogues. *Program*, vol. 5, no. 2, May 1971, p. 194-195.

5. London and South Eastern Library Region. List of members and annual report. 1969/70, 1970/71, 1971/72. London, 1970-72.

6. New York Public Library. The Use of microfilm in relation to the retrospective and prospective catalogs of the Research Libraries of the New York Public Library: a report to the Council on Library Resources (CLR Grant No. 516). N.Y., 1972. Unpublished.

7. Ibid., p. 12.

8. Great Britain. Department of Education and Science. The Scope for automatic data processing in The British Library. London, HMSO, 1972. p. 539.

9. Bryant, Philip, et al. The Bath mini-catalogue: a progress report. Bath, Bath University Library, 1972. p. 3.

EXCERPTS FROM *AN APPRAISAL OF*
COMPUTER OUTPUT MICROFILM
FOR LIBRARY CATALOGUES

by John R. Spencer

Implications of COM Library Catalogues

Catalogues of stock provide the key to the exploitation of libraries of all
types and sizes. The maintenance of catalogues has consistently posed
problems for libraries and these problems increase as the size and content
of the collection (in terms of additions, deletions and number of references) increases. The more important libraries in the nineteenth century
attempted to provide printed bound catalogues of their stock. These
printed catalogues had the substantial advantage that copies could be distributed to users and other libraries and thus further the exploitation of
the collection. Unfortunately these catalogues passed out of date at a
speed proportional to the libraries' turnover of stock. The cost of maintaining and reissuing such catalogues for most libraries rapidly became prohibitive and the printed book catalogues ceased to be used.

The solution to the problem of updating came in the form of the card
or sheaf catalogue. Single entries were made on individual cards or sheafs.
Such entries could then be individually interfiled into (or deleted from)
the main sequence. Provided sufficient resources could be devoted to
catalogue maintenance, such catalogues could solve the updating problem.
They were successful and for many years became the norm in virtually all
libraries. They had however one major disadvantage—a duplicate or satellite catalogue could only be maintained by duplicating all the updating
work associated with the main catalogue. Taken with the substantial space
and furniture requirements, this effectively precluded most libraries from
duplicating their catalogues. Thus, it was only possible to seek information

on a library's stock by visiting or contacting the library on each occasion.

The increasing use of computers held out a promise that for the first time libraries could turn to automation to maintain their catalogues. Such use of computers would seem to be well suited to replace the human factor in updating and purging of catalogues, the generated data could also be used for ancilliary activities.

The earlier systems of computer generated catalogues provided paper output via a line printer, this paper output was then bound into a book form catalogue. In its basic form the book form catalogue takes the information which would normally appear on several catalogue cards and produces one page of information with multiple catalogue entries. One volume of a book form catalogue may contain the equivalent of 20 to 25 trays of a card catalogue. Unfortunately the book form catalogue can only be updated by producing accumulations (i.e. by reissuing old entries with the addition of newer ones) thus confronting libraries with a catalogue which increased in bulk and cost with each update. The problems of entry additions and deletions is often the cause of the book form catalogue falling into disuse. Typical costs for the production of a book form catalogue are illustrated in figure 14 and reference 5. If the computer had solved the updating problem, it seemed that the end product, like the card catalogue, was to remain bulky and costly (albeit for different reasons) to maintain. It was certainly possible to reduce costs and bulk of duplicate catalogues by photo-reduction but, for most purposes, such catalogues offered no real advantages for the maintenance of satellite catalogue collections.

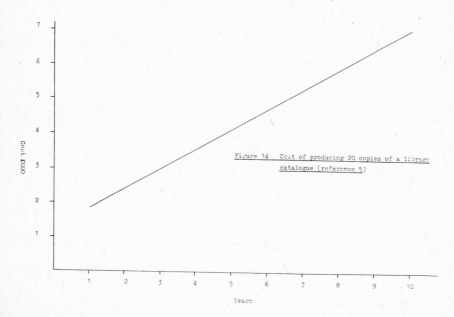

Figure 14   Cost of producing 20 copies of a library catalogue (reference 5)

As large libraries have progressed to storing information on computers, systems have been developed whereby that information may be consulted directly by the use of an on-line terminal. The use of on-line computer catalogues is somewhat limited as the cost of such systems is high. The basic advantage of an on-line catalogue is the ease with which data may be changed or updated. Information gained from an on-line system will always be up-to-date. In use, the on-line catalogue requires trained operators to gain maximum information and benefit from the system.

The development of COM has solved many of the problems associated with mechanised cataloguing. COM has almost the flexibility of the on-line system yet still offers an inexpensive alternative to the card or book form catalogue.

Consider the qualities of a library catalogue—

A public library catalogue is often required to cover a wide range of material; the users of such a catalogue tend to have relatively low motivation, while a special library catalogue covers a much smaller subject area and its users have high motivation. Thus to gain maximum information from a given catalogue, the criteria listed below must be given careful consideration.

Layout and presentation

First, the visual presentation of the catalogue information should be in such a form that is easy to use. Character requirements, page layout, etc., are factors which can affect the performance of a library catalogue. A catalogue entry burdened with unnecessary data would be less effective than a carefully planned concise entry.

Form

Second, the catalogue must be presented in a convenient form to the users of the library. Both card catalogues and book form catalogues offer user convenience but the on-line computer terminal because of its unfamiliarity may prove difficult to use for the casual library user. An essential feature of user convenience is that the catalogue should be able to be used without supervision or concentrated training.

Updating

Third, the catalogue must be able to be updated. The card catalogue and on-line catalogue are both easily updated; single items may be added or deleted with relative ease. The book form catalogue unless short-term hand written entries can be tolerated, must be totally reissued. Even with handwritten entries, the book form catalogue would need to be reissued at regular intervals.

Cost

Fourth, the catalogue must be cost effective. The card catalogue requires intensive staff time to provide an up-to-date system. The typing, duplication and subsequent filing of catalogue cards are all costly in terms of staff time. The computer produced book form catalogue requires less dedicated staff time but is costly to duplicate and requires constant reissuing to maintain an accurate record of stock additions and deletions. The on-line computer catalogue can provide the most up-to-date information but is very costly in capital equipment. The computer must have a dedicated store available to the library users; this is often very uneconomic use of computer power.

The conventional methods of generating catalogue information all suffer from the basic disadvantage of being too costly. The increasing use of computers by libraries has provided scope for a more effective method of producing catalogue information.

The use of COM in commercial applications has been steadily increasing over the last five years, but the first U.K. library to utilise COM as a catalogue media did so only two years' ago. At the time of writing this report, the number of libraries in the United Kingdom active in the field of COM cataloging is approximately twenty.

The potential of COM as a catalogue media is far reaching; it can provide, if correctly designed and applied, an easily updatable inexpensive library catalogue with user appeal.

The use of COM as a library catalogue media has several specific advantages.

1.   Space saving: up to 98% over a conventional hard copy catalogue;

2.   Speed: the throughput of a COM recorder is typically 10 to 20 times faster than a line printer, this itself does not have any great significance until the total time taken by a computer to produce a hard copy catalogue is considered. The saving in computer time for the production of multiple copies represents a large saving in overall cost, since computer time is an expensive commodity;

3.   Character repertoire: Most line printers have a very limited range of characters, usually in upper case only. The COM recorder can have the capability of producing characters in upper and lower case as well as in different type sizes and intensities. In a library catalogue application the availability of these different characters can enhance the final product to a point where the microform catalogue is superior to the conventional hard copy;

4.   Costs: A COM produced library catalogue makes it viable to provide satellite libraries and even the smallest branch with a complete copy of the catalogue, this has obvious advantages—the inter-library loans system may be simplified—books may be sent from branch to branch rather

than via a central service area. Users of the catalogue may also benefit from the ability to consult a full catalogue at every service point;

5.   Updating: The low cost of COM makes it suitable to update catalogues at regular intervals;

6.   Centralised cataloguing: The increasing use of computers for library catalogues, mainly due to the advantages offered by COM, promotes the use of centralised cataloguing services such as the British National Bibliography MARC tape service.

Consider in some detail the advantages of COM as a catalogue media as listed above—

Space savings

The space savings obtained by using microforms are typically 95% to 98% compared with that of paper. The space required for the storage of cassettes or microfiche and siting of the microform reader are omitted from the above figures. The total space requirements for a library catalogue using microform are significantly less than those required for a conventional hard copy alternative.

Speed

The speed of operation of a COM recorder is its basic advantage, this speed of operation provides several secondary advantages. The computer is relieved from the condition often referred to as 'printer bound' (the computer can process information at speed in excess of the printout capability of the line printer, thus information may be queuing to be output on the line printer hence restricting the CPU until the backlog has been cleared). This problem becomes more acute when multiple copies are required, the use of multi-part stationery for up to four copies may provide a solution for some applications, but a library catalogue often is required to be in many locations, hence the computer may be forced into making several runs just to provide duplicate copies. The use of the COM recorder eases the 'printer bound' situation by working at speeds approaching the data processing speed of the computer and the master film generated may be used to provide duplicate copies independently from the computer.

The use of an off-line COM recorder, e.g. at a commercial bureau, can offer substantial saving of host computer time, the time taken to generate a magnetic tape is only a fraction of the time which would be required to output the information contained on such a tape via a line printer. Typical values may be—

Output via line printer = 5 hours
Produce magnetic tape, 5 minutes plus time on COM recorder,
say 30 minutes.

This represents a saving of 4 hours 55 minutes of host computer time as time on the COM recorder is completely independent.

The saving of host computer time represents considerable savings in the cost of producing duplicate copies of computer generated information.

Character Repertoire

COM machinery available at commercial bureaux is generally not suitable for the production of library catalogues. Character repertoires are limited and additional characters are not easily substituted. The range of characters available from most commercially operated COM recorders is restricted to one font upper and lower case with any special characters favouring computer applications. New COM recorders being introduced are tending to have a larger range of characters with the accent on commercial printing by providing more specialised characters not normally associated with computers. This move by the manufacturers will aid the production of library catalogues by providing at least some of the more specialised characters required by many libraries for the production of catalogues. It must be remembered that a COM recorder with graphics facility is more likely to be able to produce special characters as may be required by a library catalogue than the more conventional types of COM recorder.

As stated above a COM recorder had the potential to produce characters in several different type fonts and intensities, this potential could well be exploited by libraries in the production of catalogues.

Cost

The cost of the COM recorder itself is probably the most specific disadvantage of using COM. A small COM recorder capable of generating upper case characters costs in the order of £20,000 to £40,000. For a machine capable of generating several different type fonts, the cost may be in excess of £60,000. To justify the purchase of even a small COM recorder, the volume of output must be extremely high; it has been quoted that the breakeven point to start considering COM as an alternative to paper is above 100,000 pages of original per month. Hence, very few libraries, if any, could justify the purchase of an in-house COM recorder for the production of library catalogues.

The cost of the COM recorder alone is not the only consideration when dealing with in-house plant, the cost of processors and duplicating equipment, specialised staff and the special environment required for COM recorders must be taken into account. Thus, even the largest library must be aware of the costs of using a commercial bureau.

In the United Kingdom a number of COM recorders are operated on a service basis, details of these may be found in Appendix 7. Although it is not possible to give absolute costs involved by using a bureau, typical values are given below—

Master film production - £7.50 to £10.00 per thousand frames (this would be a medium cost COM recorder producing one font of upper and lower case characters, master film produced on a graphics machine in several different fonts would cost £20 to £60 per thousand frames).

Duplicate films are charged at about 10% of that of the master.

Other charges may include a minimum charge for low volume production, re-formatting of magnetic tape if it does not meet the specification of the COM recorder, magnetic tape handling charges and loading and supplying of film containers.

The actual production of the microfilm on the COM recorder is only one stage in the total production of a COM catalogue. Data must be entered into the computer, that data sorted and formatted and output onto magnetic tape before it can be used on an off-line COM recorder.

Data preparation costs for the production of COM library catalogues may be significantly lower than by conventional computerised cataloguing systems. Typical costs may be those experienced by International Nickel Limited (reference 6).

Conventional	p	COM	p
Typing	20	Typing	25
Input sheets	3	Final run	3
Key punch	10	Conversion and Coding	13
Proof reading	3	Machine service	3
Punch corrections	1		
	37p		44p

At first sight the above table would seem to show an unfavourable cost comparison; there are, however, a number of counter-balancing factors. First, about four times as much data is being put in to the computer as a result of entering the whole abstract as distinct from the original system of providing a condensed version. So comparing like with like, the figure for conversion and coding should be reduced to 3p. Second, improvement in the turnround time by the elimination of proof reading of the key punching is an unmeasurable benefit but must be included in any comparison.

The costs involved in having to reprogramme to obtain compatibility with a specific COM recorder are not available but it has been suggested that any increase would be in the order of 5% or less.

A typical library catalogue production flow chart is illustrated in figure 15, this chart shows the various stages of production up to the magnetic tape prior to use on the COM recorder.

A flow chart illustrating the microform production of a library catalogue is given in figure 16.

Updating

Two basic methods may be used to update a library catalogue—

1.   Produce full cumulations at regular intervals;
2.   Produce cumulating additions until a sufficient number is obtained to require a complete cumulation run to be made.

The first of these two methods offers most user convenience since there is only ever one place to seek information. The disadvantage of this system however is the high cost involved in say producing a complete catalogue incorporating a small number of additions at monthly intervals.

The second method of producing a number of cumulating additions may be more economic but users of the catalogue are faced with the problem of having two places to look for information before the full cumulation is produced, say at six monthly intervals.

The operation of a minimum charge by many commercial bureaux may provide the incentive to all but the largest of libraries to opt for the full cumulating system of updating catalogues.

The widespread use of microforms by librarians may promote the use of large area union catalogues such as the LASER Catalogue (described in Appendix 2 and Reference 7). The low cost of COM for distribution copies would provide for large scale information exchanges between libraries, until now unrealistic because of prohibitive costs of conventional methods of reproducing computer output.

The steady increase of the use of microforms in libraries may well accelerate with the advent of COM catalogues. Little work has been conducted in the past on the acceptance of microforms in libraries or the presentation of information. It is suggested that these areas should receive attention before the explosive growth in the use of such microform materialises. The acceptance of microforms depend on many factors, but probably the most important is the slow process of education, perhaps the next generation of library users will show a preference for microforms rather than the expensive, cumbersome and often difficult to read alternative of hard copy.

Figure 15   Simplified Library Catalogue Production Flow Chart

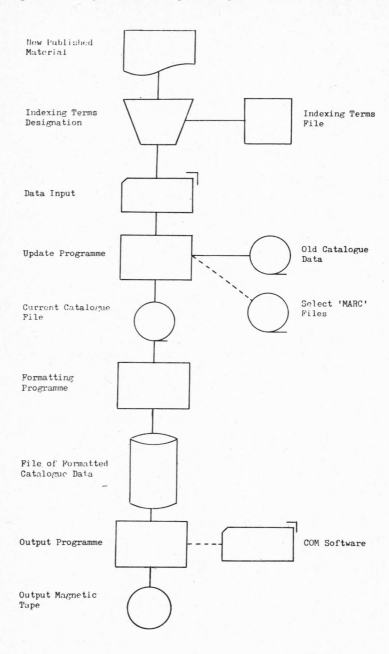

Figure 16 Microfilm Production of a Library Catalogue Flow Chart

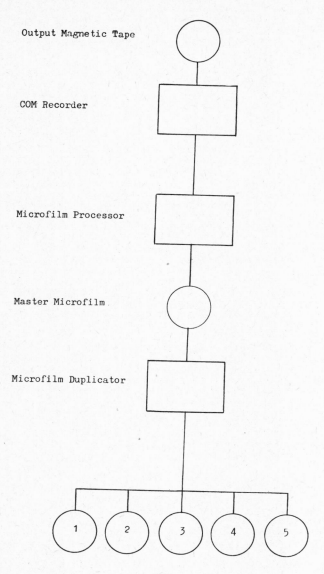

Output Magnetic Tape

COM Recorder

Microfilm Processor

Master Microfilm

Microfilm Duplicator

Distribution Copies

Case Studies

Approximately 15 libraries in the United Kingdom are using COM catalogues at present and most of these libraries have designed the COM system for their own specific needs. The case studies below give an indication
of how five of these libraries have used COM as a cataloguing tool and
what advantages COM has provided over conventional cataloguing systems.
The case studies cover the three basic areas of library cataloguing in the
United Kingdom—

1.   Public Libraries;
2.   University Libraries;
3.   Special Libraries.

Case Study 1: Westminster City Public Libraries

Westminster and Kensington and Chelsea Joint Computer Committee
started planning a computer based library catalogue early in 1967. At
that time the only methods of producing multiple copies of computer output were - photocopying; offset litho; or multi-part stationery, all of which
proved rather expensive. The development of COM and the setting up of
COM service bureaux in the United Kingdom presented an attractive alternative to paper output. In April 1971 Westminster City Libraries changed
to a COM produced catalogue, thus avoiding paper printout altogether.
    It was decided at an early stage that COM catalogue should be used by
the general public, so particular emphasis was placed on ease of use by the
general public with only minimal assistance from library staff. For these
reasons microfiches were rejected as close supervision would be required in
the loading and subsequent re-filing of the microfiches. The ideal form was
considered to be closed cassettes and this system was in fact chosen. The
choice of reader reflected the need for simplicity and ease of operation.
Westminster selected Memorex 1642 readers which are very easy to operate, their only problem being the constant need for re-focussing. Cine mode
was chosen for film orientation, again for simplicity as no film centering is
required to view the entire image area. This factor was considered to be of
prime importance as the catalogue was to be used in public areas. The
question of power operated readers was discussed at some lengths, but it
was decided that hand operated readers would be simpler to operate.
    The film used is thin based polyester, which is half the thickness of con-
ventional acetate based film and thus provides a greater capacity per cassette. With polyester based film the Memorex cassettes can hold up to
3,000 frames, representing 60,000 entries. The use of polyester based film
was prompted by Westminister's policy of providing one reader per cassette of film in public areas so avoiding the need for members of the public to change cassettes.

The sample page of the Westminster catalogue shows books 'on order' are contained within the system; this provides a useful backup whereby if a book on order appears on two consecutive monthly updates, a card is automatically sent to the supplier to expedite the order.

FOR STAFF USE / CENTRAL REF / CHURCH St / MARYLEBONE / QUEENS PARK / OULTHS PARK / PROJECT St/R / MAIDA VALE / PIMLICO / PORTLAND / CHARING CROSS / Gt SMITH St / S. AUDLEY St / A.A Road

CLASS No.	AUTHOR AND TITLE
629.13335	STEVENS, ALFRED HULL — HISTORY OF THE HELICOPTER. CORNELL MARITIME P., 1946
541.39	STEVENS, BRIAN — CHEMICAL KINETICS FOR GENERAL STUDENTS OF CHEMISTRY. CHAPMAN, 1961
658.788	STEVENS, EDWARD FRANK — SHIPPING PRACTICE. PITMAN, 1957
375.4	STEVENS, FRANCES — ENGLISH AND EXAMINATIONS. HUTCHINSON, 1970. <R.I.>
	STEVENS, J. — DOME TREASURY. SEE- DORE, GUSTAVE
620.LE COUTEUR	STEVENS, JOAN — VICTORIAN VOICES:... THE PAPERS OF SIR JOHN LE COUTEUR. SOC. JERSIAISE, 1969
387.243	STEVENS, LEONARD A. — THE ELIZABETH: PASSAGE OF A QUEEN. A. & U., 1969
616.980213	STEVENS, PETER J. — FATAL CIVIL AIRCRAFT ACCIDENTS: THEIR MEDICAL AND PATHOLOGICAL INVESTIGATION. WRIGHT, 1970
613.64	STEVENSON, ALAN CAPPUTH- AND DAVISON, B.C. CLARE — GENETIC COUNSELLING. HEINEMANN, 1970
F 759.9463 RUBENS	STEVENSON, ROBERT ALAN M. — PETER PAUL RUBENS. SEELEY, 1898
996.13	STEVENSON, ROBERT LOUIS — FOOTNOTE TO HISTORY: 8 YEARS OF TROUBLE IN SAMOA. DAWSONS, 1967
635.966	STEVENSON, VIOLET — ENCYCLOPEDIA OF FLORISTRY. COLLINGRIDGE, 1954
635.965	STEVENSON, VIOLET — INDOOR GARDENING. BARKER, 1970
375.42	STEVICK, EARL W. — HELPING PEOPLE LEARN ENGLISH. ABINGDON, 1957
614.0942	STEWART, ALEXANDER P., AND JENKINS, E. — MEDICAL AND LEGAL ASPECTS OF SANITARY REFORM. LEICESTER U.P., 1969
613	STEWART, ANDREW — LIVE TO NINETY AND STAY YOUNG. HEALTH SCIENCE P., 1969
711.409	STEWART, CECIL — PROSPECT OF CITIES: ... A HISTORY OF TOWN PLANNING. LONGMANS, 1952
	STEWART, CECIL — EARLY CHRISTIAN, BYZANTINE AND ROMANESQUE. SEE-SIMPSON, FREDERICK MOORE
387.5	STEWART, COLIN, AND STYRING, JOHN S. — FLAGS, FUNNELS AND HULL COLOURS. REV. ED. CCLES, 1963
F 956.1T	STEWART, DESMOND — TURKEY. TIME-LIFE, 1967
621.2	STEWART, HARRY L., AND JEFFERIS, FLOYD D. — HYDRAULIC AND PNEUMATIC POWER FOR PRODUCTION. 2ND ED. MACHINERY PUBL. CO.,

Each entry in the catalogue has a location code, this has proved to be a useful addition for inter-library loans as each branch library in the Westminster group has a copy of the full catalogue. The fixed data on each frame is provided from a forms slide.

The cost of COM catalogues compared with paper printout show considerable savings. The master COM film produced by Westminster is estimated to cost only 0.71p per frame, each frame may hold up to 20 entries, the cost of diazo duplicate film is estimated at £1.25 per 100 feet (2,000 frames). These figures do not include the cost of reading equipment, the Memorex readers used by Westminster cost £135 each plus £1.00 for each cassette. The cassettes may be returned for use with updated films. Maintenance charges are estimated at 5% per annum of the purchase price of the readers.

Figure 25 shows a cost comparison for a COM produced catalogue against photocopying. The comparison is for a catalogue consisting of an annual full cumulation plus monthly cumulating author supplements. The catalogue starts at 1,000 pages and increases to 20,000 pages in ten years, this represents in the tenth year a maximum of 200,000 author and classified entries. In this costing Westminster has assumed that 12 readers are for public use and one reader plus multiple cassettes are for staff use. (Reference 5)

It should be noted that work processed at a COM bureau often carries a minimum charge, so as with the case of Westminster monthly supplements are supplied at the minimum charge rather than the true cost of the work involved.

The reaction of the public to Westminster's COM catalogue has been encouraging. Many of the users found that after only a few minutes at the catalogue, its operation was very easy, in fact some people thought that the COM catalogue was easier to use than the conventional card or paper printout catalogue. It has been suggested that the public actually tended to use the COM catalogue because it was in machine form. Staff reaction has also been favourable, although some staff complained of eye strain after long periods of catalogue use, other staff however can use the system for 1 to 2 hours with no ill effects. This problem is not as serious as first thought, as in normal use the catalogue is not consulted for long periods.

The only basic problem remaining unanswered is the life of microfilm readers in public areas. Westminster has estimated the life span of a reader to be 10 years, but remain uncertain of the accuracy of this estimate.

Case Study 2: Cornwall County Public Libraries

Cornwall County Libraries changed to computer cataloguing in January 1971, at that time paper printout was being used. A total of 30 copies of additions to stock were produced once a quarter by offset litho. The problem of increasing costs led to the changeover to COM cataloguing in March

1971 and by June of the same year the system was operational throughout the county.

Cornwall County Libraries use an ICL 1902A computer, hence, a conversion programme was needed to generate magnetic tapes in the correct format for the particular COM recorder being used. Quarterly magnetic tapes are forwarded to a COM bureau for the production of 16mm comic mode film containing the additions to stock.

As with Westminster City Libraries, it was decided at an early stage that the COM catalogue should be used by members of the public, hence the reading equipment should be easy to operate. The microfilm reader chosen by Cornwall was the Scottish Instruments NCR Satellite 2W comic mode since this appeared to have all the qualities required—it was easy to operate; manually operated; reasonably cheap and cassette loaded.

The page format used by Cornwall is shown below, a non-standard 76 line page is used but this may be changed to the standard 64 line page at some later stage. The entries are arranged in a similar format to conventional cards each entry being numbered to aid searches. A useful feature of this system is a location code for each entry for use with inter-library loans.

The cost savings by using COM estimated over three years are given below (reference 13).

Printed Form (Quarterly cumulations) 30 copies

		Total
1970 Actual (616 pages)	£46.18 + £45.00[1]	£91.18
1971 Projection (1,228 pages)	£119.84 + — [2]	£119.84
1972 Projection (1,840 pages)	£196.24 + £45.00[1]	£241.24

Notes

1.   Cost of cassettes.

2.   No cassettes required during this period.

User reaction to the COM catalogue has been very favourable; a small survey conducted showed that all people interviewed thought that a microfilm catalogue was acceptable. 92% of those interviewed had no difficulty in using the catalogue and 76% preferred the COM catalogue to a conventional card system. Several of those interviewed thought so highly of the COM catalogue that a full explanation of the system was asked for. Of all the people questioned, only one thought that the microfilm catalogue was difficult to read.

Case Study 3: Birmingham University Library

The University of Birmingham Library closed its card catalogue at the end

Figure 25   Cost of producing 20 copies of a catalogue

by photocopying and COM

Photocopying

Year	Paper masters £	Copies[1] £	Total £
1	280	1,583	1,863
2	360	2,103	2,463
3	440	2,662	3,062
4	520	3,143	3,663
5	600	3,663	4,263
6	680	4,183	4,863
7	760	4,703	5,463
8	840	5,303	6,143
9	920	5,743	6,663
10	960	6,003	6,963

COM

Year	Master film £	Copies £	Readers[2] £	Total £
1	50	313	2,898	3,261
2	64	335	1,872	2,271
3	78	363	3,690	4,133
4	92	390	378[3]	860
5	106	415	3,785	4,306
6	120	440	473[3]	1,033
7	135	465	473[3]	1,073
8	149	487	3,947	4,583
9	163	515	2,153	2,831
10	170	525	2,153	2,848

Notes –   1. including binding

                 2. including maintenance

                 3. no readers purchased maintenance only.

of 1971, proposing that a microfilm version would be made available. Additions to stock after January 1972 would form a new MARC based mechanized catalogue, the output format for this being COM. The two systems combined would provide a complete microfilm catalogue for the University of Birmingham Library.

Microfilming of the card catalogue began in April 1972 and was completed by the end of the same year. Several quotations were obtained for the microfilming of the 1,000,000 cards of the catalogue, these quotations ranged from over £6,000 to a little over £1,000. The format chosen for the card catalogue microfilm was 8 entries (cards) per frame on 16mm comic mode orientation film. The card catalogue was housed on 63, 100 foot reels of film using this format.

The main aim of the Birmingham University Library was to provide a compatible microfilmed card and COM generated catalogue; hence, the choice of reader, microfilm format and image presentation were considered of prime importance to maintain this compatability. The use of 16mm film for both the microfilmed card catalogue and the COM generated film promoted the use of cassettes for holding user film. Cassettes were thought necessary for ease of handling, particularly for the casual library user. The microfilm reader and image orientation were linked factors in the early stages of the Birmingham experiment. The reader chosen was the CIL 600 which only accepts comic mode orientation images.

Birmingham University Library is a member of a group of Libraries cooperating in the production of mechanised catalogues. The libraries in the group participate in the Birmingham Libraries Co-operative Mechanisation Project (BLCMP). The aim of BLCMP is to produce magnetic tapes containing various catalogue entries and formats; this allows member libraries to use these specially produced tapes to generate catalogue entries in any desired format. The data on these magnetic tapes is so arranged to be able to produce either a unit card entry or multiple entries on computer stationery. The cost of card catalogues and computer stationery for multicopies of a catalogue, as would be required by Birmingham University Library, prompted the use of COM as an output media (reference 14). The total number of service points for the microfilm catalogues at Birmingham is 33; of these six are reserved for staff use only. Each of the reader stations would have a full set of the catalogue cassettes. The total costs for the system are estimated at £7,263 for the first year of operation and annual recurrent costs at £3,091.

The acceptance of microfilm catalogues at Birmingham University Library is very encouraging; although the system has only been operational for relatively short period, library users have changed to the large scale microfilm catalogue with no basic problems.

ANNABELL, ROSS

THE URANIUM HUNTERS.
LONDON, HALE, £1.80, 1971
[7],172P,12PLATES; ILLUS, PORTS.
338.27493   /71-19255 /7091 2076 5   1
H J K

ANNAND, A. MCKENZIE

CAVALRY SURGEON...EDITED BY A.
MCKENZIE ANNAND...
SEE SYLVESTER, JOHN HENRY
                                           2

ANNESLEY, J.E.C.

BOOK BOOK.
ILFRACOMBE, STOCKWELL, £0.78, 1970
141P; BIBLIOG.
222.11   /70-15107 /7223 0103 0   3
H

ANNIS, PHILIP GEOFFREY WALTER

NAVAL SWORDS: BRITISH AND AMERICAN
NAVAL EDGED WEAPONS 1660-1815.
LONDON, ARMS AND ARMOUR P.,
£1.50, 1970
80P; ILLUS, DIAGRS, PORTS,
BIBLIOG.
[ILLUSTRATED MONOGRAPHS]
623.444   85368 046 9   4
A.

SWORDS FOR SEA SERVICE, BY W.E.
MAY + P.G.W. ANNIS.
SEE MAY, WILLIAM EDWARD
                                           5

ANNUAL

ANNUAL ABSTRACT [OF] HOTEL
CATERING AND TOURIST STATISTICS
1967. NO 2; [PREPARED BY] RESEARCH
UNIT, DEPARTMENT OF HOTEL AND
CATERING MANAGEMENT, UNIVERSITY OF
SURREY.
GUILDFORD[SY.], UNIVERSITY OF
SURREY, £1.05, 1967
VII,95,VII LEAVES
647.94   /69-23881 /9021.6 00 2   6
A AR
SURREY UNIVERSITY. DEPARTMENT OF
HOTEL AND CATERING MANAGEMENT.

ANOUILH, JEAN

HUMULUS THE MUTE, BY JEAN ANOUILH
AND JEAN AURENCHE.
IN MODERN. MODERN FRENCH PLAYS.
842.91   8
AURENCHE, J.

ANSDALE, RICHARD FRANZ

THE WANKEL RC ENGINE: DESIGN AND
PERFORMANCE, BY R.F. ANSDALE, WITH
A SPECIAL CONTRIBUTION BY D.J.
LOCKLEY.
LONDON, ILIFFE, £2.88, 1968
8,158P,6PLATES; 99ILLUS.
629.2514   /68-19815   9
A

ANSON, SIR WILLIAM REYNELL

ANSON S LAW OF CONTRACT. 23RD ED.,
BY A.G. GUEST.
OXFORD, CLARENDON P., £3.75, 1969
XLV,655P; FORMS.
347.4   /69-23899 /19 825183 1 ˉ 10
A
GUEST, A.G.

ANSTEE, MARGARET JOAN

GATE OF THE SUN; A PROSPECT OF
BOLIVIA.
LONDON, LONGMAN, £2.75, 1970
XVIV,281P,16PLATES; ILLUS, MAPS.
984   582 10625 0   11
E G H J

ANTHONY, F.R.

THE TOWN AND COUNTRY PLANNING ACT,
1968, BY C.H. BEAUMONT, ASSISTED
BY E.R. ANTHONY...
SEE BEAUMONT, CHRISTOPHER HUBERT
                                          12

ANTHONY, ERNEST

A GUIDE TO LICENSING LAW FOR
BETTING SHOPS, BOOKMAKERS, CLUBS
AND LICENSED PREMISES, BY E.
ANTHONY AND J.D. BERRYMAN. 2ND ED.
LONDON, BUTTERWORTHS, £1.50, 1969
VII,204P; FORMS
338.476631   /69-12687 /406 10811 0   13
A
BERRYMAN. J.D.

Case Study 4: Imperial Chemical Industries Limited
(Mond Division) Special Library

I.C.I. Mond Division is one of the larger divisions of I.C.I. manufacturing basic chemicals for industry. The number of regular staff users of the library is estimated to in excess of 1,500; hence, an efficient system was required to disseminate information. The growing library of company published reports prompted I.C.I. to move from an optical coincidence system to a computer to produce lists of company held documents. The early stages of computerisation involved the creation of a KWOC catalogue to provide library users with a rapid look-up system for company reports. The hard copy printout from the computer was found to be satisfactory for the yearly lists of additions to stock which numbered approximately 2,000. To provide cumulations of these yearly lists would involve almost 20,000 documents; the cost of producing such lists on paper printout was thought to be prohibitive. As these cumulations were to be an essential part of the library service, COM was chosen as the output media, primarily on the grounds of cost.

A secondary advantage of the COM catalogue found by I.C.I. was that the catalogue could be decentralised, providing the satellite branches of the Mond Division with full catalogue data. The cost of providing a microfilm reader and a copy of the catalogue is estimated at £100.

User reaction to the microform catalogue at I.C.I. have been favourable, particularly in the provision of eight satellite libraries. No real problems have been encountered with the exception of occasional breakdowns of reading equipment, causing slight inconvenience to the library users, although backup machines are available.

Case Study 5: Unilever Research Limited Special Library

Unilever is a collection of individual companies, working in the food, edible fats and oils, and soaps and detergent field. The research division of Unilever is a central service provided for the use of all companies within the main group.

As Bedford and Welwyn libraries had been merged, the basic problem existed of producing a joint catalogue. The difficulty of producing and subsequent filing of catalogue cards for this exercise prompted the library to use a computer to sort entries and produce a joint catalogue. The first production run of the joint catalogue was the deciding factor in the use of COM. Of the four copies of the catalogue produced on paper via a line printer, only three were legible. The next edition of the catalogue was produced via COM.

The COM catalogue has provided the opportunity for users to print in hard copy specific sections of the catalogue; this is found to be particularly useful for those working away from the main library or several satellite sub-libraries.

As with all the libraries in this section of case studies, Unilever use 16mm roll film rather than microfiche for the catalogue. Other libraries have tended to standardise on readers and cassettes but Unilever use several different cassettes and even open spools with no major objections from the users.

Four catalogues are produced at Unilever: author, classified, subject and accession number. The accession number catalogue, although freely available, is used mainly by staff for checking entries and re-indexing duplicate volumes.

Reliability of microfilm equipment is the only factor which concerns users at Unilever. The microform catalogue has been fully accepted as a considerable advance from the often illegible line-printout.

LIBRARY CATALOGUES
ON MICROFILM

by Graham Larkworthy and Cyril G. Brown

In June this year Westminster City Libraries began to use microfilm as the means of reproducing and displaying computer formulated catalogues for public use. The purpose of this move was to cut the very considerable cost of reproducing this type of catalogue by normal photocopying methods, and it was preceded by a long search for cheaper means of catalogue reproduction.

When the Westminster and Kensington and Chelsea Joint Computer Committee began the planning of a computer catalogue project early in 1967, the only economic methods of reproducing computer print in small quantities were photocopying, offset litho, or, for very small numbers, multiple paper prints from the computer printer; most computer catalogues have been reproduced in one of these ways. During the last two years, however, the introduction of COM (Computer Output Microfilm) equipment into this country and, more recently, the setting up of commercial bureaux offering COM services, have made another and much cheaper method possible, that of producing microfilm direct from computer tapes and by this means avoiding a paper printout altogether. With a number of libraries in this country either adopting the method or considering its use, it may be helpful to outline Westminster's experience so far in applying COM to catalogues in public departments.

After comparing the cost of COM with that of photocopying, which was the previous method of reproduction, and after carrying out a practical trial of a catalogue on microfilm in one of the busiest lending libraries, it was decided to discontinue the printed catalogue with the first annual cumulation and substitute copies on film. Memorex 1642 Microfilm

Viewers were bought for public departments and for the Cataloguing and Inter-lending Sections, and the May cumulation of the catalogue was produced in microfilm form. At the same time, the method of cumulating the catalogue was changed; instead of an annual cumulation with monthly author supplements, the catalogue is, for the present, to be continuously cumulated.

Each copy of the catalogue is being replaced at monthly intervals with a new updated film of both author and classified sections, and, except for the subject index which is to remain in printed form, there is no longer a current printed version of the computer catalogue. All copies are on film.

In its present size of approximately 2500 pages, this catalogue is small enough to be held in a single cassette of film. As it grows with the addition of new and older stock, the copies for public use in the larger lending libraries will be divided over several microfilm readers, so that the enquirer will go to whichever machine holds the section of the catalogue he requires and he will not have to change cassettes. On the other hand, copies which are used behind the scenes by staff will be contained in multiple cassettes used on one or two machines. The ability to provide these staff catalogues in branch workrooms at small cost, and with little expenditure of space, is one of the advantages of this method. Microfilm readers with multiple cassettes will also be tried out for public use in one or two smaller branch libraries.

Cost

Compared with the methods mentioned above of reproducing a normal computer paper print, COM offers a considerable saving in cost. Both the master film and the copies are cheap to produce and there is also a saving in computer costs as no paper printout is required. This latter fact accounts for the bold plunge into this medium; there is little to be gained from a half-and-half situation with print in addition to microfilm.

Some idea of the savings in cost to be gained by using COM can be seen in the comparison between this method and photocopying shown in the table below. These figures, which are based on Westminster experience, show the comparative reproduction costs for twenty copies of a catalogue consisting of an annual full cumulation plus monthly cumulating author supplements. The size of the catalogue is 1000 pages at the start, increasing over a period of 10 years to 20,000 pages and representing, at its maximum, author and classified entries for 200,000 titles. Costs for smaller or larger catalogues would be in proportion. In the costing it has been assumed that twelve of the catalogues would be public catalogues and that, for these, one microfilm reader would be provided for each cassette of film. The other eight are assumed to be staff catalogues consisting of a single reader with multiple cassettes. The cost of microfilm readers is £135 each plus £1 for each cassette. Maintenance charges are estimated at 5 percent per annum of the purchase price of the machines.

CATALOGUE REPRODUCTION—COMPARISON OF COST BETWEEN PHOTOCOPYING AND COM

	Photocopying			COM			
Year	Paper masters	Copies (20) including binding	Total	Master film	Copies (20)	Microfilm viewers including maintenance	Total
	£	£	£	£	£	£	£
1	280	1 583	1 863	50	313	2 898 (20)[1]	3 261
2	360	2 103	2 463	64	335	1 872 (12)	2 271
3	440	2 622	3 062	78	363	3 690 (24)	4 133
4	520	3 143	3 663	92	390	378[2]	860
5	600	3 663	4 263	106	415	3 785 (24)	4 306
6	680	4 183	4 863	120	440	473[2]	1 033
7	760	4 703	5 463	135	465	473[2]	1 073
8	840	5 303	6 143	149	487	3 947 (24)	4 583
9	920	5 743	6 663	163	515	2 153 (11)	2 831
10	960	6 003	6 963	170	525	2 153 (11)	2 848

[1] No. of machines purchased in that year.   [2] Maintenance only.

As one can see from these figures, the charges for photocopying rapidly outstrip those for microfilm until in the 9th and 10th years; when a programme of machine replacement begins, the difference is over £4000 a year.

Nor is this all. To provide a direct comparison between the two media, it has been assumed that the same catalogue is being reproduced in each, but we would point out that the method of cumulating the catalogue which is used with photocopying is not necessarily the best to use with COM. Bureau charges for microfilm copies tend to be so much per 1000 frames, or so much per 100 feet of film, with a minimum charge for each job. The result is that, in producing a monthly supplement, the payment for copies will be the minimum charge rather than the actual cost of the job and it is possible to provide more at very little extra cost. For example, if a monthly cumulating *classified* supplement is provided for this catalogue, in addition to the author supplement, the photocopying charges would be increased by £950 per year, whereas the microfilm charges would increase by less than £100.

To take full advantage of this method of charging, one needs either to cumulate supplements over a long period, taking the view that since a supplement has to be consulted most of the time, it does not matter how large it is, or better still, to cumulate the full catalogue more frequently and do away with supplements altogether. The latter course, however, means forgoing much of the saving in the interests of a better catalogue. Remember that these are only reproduction costs. The effect on computer costs of any decision on cumulation must be borne in mind.

Several other factors may alter these comparative figures. All calculations in this example are taken from the point at which computer tapes are ready for the production of a catalogue. Should these tapes be in the format for producing a paper print of the catalogue rather than a microfilm, they will need to be reformatted for COM at a charge, if done commercially, of approximately £1 per 100 frames of film. This would affect a library changing from print to microfilm. Computer programs, however, can be amended to provide finished tapes in the correct format or, if one is starting from scratch and with sufficient confidence, the program can be written initially with microfilm in view as the end product.

The cost of microfilm readers is another factor. On one hand, cost is likely to come down. This is a highly competitive field and there are already microfilm readers on the market cheaper than those used by Westminster. On the other hand, we do not know the life of a machine under these circumstances. In estimating, we have allowed a life of ten years; this could be wildly optimistic.

Finally, there is the reaction of the user. Experience may show that members of the public can be left to select and change cassettes. If so, this would influence cost because the number of microfilm readers required is then dictated, not by the size of the catalogue, but by the number of people likely to consult it at the same time, and can vary according to the service point. A further advantage in this situation is that the catalogue itself could be spread over more cassettes with less risk of two people requiring the same section at the same moment.

Microfilm readers

In the choice of a microfilm reader, the main consideration was given to ease of operation. The machine had to be such that the least mechanically-minded person, whether staff or public, could walk up to it and work it without difficulty; and for this reason, after testing both motorized and hand-operated model, it was decided to use the latter. The Memorex 1642 Viewer which was chosen is very satisfactory from this point of view although it has weaknesses in other directions.

It was also considered important to have the film presented in cinemode, that is, with the frames moving up and down the screen rather than in comicmode, with frames moving from side to side. Cinemode in this application allows more frames to be included on each reel of film, and it also means that the factor by which the catalogue is arranged, namely, the author or the class number, is always in the same position on the screen whenever the film is stopped. With comicmode it is necessary to scan the screen to find which section you have reached.

Cassette loading was a requirement because of the need for a rapid change of film. With the full author and classified catalogue estimated to require eight reels of film, the facility to remove one and insert another easily and quickly is most important and, in this respect, cassette loading machines were preferable to the cartridge loading type, which require the film to be wound back into the cartridge before it can be changed.

Microfilm

Microfilm was chosen in preference to microfiche. Although there is a wide choice of readers for the latter form, many of them quite inexpensive, it was felt that for public use this advantage would be outweighed by the difficulty of handling and controlling the number of fiche required for the full catalogue.

The film used is a thin polyester film which is half the thickness of the usual acetate film and consequently allows a greater quantity to be held in a cassette. With this film the Memorex cassette will hold up to 3000 frames which represents approximately 60,000 entries. This was important in view of the intention to provide one microfilm reader per cassette for catalogues in public departments.

The COM equipment used by Lowndes-Ajax Computer Services Ltd. of Croydon, the bureau used by Westminster, produces a film with a negative image; the one in current use has white characters on a very dense blue background. Opinions vary from one member of staff to another on whether or not the use of this film imposes a strain on the eyes. Some have found a strain after prolonged consultation, whereas others have used the catalogues for 1-2 hours at a time without ill effects. The problem is certainly not as serious as we thought it might be. It does not apply to normal use of the catalogue but only to continuous use over a long period and then only to certain individuals.

User reaction

The reaction of the public to the new form has been most encouraging. Our early fears that they would be deterred from using a machine have proved to be unfounded. People today are fairly sophisticated about mechanical things and we might have realized that a microfilm reader, which looks like a television set and operates like a "What the butler saw" machine, would not cause much alarm. All kinds of people have used it including the very elderly.

It must have taken many years for the card catalogue to be accepted and it will obviously take time for the public in general to realize that the new piece of equipment is the future catalogue, but there is evidence that people are attracted to it *because* it is in machine form. There is an element of enjoying a novelty about current use. One comment was that it was "fun" to use the catalogue; another comment was: "I see you have a catalogue now!"

On present experience we no longer have reservations about a catalogue on microfilm or about the use that will be made of it. Our only reservation concerns the machines themselves: whether or not the microfilm readers now being manufactured are sufficiently robust to stand up to general public use. This may be the deciding factor in the success or failure of the project.

LIBRARY COM APPLICATIONS

by Samuel Memberg

This discussion deals with Computer Output Microforms in general and specifically with COM technology as it may apply to the future of library catalogs.

The success and acceptance of MARC and other automated data bases in the past ten years has opened the door to a re-examination of the traditional card catalog. We are now presented with several viable forms for the library catalog. Not only are there cards, more and more being produced by computer, but book catalogs, microfilm catalogs, microfiche catalogs and, that ultimate vision of the future, on-line catalogs.

While this paper deals with COM, it must be remembered that all of the display media have their own strong and, of course, weak points. Also, one must bear in mind that just because one application is best suited to a particular medium, it does not necessarily follow that other applications are equally well suited.

Everything that follows presupposes access to an automated data base containing all the information to be included in your COM product—whether it be catalog or in-house technical services listing. Let us assume such access or possible future access, since if we do not, this paper ends here.

In any case, more and more libraries are using catalogs derived from automated data bases. Librarians are realizing (or are being forced to realize) that it is far cheaper to pool cataloging resources than to continue to go it alone. Particularly helpful incentives in this area have been the Library of Congress' MARC program and OCLC. While it is obvious that the computer provides an ideal medium for cooperative effort, it may not be quite as obvious that once data is magnetically encoded, there are a multitude of forms which the finished catalog may take. No longer must hard copy (paper) be the only vehicle for catalog production as it has been for the past two thousand years. We now have two nonpaper options for end products.

The most obvious is the computer terminal, which while an impressive tool in certain areas, has yet to show itself to be a viable replacement for a public catalog. While it is indeed probably that the computer terminal will play an ever-increasing role in libraries and in all aspects of our everyday lives, the prospect of having an on-line catalog of a library's holdings, as accessible to the average reader as the present hard copy catalogs, is at least several years away.

The cost of a computer terminal, the cost of on-line storage and the cost of the computer itself, all combine with the attendant costs of communication lines and equipment to virtually rule out the possibility of an on-line catalog for the general public in the immediate future. For the time being, terminals will continue to be few in number and will have to be tended by trained personnel.

The second alternative to hardcopy, be it card or book, is Computer Output Microform. Computer Output Microform, as it is ubiquitiously known, COM, provides something of a middle ground between paper and electronic catalogs. It substitutes film for paper, and opens the door to substantial savings, if film or fiche is acceptable to both librarian and patron.

COM is also an easily updatable medium, not as immediate as the on-line terminal, but much more quickly updated than paper. Computer Output Microforms, because of their low cost, can permit more frequent cumulations and supplements, and can also permit the inclusion of large amounts of holdings and in-process information with the body of the catalog.

Once you have access to the data base, the first and probably most important question to be answered is where is the COM to be used, or rather by whom. Is it to be used by public or as a processing tool? If by the public, then is that public to have hands-on access or will a staff interface be provided, if only for instruction in the use of the COM catalog? Also, what will be the user's age, educational background and needs?

One sort of COM may be fine in a university library, not quite as useful in the adult room of a neighborhood library, and totally useless in the juvenile reading room. As simplistic as this sounds, there have been too many cases where even the printed catalog could have been much more useful had it been more suited to its specific readership.

This is even more important when we consider, for example, the destructive potential of a jelly donut to a fiche catalog or, worse yet, an ultrafiche catalog. Giving the user the ability to obscure hundreds of entries with one thumbprint tends to be a bit mind-boggling. However, concurrent with the type of user is the volume or traffic of those users. Bearing in mind the fact that a card catalog offers, at least in theory, one access point for each of its drawers, the compactness of microform could prove to be a major drawback.

For example, if the entire catalog is put into single film readers or single sets of fiche, how many machines are required to service the lunch-hour

crowd in a large urban library when compared with the access potential of
the hundreds of card drawers previously available? To my knowledge, no
one has yet come up with an equation to determine the point at which the
long-suffering patron stalks out in disgust after spending 10 or even 5
minutes behind some compulsively thorough student preparing for a term
paper, or for that matter, someone looking up pornographic books.

Hopefully, the current experiments going on across the country will provide useful data as to the number of viewing machines necessary for a given
number of readers. When this happens, the library community should be
better able to judge the cost and desirability of COM catalogs for the public
sector.

While most COM catalogs produced for public use are in 16mm film
format, academic and special libraries seem more willing to try microfiche.
There are several reasons for this. Fiche readers are a good deal cheaper than
motorized film readers, and the user tends to be able to cope with the not
too demanding task of putting a fiche into a reader and refiling it when he is
finished. Also microfiche lends itself to supplementation much more readily
than does film. In fact, one of the major problems in using film is the fact
that in order to supplement the catalog and keep it in the same place as the
cumulation, the entire file must be recreated. This costs a good deal more
than simply producing one or several fiche which can be tucked into the
empty file slots behind each fiche cumulation. Furthermore, with film, the
temptation to cut costs by having infrequent or nonexistent supplements is
far more appealing than the thought of trying to splice ten feet of film on to
the end of a 400-foot roll. If you think about the potential problems of that
for a moment, you too may be tempted to use, horror of horrors, that
ancient tool of the dark ages, the manually filed card catalog, as a supplementing vehicle until the next reaccumulation of the film. This is clearly not
quite the best of all possible worlds. But it is better than having a totally
outdated catalog or one which requires an ever-growing commitment in staff
and money in order to stay as current as a COM catalog.

With the above in mind, we shall continue to look at COM as a less than
perfect but nevertheless useful and affordable alternative to the other
media.

Another area in which COM offers cost effective utility is that of behind-
the-scenes listings. The original use of COM in the real world was to provide
very quick turnaround of voluminous amounts of information that was not
looked at very often. The commercial sector, having discovered the in-
credible potential of computers (and their ever so detailed reports), began
choking on those selfsame reports. COM became (and is still becoming at an
exponential growth rate) the answer to the warehouses of listings which
computers spew forth whether they are doing productive work or not. It is
perhaps in this behind-the-scenes environment that COM can be experimented with most easily. It is here that the most current information is
needed to help eliminate repetitive searches and backlogs which accumulate

with unbelievable speed. The staff, once any initial reluctance is overcome, quickly learns to use the microform and just as quickly appreciates the time savings in having a copy of an in-process, authority, or order list either at their desks or just a few steps away.

We at NYPL have observed, unofficially of course, lest there be a shop steward lurking nearby, that the staff far prefers fiche to film. The reason for this is the speed and ease with which a title can be searched with fiche. Since film must be searched sequentially, much more time is required to locate an item than with a direct access tool such as fiche. Not only is the investment required for a few microfiche readers quite small, but the experience gained in this endeavor can be very beneficial when larger COM applications are undertaken.

Before embarking on any COM venture, even if the entire operation is to be handled by a service organization, one should have an idea of how it is produced. This knowledge may help you get a product more suited to your needs than you would have believed possible. To this end I offer a short explanation of how COM is created:

Keep in mind that because of the wide variety in degrees of sophistication of COM recorders, what follows is a general schematic, rather than a detailed account of what takes place in a COM device. The initial step in the creation of a computer output microform is the proper formatting of the magnetic tape containing the data which is to be "printed" on the film. Some COM recorders can take a simple print-image tape (or be plugged into the computer in place of a mechanical printer), while others require an extensive reformatting of the tape, complete with complex instructions before they can operate. But, before horrifying visions of expensive programmers with bizarre work habits come to mind, relax, the vast majority of COM recorders function quite well with the print image tape. For most of the others, the COM service bureau will provide and install the software package required by their recorder on your computer at no charge. The tape is then read by the recorder and ultimately converted to visible light that produces man-readable characters on the film.

There are several ways in which these characters are created and transferred to the film. The most popular method involves display of the man-readable characters on a cathode ray tube, or CRT, similar to a television screen. Once the characters appear on the CRT screen, a camera photographs the image through a lens system which has been set for the desired reduction ratio.

In one type of CRT an electron beam is shot through a metal plate with cutouts of the characters of a particular type font. After the beam passes through the desired cutout, it hits the inside of the screen and illuminates the character's image.

The second method involves the stimulation of the proper sections of a dot matrix in order to produce the desired character. If for example, the matrix is composed of four vertical rows of five "dots" or potential sources of light, when the COM recorder reads an uppercase "H" on the tape, the dots on the outside portions of the matrix, as well as those dots representing the crossbar, are stimulated. This pattern of twelve points of light is then transmitted to the screen.

The third manner in which a character may be generated on the screen is via a moving electron beam which "paints" the character on the CRT with a series of short strokes. Two types of COM recorders generate an image in this manner. One uses short vertical strokes which are moved along the vertical and horizontal coordinates as defined by the type font being used. The other "painting" recorder is capable of beam movement in any direction and is thus particularly well suited to the production of graphics COM.

The remaining methods of image creation, while not using CRT's, depend on the dot matrix, and transfer characters to film either by optical fibers or by the focusing of a light beam directly onto the film. After the film has been exposed, it must be developed (except in the case of one COM recorder in which the film is burned by a laser beam and need not be sensitive to normal light). If fiche rather than film is the required end product, 105 millimeter film will have been used and cut to form the standard "4 x 6" inch fiche.

Since today's COM recorders can produce a wide variety of products, it is perhaps time to take a look at the various items which must be considered before a decision on the advisability of replacing all or part of the hard copy catalog is made. The first piece of information is the size of the catalog which must be replaced by the microform. At this time it might be pointed out that a library having a large catalog in book form might want to consider the possibility of retaining the retrospective catalog in hard copy while using a COM catalog for new acquisitions. Remembering that even the least sophisticated of COM generators are generally able to produce both fiche and film, the choice of format is entirely dependent on the kind of microform reading equipment which would be desirable for the user. Microform readers have diversified to such an extent that prices vary from the one hundred sixty dollar range for a good fiche reader to the more than two thousand dollar fiche cassette readers. Since any library system thinking of switching from a non-microform catalog will probably require a great many COM readers, the cost of this equipment presents a major, if not insurmountable, obstacle. And, while all sorts of figures can be produced to show that over a period of time the switch to COM will more than repay the investment in equipment, capital is still hard to come by.

It is unfortunate that microform reader technology is still at a stage of development which lends some measure of truth to the homily, "The simpler the better." The ideal viewer for a library serving a wide variety of users, one which contains the entire catalog (or logically separable sections of it) locked away from prying hands, seems to be finding increasing acceptance among public libraries. Motorized, enclosed film readers, while significantly below the thousand dollar per unit level, have had more than their fair share of difficulties. However, it seems that both machine and film are heading towards a happier union which will do much to prevent the curious patron from causing as much damage as he has in the past. We should soon have a better idea of some of these readers usefulness and durability because of the large number now in everyday use. If these prove to be nearly as good as their manufacturers claim, I have a feeling that we shall soon see a great proliferation of these devices. Viewers which handle multiple fiche, while potentially able to hold vast amounts of data, are the most expensive of microform readers and have not, to my knowledge, been heavily exposed to use by the ultimate testing device, the general public.

The ultrafiche reader, while perhaps the newest on the scene in terms of wide distribution, is intimately linked with the technology of the fiche's creation. And while presenting perhaps the cheapest of alternatives for certain applications, it is only at present coming to grips with the indexing problems inherent in having upwards of two thousand pages on a 4 x 6" fiche. Furthermore, the very density of the information requires minute movements of the controls if one hopes to get to, and stay at, a specific location. In other words, ultrafiche is not for the nervous reader. In any case, while this technology must still be considered rather exotic when compared to normal COM, both the readers and the fiche preparation have become progressively less expensive.

The last major type of reader left for consideration, the simple fiche reader, is the least expensive and possibly most durable. Its big drawback, the relatively large number of fiche required for sizable catalogs and the concurrent necessity of having the user constantly load, unload and refile fiche, seems to limit its use to behind-the-scenes operations, small specialized collections with limited users, and perhaps university libraries where students may adapt more readily to the above requirements.

Regardless of the format chosen, the problem of locating an item buried in thousands of frames of microform requires an easily used index. It is in this area that COM shows some of its versatility.

Computer Output Microform affords the possibility of automatic index generation along with the main body of information. On fiche, for example, a simple instruction to the COM vendor that indexing information is encoded in the magnetic data at a certain position on each page, results in the creation of an index frame on the fiche. This index is usually located in the last frame position (or extreme lower right corner of the fiche) and corresponds to the index on the locator grid on the face of the reading machine. The index will normally contain the first 20 or so characters starting with the position which has been specified, and the grid coordinate where that page is to be found. This "automatic" indexing can also provide the information for the "eyeball" or eye readable heading at the top of each fiche. This heading can not only contain the fixed information identifying the fiche, but the first line of index information from the first frame of the fiche. One note, since any bad or incorrectly entered records tend to collect at the front of the file (because of leading blanks, etc.), it is advisable to

keep the eyeball index blank on the first fiche so as not to provide misleading information to the user. As an added filing aid, the fiche are numbered
in eye readable numerics as they are produced. Some interesting games can
be played with the eyeball heading. For instance, the variable information
can be put in larger characters than the fixed data, thus making retrieval a
bit easier. Also, with Diazo copies, the film can be striped with various
colors so that supplements and cumulations or titles and authors, for example, can be differentiated more readily. Vendors will seldom volunteer
the color-striped film, but it does exist.

The indexing of microfilm may be done by generating a separate index
tape and using this to produce a hard copy index; by putting blips on the
film so that a mark relating to an alphabetical marking on the viewer is seen
as the film is used, or by using odometer-like readings which relate to a hard
copy index. There are of course readers and film which survive and function
with no indexing scheme at all, other than having the data in alphabetical
order and depending upon the user's intuition and perseverance.

Almost all COM recorders can produce sixteen, and one-hundred and five
millimeter output copy. I shall assume that all creation and processing of
the COM is done by a service bureau. Several factors lead to this assumption. An extremely large number of pages must be produced monthly in
order to justify the cost of even the least expensive COM recorders. Developing and duplicating the film requires additional equipment which, while
neither very expensive or complex, does require a certain amount of attention. And lastly, the benefits of more sophisticated equipment are unattain-
able unless one is willing to spend upwards of one hundred thousand dollars
for a piece of equipment which will not only spend most of its time doing
absolutely nothing, but also require skilled and inexpensive operators who
will also spend most of their time doing nothing. Furthermore, going to a
service bureau permits constant comparison shopping as well as the ability
to switch vendors and equipment with relative ease should changing requirements of poor performance make it necessary.

As an example of the flexibility which use of COM service bureau permits, the New York Public Library is now using five service bureaus, and
two produce standard upper/lower case fiche. Two others provide not only
the standard upper/lower case character set but a full range of diacritics as
well, enabling the library to produce COM containing every character in the
ALA character set. A fifth vendor photocomposes thirty-five millimeter
film. This, hopefully, can be used as an interim step in the production of
either ultra-fiche, or a printing plate for the production of books at a sizable
saving. The use of all these vendors is admittedly a little paranoid. However,
it has enabled us to keep prices down. Not only do our vendors know about
each other but they also know that we are continually testing other service
bureaus. The amazing thing about all of this is that our volume is not nearly
large enough to offer visions of instant wealth to any of the vendors. They
all apparently want our business and are, within limits, willing to try and
underbid each other.

In shopping for a vendor do not hesitate to ask competitors about each other's capabilities. After a few sessions of "He said this, you said that," the vendors should have revealed a good deal more about their abilities than on the first go-around. Ask for any options that occur to you even if they are not offered. The worst that can happen is that you will be thought a bit strange; at best you may even get some of your strange requests. If fiche is produced, ask for large eyeball characters as well as back striping to make the eyeballs easier to read. And remember, if a stroking machine is used to generate the COM, there is a possibility of having several different characters added to the machine's repertoire without too much difficulty. There is also the possibility of reformatting your print tape and/or using a different character size at the same reduction ratio to improve the legibility of the final product.

Since almost all COM recorders provide the three most popular reduction ratios—24, 42 and 48X, the choice is dependent on the format and viewer selected for the catalog. Bear in mind that the reduction ratio of the film need not necessarily be the same as that of the viewer. This means that depending on the screen size, and design of the viewer, a 42 X fiche could be read at 32 X as well as 48 X and still have an entire frame displayed on the viewer's screen. As a matter of fact, the games which can be played by altering both the number of characters on a line and the number of lines on a page of the original print image tape, together with the variety of character sizes available on many COM recorders, can often provide the user with the ability to "custom tailor" his final product. For example, we are currently producing 42 X fiche with something like 38 X characters which is being read on both 32 X and 42 X readers. In order to do this, the number of characters per line has been reduced from 132 to 112 and the number of lines per frame (or page) from 60 to 48; the resultant COM not only provides enough room for the wide variety of diacritics which are essential for some applications, but is markedly easier to read, and consequently more acceptable to the user.

In our search for the ideal alternative to hard copy, we have tried 24, 42 and 48 X COM in both the 112 character forty-eight line, and the more conventional 132 character sixty line formats. These, together with a variety of character sizes within each magnification ratio, have shown us that a greater number of options exist in COM generation than is apparent at first or even second glance. As a matter of face, we are now using several different fiche formats and reduction ratios for different applications.

The above examples represent established and fairly straight forward techniques which, although volunteered by a few vendors, are securable with a little persistence. The reluctance of service bureaus to offer options is understandable because it is obviously easier for them not to make changes in their equipment settings. It cannot, however, be stressed too strongly that no service bureau utilizes 100% of its COM recorder's capacity. If they did, they would run out and buy another recorder which would then be underutilized; and unless your requests are beyond the machine's capabilities, the vendor will be not only willing to help, but surprisingly knowledge-able.

The economics of COM are such that even though some of our reformat-ting reduces the data in each frame by 30 percent, the total cost of pro-ducing fiche is often only slightly more than half the cost of the blank paper which would be required to print the number of copies which are distributed. These savings are often sufficient to pay for the viewing machines in a short time.

For example, at The New York Public Library, a weekly in-process list is produced, for which the savings over blank paper costs alone paid for four-teen fiche readers in less than a year. And it must be remembered that all of the above comparisons have excluded computer costs. If these figures are taken into account, COM becomes even more attractive, since creation of a COM tape takes only a few minutes as compared to the minimum of the three and a half hours of print time required to produce just one copy of this same list.

An even more dramatic example is taken from a recent estimate for an 80,000 title catalog. The cost for printing and binding of 50 copies of the 8-volume set would be about $20,000. The same catalog produced in 42 X fiche would cost $1500. Of course, the cost of 50 readers and 3 Reader/Printers would raise this to $14,000, a savings of only $6,000. But on the next run, the savings are on the order of 90% of the cost of a printed book. The cost of 16mm film in 50 motorized readers would be in the neighbor-hood of $36,000, and although this is $16,000 *over* the printed book and $22,000 over the fiche option, the savings on the next run would be 80% of the printing costs.

With these figures staring one in the face, there is sometimes a tendency to become overly enthusiastic about COM and perhaps overlook some of its shortcomings. First on the list of drawbacks is the problem of getting the library patron used to the microform and viewer. It is possible that for cer-tain libraries (or branches) a staff member might have to be assigned to the viewing station to do nothing but instruct users (and have abuse heaped on his head for it) in the use of the microform catalog.

Secondly, as was mentioned earlier, while a card catalog potentially offers many access points, and a book catalog as many access points as volumes, each user can tie up an entire microform catalog. So that, while the number of copies of a catalog may remain constant, one machine con-taining five volumes of information serves one user instead of five. The number of viewers must therefore be considerably greater than the number of hard copy catalogs presently in use.

Another drawback to COM is its inability to change type fonts and sizes in the course of a run. And while there seems to be some hope on the hori-zon, the only way to get COM with the benefits of mixed type at present, is to photocompose it on a very sophisticated device such as a Videocomp, Comp 80, or Singer 6000. Use of these devices for photocomposition re-quires extensive programming and is, for all practical purposes, reserved for larger institutions.

Finally, something often overlooked is the fact that all microform readers need bulbs every so often and the more complicated machines require more complicated maintenance. Furthermore, in order to realistically budget for the future, one must assume periodic replacement of equipment. To date, no one knows the life expectancy of the current crop of microform readers, especially in a public environment. This fact, more than any other we have explored, is the unknown quantity in any equation we try to formulate in order to analyze the potential costs of COM.

Before closing, I would like to present, just for comparison's sake, some relative costs of various COM formats. Prices used are approximate and may or (rather will) vary with vendor, quantities of frames, geographic locations, etc. Also, all equipment costs are disregarded. Assuming 20 copies of an 80,000 title catalog with 10,000 titles added during the year, the following would be one year's costs for one cumulation and 11 cumulative supplements:

> 16 millimeter film (42 X) $3100
> 42 X fiche $1350
> 48 X fiche $1100

Alternatively, we could produce 4 complete cumulations (especially important if microfilm is used) during the year and dispense with supplements entirely. This method would cost between two and a half and three times as much as the above schedule. While at first glance this seems to be an exhorbitant increase in cost, the low absolute costs of COM mean that we could have the quarterly cumulations on 42 X fiche for only $4,000 a year.

In the few years that COM has been used for library applications, the end product, once a piece of barely legible microfilm with only one set of fuzzy uppercase characters, has become capable of providing crisp images of not only alphanumerics, graphs and diagrams, but also of the weird set of markings which are indispensible to large segments of the library community. And, though the above figures seem to indicate substantial savings via COM, we are in a period of experimentation. Trapped between the unwieldly card catalog and the expensive, not-yet-perfected, on-line catalog, we continually search for alternatives. Some libraries using fiche are suddenly finding film preferable while others have rejected their film outright and are ecstatic about the switch to fiche.

Unfortunately, one of COM's mixed blessings is the variety of output alternatives offered to the user. And while the possibility of saving as much as 80% of the cost of each catalog produced is tempting, a good deal of time must be spent in studying not only the pot of gold at the rainbow's end, but the attendant thunderstorms as well.

REGIONAL NUMERICAL UNION CATALOG ON COMPUTER OUTPUT MICROFICHE

by William E. McGrath and Donald Simon

Twenty-one Louisiana libraries have produced on Computer Output Micro-fiche (COM) a Union Catalog containing locations for 1,100,000 books. About 150,000 of these are current acquisitions (books acquired in the last two years); the rest are volumes in the retrospective collections of ten of the twenty-one libraries. The *Numerical Register of Books in Louisiana Libraries*, as the catalog is now entitled, is the second step toward what is hoped will be a comprehensive current and retrospective list of over two million volumes, the estimated holdings of the participating libraries. The first was a conventionally printed *Register* of 550,000 books, issued in 1971 and distributed to fifty Louisiana libraries.

The new *Register* is not a bibliography. It includes no bibliographic in-formation. It is a location device for books whose bibliographic informa-tion is already known and includes nothing that is not also listed by the Library of Congress. The title was deliberately chosen to distinguish it from an older bibliographic *Louisiana Union Catalog*. All books listed in the *Register* are those having a Library of Congress (LC) card number; indeed the LC card number is the entry. The term "numerical" was chosen because we anticipate using other numbers besides the LC number—e.g., the Mansell number, and the International Standard Book Number (ISBN).

The LC card number is the most widely used book number we now have. This fact is put to good use by the Library of Congress in its own *NUC—Register of Additional Locations*. There are other LC number in-dexes, but they are not union catalogs. (The Mansell number, of course, will be very useful when publication of the *NUC—Pre-1956 Imprints* is complete.)

Reprinted from the *Journal of Library Automation*, 5: 217-29 (December 1972) by permission of the publisher. Copyright © 1972 by the American Library Association.

Many more titles can be represented on a page by number codes than by complete bibliographic data, at a ratio of perhaps 600 to 9. Unit costs are, therefore, much less. The first edition (1971), containing 550,000 volumes, was produced for an estimated total cost of $22,600—$8,600 grant plus $14,000 absorbed. One hundred copies of the *Register* were printed in hard copy form with approximate overall unit costs for keypunching, computer, travel, salaries, and printing, as follows:

	In terms of actual expenditures (grant funds)	*In terms of total funds, expended plus absorbed*
Per title entry	2.5¢	6.0¢
Per volume entry	1.6¢	3.8¢

The second edition (November 1972) contains over 1,100,000 volumes and in terms of the second grant, was produced on Computer Output Microfiche for an estimated total cost of $31,200, i.e., $10,000 grant plus $21,200 absorbed. (Reproduction costs for the COM are negligible. For an original copy of 5 fiche, containing all 1,100,000 volumes, we were charged $25 by a commercial firm, and for extra copies, $3 each. Copies for distribution will be sold at a slightly higher price.) Unit costs for the COM edition are:

	In terms of actual expenditures (second grant funds)	*In terms of total funds, second grant expenditures plus absorbed*
Per title entry	1.8¢	5.6¢
Per volume entry	.9¢	2.8¢

Unit costs computed on the basis of total costs to date suggest that they remain relatively constant from cumulation to cumulation.

The concept of a numerical register is not new. The idea was discussed at length in a proposal by Harry Dewey (1) almost a generation ago in which he espoused all the essential ideas, and again in 1965 by Louis Schreiber (2). Both argued that if the bibliographic data including the LC card number were already in hand, one could then merely look up the number in a numerical union catalog to determine a location. Goldstein and others (3) have also studied what they called the "Schreiber catalog" and have produced a sample computer printout of LC numbers. Computer output microfiche, on the other hand, was not anticipated in the original concept. It has made reproduction and distribution cheap, fast, and eminently feasible. The history of the *Register* and its rationale have been discussed more fully by McGrath (4).

Programs Comprising the Union Catalog System

The Union Catalog data record is shown in Table 1. The first three fields are the familiar LC card number, and the fourth, the library location.

Table 1. The Data Record

(1) *ALPHA series*	(2) *Year or numeric series*	(3) *Serial number within numeric series*	(4) *Library*
Agr	C	2354	69

(1) Alpha series prefix—this data field may contain from 1 to 4 alphabetic characters denoting a special series.
(2) Numeric series prefix—this data field may contain 1 or 2 digits.
(3) Serial number—this data field may contain up to 6 numeric digits.
(4) Alphabetic library designation code—this field contains a preassigned alphabetic code (up to 26) designating the participating library.

The three programs which use this data record and comprise the Union Catalog System are shown in Figure 1 and described below.

LNREDT Program

LNREDT is an editing program which examines all card input data to determine whether they are acceptable or not.
Each data field as shown above is examined as follows:
Field 1 for the presence and rejection of nonalphabetic characters, and also to determine if the alphabetic code is a member of the accepted set of codes obtained from the Library of Congress; the accepted records are transferred after checking all fields to a magnetic tape file for subsequent use; rejected data records are printed and visually scanned for the source of error;
Fields 2 and 3 for the presence and rejection of nonnumeric characters;
Field 4 to determine if alphabetic.

LNRSRT Program

LVRSRT sorts all records on the above mentioned tape file. The major sort key is the numeric prefix, Field 2. The minor sort keys in order of the sort sequence are:
Field 1—the alphabetic special series indicator;
Field 3—the book serial number.
Field 4—the library code designation.

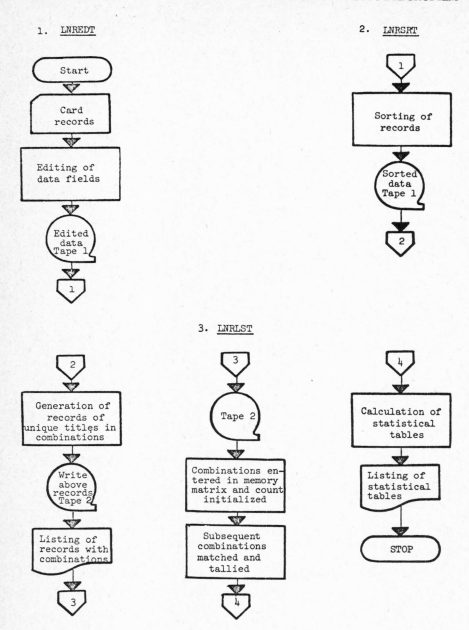

Fig. 1. Flow Chart of the Programs Comprising the Register System.

LNRLST Program

LNRLST is the main program which uses the sorted data tape to:

a. create a single record for each unique LC number containing the library code designation of each library having this particular book;
b. produce a listing of the above records in LC card number order;
c. generate records of unique titles in combinations of libraries owning the titles;
d. enter into a memory matrix the combinations of libraries created in part (c); combinations are then counted; each time a combination is encountered, the matrix is searched for a match; if a match is found, the corresponding matrix position is incremented by one; if no match is found, a new matrix position is created with the new combination and the corresponding count initialized to one; this routine also provides for a total count of each library's contributions plus a grand total of all libraries' contributions;
e. tabulate, from the data compiled in (d) above, several elaborate tables of summary statistics; these statistics are described later in this paper.

The number of libraries the program LNRLST can accommodate is a variable and is entered as an execution-time parameter along with the library names and code designations. The main program occupies approximately 150,000 bytes of core memory.

The Output

A sample of the *Register* entries appears in Figure 2. A simple one-letter designation was used to identify each library rather than the usual National Union Catalog (NUC) designation in order to save space in the printout. These letters appear alphabetically to the right of each LC number. A typical page of the *Register* contains ten columns of up to six-digit LC numbers, with the two-digit series number appearing only once at the beginning of each series. Thus each page contains about 600 LC numbers. The latest cumulation of 1,100,000 volumes (560,000 LC numbers) consists of nearly 1,000 pages. The entire output was produced on five pieces of fiche directly from the cumulated tape. The COM program was written by the commercial firm which contracted to run it.

The computer output microfiche was issued on five 4 x 6 pieces in 42X. Each piece contains 208 frames and each frame contains an average of 1,126 volumes and 573 titles. The data can be produced on 24X fiche as well as roll film.

Statistical Summary

The large samples of holdings (from an initial 5,000 volumes, through successive cumulations to 90,000 and, the most recent, 1,100,000) provide an excellent data base for statistical analysis. We believe the samples may be the largest title by title comparison of monographs ever tabulated in this format. Very little analysis is presented in this paper, but the data base and its format will be explained. Even without analysis, many interesting observations can be made.

```
973109 0        4449 E          9097  0        15440 P        75448 AEZ
973606 0        4587 CE         9157  AE       15503 C        75456 AZ
                4607 E          9236  B        15972 O        75500 EZ
                4690 BCEN       9314  Z        15980 E        75527 EJ
  PS   76       4729 M          9611  E        16003 E        75535 BO
                4788 E          9717  O        16109 E        75551 E
 15168 J        4859 C          9792  BE       16141 EO       75578 M
112600 J        4891 E          9944  Z        16393 A        75586 A
                4903 ACEO      10294  O        16405 E        75614 E
                4911 E         10349  E        16472 E        75630 ELMO
        77      4938 E         10354  Z        16649 E        75728 A
                5087 BJLO      10357  E        16681 E        75736 Z
     5 A        5158 AB        10361  J        16728 E        75779 AI
    56 I        5190 A         10365  E        16752 E        75787 AE
   100 0        5296 O         10460  E        17260 CE       75823 AE
   214 BP       5564 C         10468  A        17567 E        75866 ABIZ
   257 BE       5568 A         10558  E        17689 E        75874 EZ
   360 A        5647 E         10631  Z        17733 O        75902 ACEGL
   407 A        5655 A         10645  E        18103 E             Z
   431 CP       5785 O         10661  AE       18154 E        75937 ABCMN
   553 C        5813 AE        10716  EO       18225 E             OZ
   632 E        5821 BP        10723  Z        19038 E        75996 C
   738 AE       5927 E         10774  B        19056 E        76051 ACIOP
   876 ABCEH    6112 E                                             Z
```

Fig. 2. Portion of a typical page of the computer printout showing the 2-digit 76 and 77 series, a typical prefix—PS, the serial numbers with the series, and letter codes to the right of each serial number. For example, Library A has the book 77-5; seven libraries—A, B, C, M, N, O, and Z hold the book 77-75937. Each page contains ten columns; only five are shown.

Most of the tabulations are designed to throw light on the various aspects of the overlap problem, since a decisive factor in determining the utility of the *Register* is a knowledge of the number of titles held in common by all the libraries. Over the years there has been continuing interest in overlap. Probably the first and most elaborate of the early studies was by Leroy Merritt (5), and one of the most recent by Leonard, Maier, and Dougherty (6). Continuing interest is expressed in such proclamations as that by Ellsworth Mason where he claims that materials are "being acquired in duplications that are rather staggering across the country" (7).

The following statistics were tabulated from input for current acquisitions, the most recent being a total of 90,302 volumes, rather than the retrospective and current totals in the production runs. The 90,302 volumes were acquired for the most part during the two year period, fall 1969 to fall 1971. The statistics show holdings for sixteen libraries.

The Basic Tabulations—Titles Held in Common by Unique Combinations of Libraries

The basic tabulation sections which are shown in Table 2 actually fill seven pages of computer printout. The tabulation is designed so that each unique and actual combination of libraries is separately listed, and the books held by each combination are counted. Thus, in the table, although the total number of books held in common by Libraries A and B is 127, the number of books held in common by them *and no other library* is only 52. The number of books held by Libraries A, B and Z, *and no other library is* 18. None of these 18 is included in the count of 52, and none of the 52 in the 18. They are mutually exclusive. But the 18, plus the 52, plus the small counts in each of the other combinations in which A and B share holdings is 127.

The percentage of common holdings for each combination is also given except when the percentage is less than .01. Thus libraries A and B have .48 percent in common of their total combined holdings of 10,688 volumes.

It is interesting to note that of the 65,535 possible combinations, in only 444 combinations did the percentage of common holdings exceed .01 percent, and in only 8 did the percentage exceed 1 percent. Of these, the highest is 5.43 percent (A and Z). This 5.43 percent means that 678 of A and Z's common holdings were held by no other library. The total of A and Z's common holdings that were also held by other libraries is 1,315, or about 10.5 percent of 12,470. Again this is the highest percentage of any combination.

Summary of Titles Held in Common

The basic tabulation of titles held in common is summarized in Table 3. Column 1 is the number of libraries from 1 to 16 in each combination. Column 2 is the total number of titles counted in all combinations. For example, 59,907 titles exist in unique copy; thus there were only 59,907 copies (column 3), but there were only 8 titles which as many as 9 libraries held, for a total of 72 copies (column 3).

Table 3. Titles Held in Common by Each Unique Combination of Libraries

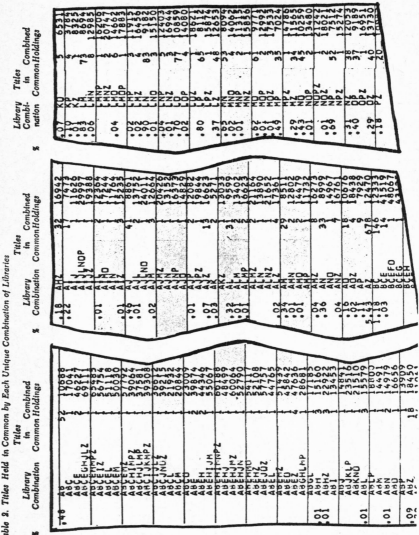

Table 3. Summary of Titles Held in Common by Unique Combinations of Libraries (Spring 1971 tabulation)

Column 1 No. of Libraries in Each Combination	Column 2 Total No. of Titles in all Combinations	Column 3 Total No. of Copies in all Combinations	Column 4 No. of Times a Combination Occurred	Column 5 Theoretical No. of Times a Combination can Occur (Binomial Distribution)	Column 6 Average Title Overlap Per Combination
1	59,907	59,907	16	16	3,774.19
2	8,766	17,532	117	120	74.92
3	2,453	7,359	356	560	6.89
4	782	3,128	360	1,820	2.17
5	279	1,395	214	4,368	1.30
6	84	504	75	8,008	1.12
7	43	301	41	11,440	1.04
8	13	104	12	12,870	1.08
9	8	72	7	11,440	1.14
10	0	0	0	8,008	0.00
11	0	0	0	4,368	0.00
12	0	0	0	1,820	0.00
13	0	0	0	560	0.00
14	0	0	0	120	0.00
15	0	0	0	16	0.00
16	0	0	0	1	0.00
Totals	72,335	90,302	1,198	65,535	60.38

Column 4 shows that all 16 libraries contributed unique titles and that there were 117 different combinations of two libraries, out of a possible 120 (column 5). Thus there were 3 combinations of 2 libraries which had no titles in common. It is also most interesting that there were only 7 combinations of 9 libraries out of a possible 11,440, and no combinations of 10 or larger.

According to the binomial distribution, there are 65,535 theoretical ways that 16 libraries can combine (total, column 5), whereas, in this sample, only 1,198 combinations occurred (total, column 4).

Column 6 is the result of column 2 divided by column 4. Thus 3774.19 is the average number of unique titles contributed by each library. 74.92 is the average number held by any combination of 2 libraries, and 6.89 is the average held by any combination of 3.

Summary of Each Library's Multiplicated Titles

The administrators of each library are especially interested to know how many of their own titles are also held by other libraries. This information for total input (i.e., for titles with LC prefixes from 1900 to the present) is given in Table 4. (Tables were also produced giving the same kind of information by decade and for the last two years, but are not reproduced here.)

The column labels are self-explanatory, but it may be observed that the total in column 5, 30,395, equals the difference between the total copies, 90,302 (column 3, table 3) and the number of titles held by one library only, 59,907 (columns 2 and 3, table 3).

Table 4. Summary of Each Library's Multiplicated Titles (1900-1971 imprints)

Column 1 Library	Column 2 Library Code	Column 3 Number of Volumes Contributed by Each Library	Column 4 Each Library's Volume as a % of Total Volumes	Column 5 No. of Titles for Which Copies are also Held by Other Libraries	Column 6 Each Library's Multiplicated Titles as a % of Own Titles (Col. 5÷Col. 3)	Column 7 Each Library's Multiplicated Titles as a % of Grand Total (Col. 5÷Total, Col. 3)
Louisiana State Library	A	4,708	5.21	2,497	53.03	2.76
Louisiana Tech University	B	5,980	6.62	2,378	39.76	2.63
University of South- western Louisiana	C	6,353	7.03	1,932	30.41	2.13
Louisiana State Uni- versity-Baton Rouge	E	29,186	32.32	6,190	21.20	6.85
Louisiana State Univer- sity Medical Center	F	580	.64	168	28.96	.18
Grambling	G	1,606	1.77	471	29.32	.52
Centenary	H	4,472	4.95	2,061	46.08	2.28
Louisiana State Uni- versity-Alexandria	I	2,765	3.06	1,087	39.31	1.20
Southeastern Louisiana	J	4,153	4.59	1,849	44.52	2.04
Northwestern Louisiana	K	563	.62	230	40.85	.25
Northeastern Louisiana	L	4,891	5.41	1,980	40.48	2.19
Loyola—New Orleans	M	3,803	4.21	1,744	45.85	1.93
Louisiana State Uni- versity-Shreveport	N	4,291	4.75	1,749	40.75	1.93
Louisiana State Uni- versity-New Orleans	O	5,968	6.60	1,783	29.87	1.97
Nicholls	P	3,221	3.56	1,048	32.53	1.16
New Orleans Public	Z	7,762	8.59	3,228	41.58	3.57
	Totals	90,302	100.00	30,395		
	Average	5,644	6.25	1,900	37.78	2.09

Distribution of Titles Published and
Multiplicated by Decade

Table 5 shows that the very largest overlap, in current acquisitions, occurs among books with recent imprints. This is to be expected since these figures do not make any comparison to older books recently acquired by one library to those already in another library, and since the acquisition of older books is from a much larger universe than that for current books.

Table 5. Distribution of Contributed Titles Published and Multiplicated by Decade (Titles acquired from 1969 to 1971)

Imprint Period	Number of Titles Contributed	% of Titles Contributed	Number of Volumes Multiplicated	% of Total Volumes Multiplicated
1900–1909	1,483	2.05	23	.13
1910–1919	1,049	1.45	29	.16
1920–1929	1,180	1.63	22	.12
1930–1939	1,816	2.51	74	.41
1940–1949	2,539	3.51	102	.57
1950–1959	5,353	7.40	361	2.01
1960–1971	58,915	81.45	17,356	96.59
Totals	72,335	100.00	17,967	100.00

Other Summary Statistics

The foregoing tables illustrate the kind of tabulations that can be made with this type of data. More detailed tables can be compiled, and indeed were—e.g., tables giving the percentage of books acquired for each year and each decade for each library, with ten year totals and averages. Other possibilities would be frequency distributions and summaries for clusters of similar libraries.

This material awaits analysis. We believe it contains many heretofore unsuspected insights.

Future Plans

Since the data can be updated so readily, plans are being made to provide funds for the extraction and keypunching of LC numbers in the remaining retrospective collections of the participating libraries. These libraries contain an estimated total of two million volumes. Succeeding cumulations will be readily produced on COM. Most of the cost has been for extracting retrospective numbers from card catalogs. Once the remaining retrospective collections are cumulated, costs for cumulating current input will be negligible.

Any final catalog, of course, can never list complete holdings since each library has many titles without LC numbers. Those titles could be listed in more conventional form. Since they are in a minority, the expense would be far more reasonable than it would be to reproduce entire holdings in conventional form.

We have said nothing about other aspects of the project. In committee discussions, however, much has been said about the feasibility of using the LC card number to access the information in other major projects such as MARC, and possibly even the data bank in the Ohio College Library Center. Technically, it is feasible to print a conventional bibliographic catalog by matching up our LC numbers with titles listed in the current MARC tapes; pragmatically and economically, of course, it is another matter.

Other possibilities are the printing of a list of specialized holdings by accessing the subject headings on the MARC tapes, assignment of specialized acquisitions, and the gathering of information which might affect development of a joint processing center.

Acknowledgments

This project was supported in part by the Library Services and Construction Act Title III funds administered by the Louisiana State Library.

The authors wish to give special thanks to Miss Sallie Farrell, Louisiana State Librarian, for her enthusiastic support and fine advice. We wish also to thank the other members of the L.L.A. Committee on the Union Catalog: Mr. Sam Dyson, Louisiana Tech University; Mrs. Jane Kleiner, Louisiana State University, Baton Rouge; Mrs. Elizabeth Roundtree, Louisiana State Library; Dr. Gerald Eberle, Louisiana State University, New Orleans; Mrs. Hester Slocum, New Orleans Public Library; Mr. Charles Miller, Tulane University, New Orleans; Mr. Ronald Tumey, Rapides Parish Library, Alexandria; and finally, Mr. John Richard, past president of the Louisiana Library Association, who saw the importance of the project, and who appointed the original committee.

Complete documentation for this project, including computer programs, has been deposited with the ERIC Clearinghouse on Library and Information Science (8).

References

1. Harry Dewey, "Numerical Union Catalogs," *Library Quarterly* 18: 33-34 (Jan. 1948).
2. Louis Schreiber, "A New England Regional Catalog of Books," *Bay State Librarian* 55: 13-15 (Jan. 1965).
3. Samuel Goldstein, et al., *Development of a Machine Form Union Catalog for the New England Library Information Network (NELINET)*. (Wellesley, Mass.: New England Board of Higher Education, 1970) (U.S. Office of Education final report, Project No. 9-0404.) ED 043 367.
4. William E. McGrath, "LNR: Numerical Register of Books in Louisiana Libraries," *Louisiana Library Association Bulletin* 34: 79-86 (Fall 1971).
5. Leroy C. Merritt, "The Administrative, Fiscal, and Quantitative Aspects of the Regional Union Catalog," in *Union Catalogs in the United States* (Chicago, Ill.: American Library Association, 1942).
6. Lawrence E. Leonard, Joan M. Maier, and Richard M. Dougherty, *Centralized Processing: A Feasibility Study Based on Colorado Academic Libraries*. (Metuchen, N.J.: Scarecrow Press, 1969).
7. Ellsworth Mason, "Along the Academic Way," *Library Journal* 96: 1671-76 (15 May 1971).
8. William E. McGrath and Donald J. Simon, *LNR: Numerical Register of Books in Louisiana Libraries; Basic Documents* (Lafayette, La.: Louisiana Library Association, Dec. 1972) (U.S. Office of Education) ED 070 470, ED 070 471.

THE APPLICATION OF MICROFORM TO MANUAL AND MACHINE-READABLE CATALOGUES

by D.G.R. Buckle and Thomas French

Abstract

At Birmingham University Library it is proposed to implement in October 1972, a complete microfilm catalogue system. This system originated from two sources. Over the past two years various means have been evaluated of converting the library's card catalogues (which were closed at the end of 1971) to a more compact form. An interim report* mentioned microfilming as one of a number of possibilities. At the time the production of hard copy was envisaged, but since then a true microform system has seemed preferable, in which the catalogue would exist as cassettes of film to be viewed by all users on reader machines. This system has been specified and costed, and details are included in this paper. The impetus in reaching this viewpoint was provided by the progress made over the last 18 months in the field of COM, which rapidly commended itself as the choice of output medium for the new mechanised MARC-based catalogue, which covers all the library's serials and all monographs acquired after January 1972. BLCMP union catalogues in these categories will also be held in COM form at Birmingham University Library.

Microform—Its Application to a Manual Catalogue

Choice of format

Basically three media were considered as the form in which the old catalogue

*Program, Vol. 5, No. 2, p. 41-66, May 1971.

Reprinted from *Program; new of computers in libraries*, 3: 187-203 (July 1972) by permission of the author and publisher. Copyright © 1972 by Aslib.

would be held in microform: fiche, 35mm film, or 16mm film in cassettes. Fiche was looked at inasmuch as it was a newer medium; at that time, for example, the *Books in English* experiment with PCMI was under way; while 35mm film was the one format in which the library's own Photographic Department could work. But considerations of file security and greater convenience meant that the choice had to be 16mm film in cassettes. Fiche seemed unsuitable for an intensely used, manually consulted situation; the one mechanised fiche handling system in existence was prohibitively expensive, and would in any case have necessitated an extra member of staff to do the searching for the catalogue user, thus inhibiting 'browsing'. Filming in 35mm raised immediately problems of compatibility with COM, which is not normally used in this format; no cassetting systems were available, and open reels of film, which can easily be wound off their spools, did not commend themselves in our situation. Finally, filming in this format, even by the library's own Photographic Department, was still more expensive than the cheapest quote received (see Table 1 below).

Processes and costs

We therefore decided that the best medium was 16mm film in cassettes, and contacted a number of microfilm bureaux to obtain quotations. The range of prices quoted for an identical process—the filming of about 1 million catalogue cards—was surprising. In the following table, the cost relates to the filming of the cards and production on one master copy:

Table 1. Range of costs quoted for filming card catalogue

	Filming† On-site	Off-site	No. of cards per frame
Most expensive	£6,300	£4,600	1
Middle range	£3,800	£2,000	1
Cheapest	£1,018	£688	8
Library Photographic Dept.	£1,307	—	21

Associated costs also varied, though less dramatically. Thus the cost of one set of duplicate films varied between £60 and £300, mostly in the £100–£250 range; the unit cost per cassette, from 75p to £1.75.

† Filming on-site implies that the bureau's staff and equipment are brought to the library premises and operate there. Off-site implies that cards are collected for filming at the bureau's premises and then returned to the library.

Most firms seemed to prefer an automatic feed camera, which basically exposes one card per frame. This is a comparatively fast method—the length of time required to complete the filming was estimated at 4-5 months, but it results in a large number of reels of film, hence a large number of cassettes and increased prices for multiple copies of the catalogue. Typical figures are 120-200 cassettes.

One or two firms suggested the 'duo-filming' technique, whereby two sequences of 8mm width are filmed side by side on a 16mm film. The sequence runs down one column to the end of the reel and then is continued up the adjacent one, so that each cassette contains a sequence twice the usual length. Each 8mm band occupies the entire viewing screen; a switch on the reader machine controls the movement from one band to another. Thus a more expensive reader machine with this tracking facility would have been required.

Filming in 35mm would have enabled up to 21 cards to be exposed per frame; but because of the different format, about as many reels of film would be produced as by the method finally decided on; and of course they could not be cassetted.

One other possibility considered was the hiring of an automatic feed camera to be operated on site by library staff. Costs for this however still came to £1108, and 134 cassettes would have been produced.

The process suggested by the firm who have been given the contract involves the use of a planetary camera. Eight cards are filmed per exposure, in two columns of four, producing something like the same page layout (in comic, not cine, mode) that we envisage for our COM catalogue (save that here there will be 20 entries per page). The total filming cost will be £688. Sixty-three reels of film will be produced, each 100 ft. in length and suitable for cassetting, and each containing 16,000 entries. Each duplicate set of films will cost £60, plus about another £60 for cassettes. In fact the master film will be retained as an archival copy, and up to 27 copies will be used—for details, see Part II, section 3.

Filming began on 6th April, and should be completed by the end of September. About 40,000 cards are filmed each week. It is hoped that there will be little disruption to users of the catalogue; evidence from elsewhere* seems to confirm this. Finally, it is intended that the whole process will be repeated annually (or perhaps less frequently), to take account of deletions to and withdrawals from pre-1972 stock.

Readers and retrieval

A variety of cassette microfilm readers is currently available. We required a machine that would be suitable both for the microfilm of the old catalogue and for COM, and which would stand up to continuous use by staff

*E.g. Newcastle U.L. report little inconvenience caused by cards being removed for keypunching (Catalogue Computerisation Project. Final report, pt. 1, p. 19-20, 1972.)

and students. The kind of equipment available ranged from simple, sturdy hand-wound machines costing about £70 to sophisticated motorised units in the £1000 price range. Financial considerations apart, we felt that motorised machines would be far more liable to breakdown in the kind of situation we are proposing.

READER

A manually operated reader was therefore selected; it is specified in this paper. It is inexpensive, hardy and compact. The purpose of quoting this equipment in detail is to familiarise the reader with modern microfilm readers. If microform is accepted as the medium for catalogue production, then a detailed analysis of the reader market must be undertaken.

There has been tremendous growth in the reader market since the beginning of 1971 and much of the equipment is untried in the real environment. Caution must be the key word when considering such a product market.

Computer Instrumentation Ltd.

CIL 600 Series Microfilm Reader—Roll Film Model:
Specification

Microforms:	16 mm roll film in cassettes.
Magnifications:	Fixed, at 18×, 24× or 38×; all lenses are interchangeable.
Screen:	380 mm × 280 mm (14" × 11"). Translucent.
Lamp:	Tungsten halogen A1/220, 12v, 50w with a life of 150 hours. Cost: 90p
Power:	115/240v.
Dimensions:	Height: 492 mm (19. 5") Width: 420 mm (16. 5") Depth: 510 mm (20")
Weight:	12. 7 kg. (28 lbs)
Accessories:	Turntable stand Wheeled stand
Film wind:	Manual—handle at front right.
Cost:	Approx. £90

CASSETTES AND CAPACITY

The microfilm cassette completely encloses the film requiring no threading or spooling. The cassette protects the film from dust and rough handling and is easy to load and unload from readers. Each cassette measures

100mm x 100mm x 25mm (4"x 4"x 1") and weighs 170g (6 oz.) when loaded. The capacity of one cassette is 100' of film, containing 2,400 frames (COM) or pages (at 24 x reduction). Our output page will contain 20 catalogue entries, so that one cassette will contain a total of 48,000 entries. This means that the Union Name Catalogue at the end of the first year could be housed on two cassettes. (These figures are for thin-based Kalvar or diazo film. The use of normal film, on a thicker base, would halve the capacity of each cassette.)

RETRIEVAL

Code line indexing can provide quick and easy access to given areas on the microfilm visually. Let us consider a simple alpha index A-Z. Each character would be marked vertically down the side of the microfilm reader screen; the microfilm, during processing, will have horizontal lines marked between each frame of film, the position of the line changing on completion of entries for each letter of the alphabet; this will result in 26 different line positions between frames. When the film is spooled quickly, the lines will appear to be continuous to the user, each line matching with an alphabetic position on the index on the reader. Immediately, the line indicator matches the given letter of the alphabet that the user wishes to search; he can show down to access each frame.

READER/PRINTER MACHINES

It is also intended that there will be at least one motorised reader/printer, to serve both as a fast access machine for staff use and as a means of providing hard copies on demand. (These would be charged to the user.)

Reports from other libraries

During the course of our studies we were being continually surprised to learn of news of developments in microfilm catalogues, especially COM, in other libraries in this country. These projects were then largely undocumented. The general impression was that microform systems were being implemented not as the results of theoretical long-term planning but out of practical necessity.

There appear to be very few developments abroad in the field of microfilm catalogues. One or two American university libraries are reported as having microfilmed their catalogue cards as a security measure (5). A further report has also been published on the COM-produced catalogue at Lockheed's (9); while there is recent news of a COM system at the Los Angeles Public Libraries (5), and of a microfilmed card system at the New Jersey State Library (7).

Table 2. Microform

| | COM | | | | |
	Total No.	Operational Now	In use by end of 1972	Planned for 1973 +	Public Reading Equipment
County Libraries	8	4	—	Definite: 3 Possible: 1	Hand Operated: 5
City Libraries	3	1	—	Definite: 1 Possible: 1	Hand Operated: 1
Polytechnic Libraries	—	—	—	—	—
National Libraries	1	1	—	—	Hand Operated: 1
University Libraries	3	—	2	Possible: 1	Hand Operated: 2

In this country the initial impetus came originally almost entirely from various county library systems. Table 2 shows that, out of eight such libraries considering COM catalogues, four now have operational systems. One city library and one national library also have COM systems now in use; while one polytechnic library has microfilmed its card catalogue and is using the cassetted film as the catalogue medium. Systems to be implemented before the end of this year include one national library, which is microfilming its cards, and one university library, provisionally, which has been experimenting with COM; while Birmingham University Library will by then have in operation both the systems described in this paper.

It may be significant that those libraries which have opted for traditional hard copy rather than microform have no firm dates for the introduction of their book-form catalogues (one library completed both microfilming and the production of hard copy a few years ago but is not using either medium).

By the end of 1972, therefore, there should be some 10 microform catalogue systems in use in this country: in 4 county libraries, 1 city library, 1 polytechnic library, 2 national libraries, and 2 in university libraries.

" catalogue systems in U.K.

FILMED CARDS						
Total No.	Operational Now	In use by end of 1972	Planned for 1973 +	Hard copy used	Public Reading Equipment	Total No. of Libraries
–	–	–	–	–	–	8
3	–	–	Definite: 1 Possible: 2	2	Type undecided: 1	6
1	1	–	–	–	Hand Operated: 1	1
2	–	1	Possible: 1	–	Hand Operated: 1	2
3	–	1	1	2	Hand Operated: 1	5

Computer Output on Microform—Its Application to a Machine Readable Catalogue

Introduction

The system designed to generate and maintain a machine readable catalogue for the cooperating libraries of the Birmingham Libraries Co-operative Mechanisation Project is completely flexible in its approach to output media. Edited magnetic tapes are produced containing the various catalogue organisation and format requirements. This flexibility allows each library to decide how it wishes to list the final product for library use. The same magnetic tape can produce either a unit catalogue entry on card or a multi-catalogue entry in page form. The unit catalogue entry would be produced on continuous card stationery and manually filed into a card catalogue. Such a catalogue would require constant filing to maintain it; it would be a permanent file maintained in parallel with the machine file and updated by the machine file. The multi-catalogue entry would be either in book form, produced in multiple copies on the computer line printer or some combination of line printer/xerox system, or microform.

Although the card catalogue is potentially the most up-to-date catalogue, it is extremely labour intensive and would require constant manual attention. Card stationery is expensive to use. As the data base of the catalogue is within the machine, the machine version clearly can be reorganised and edited at will, but the cost to reproduce it in card form would be prohibitive; similarly, so the costs of producing multiple copies of the card catalogue. Access to the catalogue data contained in a card catalogue is also restrictive, firstly because of the nature of a unit record system, which only allows one entry to be seen at a time, and secondly because of the size constraints upon the amount of data that can be entered onto the card. However, the breakdown of the catalogue into drawers of cards can offer greater access to users in reducing queuing problems. Although there are access and up-to-dateness advantages, the card catalogue is an expensive and inflexible medium.

It had been assumed in the past that Birmingham University Library would have a book form catalogue produced from the machine data base. As a consequence of costing the production of a book form catalogue on a computer line printer to the specifications and quantities we require, it became apparent that alternative methods of output and reproduction must be evaluated. The book form catalogue clearly offered flexibility of organisation and format, but at the cost of potential up-to-dateness as compared with the card catalogue. The book form catalogue implies no filing, but only because it is a reflection of the state of the catalogue at a given time, the full catalogue having to be reproduced at intervals possibly with intervening cumulative listings—clearly a captial intensive catalogue. Although it has the access advantages of a multi-entry system, its physical access is not that of a card catalogue, unless an individual volume was produced for each drawer equivalent.

Both card and book form catalogues produced on a computer line printer suffer from character set restrictions. The costs of production and reproduction move upward quite dramatically the greater the character set availability on the print chain of the line printer.

There is a severe cost/speed relationship in using a computer which is reflected in the use of the central processing unit and the peripherals: the more you can maximise the use of fast peripherals, the less cost incurred. Slow peripherals are expensive to use, particularly for vast amounts of data. The line printer is a slow peripheral and this is reflected in the costs of line printer output. Magnetic tape is a fast peripheral medium; if this can be associated with an output medium of similar speeds, significant savings should be achieved. This search for such a medium directed us to Computer Output on Microform (COM).

COM has the same format, flexibility, and access constraints as a book form catalogue, its most obvious advantage over a book form catalogue lies in the cost of reproduction, because of the speed of data transfer.

Let us list some of the advantages of COM:

1. The maximisation of data transfer speeds, implying reduced output costs.

2. Handling intensity is reduced—problems of decollating, bursting and bulk distribution disappear.

3. Minimum character set requirements of upper and lower case are satisfied with the added availability of variable print fonts.

4. Low cost of raw materials and reproduction.

5. Approximate ratios of paper to microfilm:

Storage volume	50:1
Weight	50:1
Postage 1st class	20:1
2nd class	30:1
Supplies cost	
Single part	1.5:1
Four part	4:1
Printing speed	1:9

The cost/benefits of COM imply that the flexibility of a computer held catalogue can be taken advantage of at reasonable cost. Multiple copies of complete catalogues, or parts of catalogues, can be produced, cheaply offering standard catalogue entries in multiple locations.

COM bureaux

Three types of bureau facility are available in the UK at the present time; independent commercial bureaux, commercial bureaux operated by equipment suppliers, and users offering surplus time on their machines.

Most of the commercial bureaux concentrate on the generation of 16mm roll film with images set in comic or cine* mode and 105mm roll film which is subsequently cut to form fiche. Two reduction ratios are in common use for fiche generation; one being an effective reduction of 24X which permits up to 98 frames to each fiche; the other being an effective reduction of 42X which permits 200 or more frames to be set on the same area of film. Microform charges are usually based on a price per 1000 frames.

COM recorders can produce variously 35mm, 16mm, or 105mm films. Many of the recorders are restricted to 16mm form.

For us the choice was between 16mm roll film in cassettes and microfiche. Both have low cost terminal readers available. Both are suitable media for recording from hard copy and via COM devices. Both have relatively low recording costs, and neither therefore requires substantial duplication to be economic.

There is little difference between the media until we consider catalogue use. At 20 entries per page a single cassette would hold up to 48,000 entries; for the same volume 33 sixty frame density microfiche would be required. In operational terms a cassette file could be left for self service while an equivalent microfiche file would demand very close supervision to avoid loss and disorder. This flexibility in use was the major factor in deciding in favour of 16mm roll film in cassettes.

Bureaux can offer a selection of output options and peripheral services, such as film duplication by alternative methods. They are also willing to assist with any programming that may be required to reformat magnetic tapes for their recorders. Many have a range of software already available to cater for common requirements. Strict production and turnround schedules are agreed and met.

Quotations were received from several bureaux who were informed of our total output requirements for the first year of processing. The output requirements were as follows:

Name catalogue   5,808 pages p.a.
Classified catalogue   7,008   ''   ''
Union name catalogue   10,416   ''   ''

All quotations were for 16mm microfilm produced at 24X reduction in cassettes.

Catalogue organisation

The packing density of entries into a cassette of microfilm plus the low cost of copies offers an extremely flexible catalogue medium. This medium gives the opportunity of de-centralising the post-1971 main catalogue by providing the opportunity of offering the complete catalogue in its various formats to departmental libraries, sub-libraries and reading rooms. The ease of editing allows inexpensive subject area catalogues to be produced from the full name or classified catalogues. Security of the catalogue is enhanced; the cheapness of reproduction takes the financial sting out of any loss or damage.

A single-cassette-to-reader dedicated system reduces user handling problems. If the cassette could be locked in, it would also be a completely secure system, however this is expensive in dedicated readers. To reduce the prospect of queuing, the catalogue would have to be broken into volumes, as would a book form catalogue; the greater the number of volumes, the less the prospect of serious queuing problems. This approach does not maximise the use of readers, and is expensive in under-utilised cassettes which would hold short strips of film which are more expensive to produce. If the local name catalogue were broken into ten volumes, each cas-

---

*'Cine mode'—images are arranged vertically. The alternative is 'comic mode'—images are arranged horizontally. This mode has microfilm reader implications.

Table 3. Comparisons of output costs in the first year for the various media under consideration

| | Microfilm Bureaux | | | | | Micro-Fiche | Line-Printer† | | Line-Printer/Xerox* |
| | | | | | | | Data Centre Machine† | In House Machine* | |
	A £	B £	C £	D £	E £	F £	£	£	£
Name Catalogue (six copies)	72	65	70	66	81	99	1399	319	530
Classified Catalogue (six copies)	87	77	82	82	98	121	1632	372	634
Union Name Catalogue (one copy)	83	70	79	79	95	44	460	212	208
Total	242	212	231	247	274	264	3491	903	1372
Order of cost	3	1	2	4	6	5	9	7	8

Notes:

The total costs for microfilm exclude loading cassettes
* Upper case only
† Upper and lower case
‡ Both line printer costings assume 3 part stationery and two printer runs

No binding costs or transit costs are included in the figures for a book form catalogue
No cassette costs or transit costs are included in the figures for a micro form catalogue

sette would only use one tenth of its capacity. A dedicated reader system
would imply a reader per volume per catalogue. The cost in money and
space would be high, for multiple copies it would be prohibitive; without
multiple copies there could be queuing problems. This is a high price to
pay to avoid the possibility of losing a cassette of film which would cost
no more than £2 to replace.

Using normal film, the annual intake to the local classified catalogue and
name catalogue will each be completely stored in one cassette of film; the
union catalogue will require two cassettes. If thin film were used, three
years' intake could be similarly stored. The complete catalogues will be
broken into volumes within the cassettes by the use of the index retrieval
system already described. It is proposed that the union catalogue be used
only by library staff.

The system will provide 33 catalogue location points, six of which will
be for library staff only, the remainder for any user.

Each reader has associated with it a full set of catalogue cassettes
housed in a bank of pigeon holes. The bank consists of four ten-deep
columns of pigeon holes, each headed by classification of catalogue over a
colour code. Each cassette is identified by content over colour code and
numbered. The user takes down the cassette required, places it on the
reader, searches and returns it. The colour code system aids the relocation
of cassettes in the bank. The specified bank gives provision for five years
union catalogue growth and ten years local catalogue growth, assuming the
use of normal film. The four columns are in two divisions representing
catalogue types; the two columns in each division house in one column the
six-monthly catalogue, in the other the monthly supplements.

This is a compact system that maximises the use of readers and provides
greater catalogue access to the user at a low cost. Costs in the tables that
follow are based on lowest acceptable quotations submitted.

Table 4 (Siting of catalogues) illustrates the system. Main library staff
departments each have one copy of each catalogue and one reader. The
sub-libraries have two reader machines each—one for staff, one for public
use. While the Law and Music Libraries have one copy each of the union
and of the old author and classified catalogues, the Medical Library has
one copy of the union and two copies of all the other catalogues, plus
one extra copy of the new classified catalogue for staff use.

For the Main Library Catalogue Hall there will be ten readers and ten
copies of the new name and classified catalogues, but only five copies of
the old author and classified catalogues. In view of the large number of
cassettes required to accommodate the old catalogues, this will represent a
significant economy. Queuing problems are unlikely in view of the availability of ten reader machines in the Catalogue Hall, plus the dispersal of
catalogue queries to other reference points, e.g. the Reading Rooms, which
will each have one copy of each catalogue and one reader. Finally, there
will be one spare copy of each catalogue held in reserve, and two spare
readers.

Since cassettes can be re-used, they represent a non-recurrent expenditure, whereas the cost of filling them with films is recurrent. This has been allowed for in the tables that follow. It has been proposed that the old card catalogue be re-filmed annually, at a basic cost of £688; this therefore represents a standard recurrent cost. The new catalogue comprises a file growing at a constant rate, so the cost of its production increases annually.

Tables 5-10 show therefore that, in the first year, total costs for the system will be £7263; thereafter, annual recurrent costs are £3091.

Tables 4-10: explanatory notes

The following abbreviations refer to specific locations at Birmingham University:

ILL =	Inter-Library Loans Office
Cat. Rm. =	Cataloguing Room (Dept.)
Sub. Libs. =	the three sub-libraries for Medicine, Law and Music
Main Cat. Hall =	the Catalogue Hall of the Main Library. Here there are ten readers and ten copies of the new catalogues, but, as an economy, only five copies of the old catalogue between the ten readers.
Campus =	ten locations at various points on the campus, usually departmental libraries, where complete catalogues will be available.
R/Rs =	the four Reading Rooms in the Main Library.
Reserve =	two readers and one copy of each catalogue kept as spares.
o =	the old (microfilmed card) catalogue
n =	the new (COM) catalogue

Table 4 Siting of catalogues

Catalogue	ILL		Cat. Rm.		Accessns.		Sub-Libs.		Main Cat. Hall		Campus		R/Rs		Reserve		Total	
	o	n	o	n	o	n	o	n	o	n	o	n	o	n	o	n	o	n
Union Name				1		1		3								'1		7
Local Author	1		1		1		4	6	5	10	10	10	4	4	1	1	27	31
Local Classified	1	1	1	1	1	1	4	7	5	10					1	1	13	21
Number of film readers	1		1		1		6		10		10		4		2		35	

Table 5. Cost of catalogues

	ILL		Cat. Rm.		Accessns.		Sub-Libs.		Main Cat. Hall		Campus		R/Rs		Reserve		Total	
	o	n	o	n	o	n	o	n	o	n	o	n	o	n	o	n	o	n
	£	£	£	£	£	£	£	£	£	£	£	£	£	£	£	£	£	£
Union Name		17		17		17		51								17		119
Local Name	58		58		58		232	30	291	50	581	50	232	20	58	5	1568	155
Local Classified	45	7	45	7	45	7	176	49	221	70					45	7	577	147
Total	103	24	103	24	103	24	408	130	512	120	581	50	232	20	103	29	2145	421

Table 6. Cost of microfilm readers

	ILL	Cat. Rm.	Accessns.	Sub-Libs.	Main Cat. Hall	Campus	R/Rs	Reserve	Total
	£	£	£	£	£	£	£	£	£
Non-recurring	87	87	87	522	870	870	348	174	3045
Recurring	15	15	15	90	150	150	60	30	525

Table 7. Numbers of cassettes required.

Cassettes	ILL		Cat. Rm.		Accessns.		Sub-Libs.		Main Cat. Hall		Campus		R/Rs		Reserve		Total	
	o	n	o	n	o	n	o	n	o	n	o	n	o	n	o	n	o	n
	47	7	47	7	47	7	189	31	236	20	300	10	120	4	47	8	1033	94

Table 8. Total cost for the first year

ILL £	Cat.Rm. £	Accessns. £	Sub-Libs. £	Main Cat.Hall £	Campus £	R/Rs £	Reserve £	Total £
283	283	283	1370	1908	1961	784	391	7263

Table 9. Total annual recurring costs

ILL £	Cat.Rm. £	Accessns. £	Sub-Libs. £	Main Cat.Hall £	Campus £	R/Rs £	Reserve £	Total £
142	142	142	628	782	781	312	162	3091

Table 10. Total non-recurring costs

ILL £	Cat.Rm. £	Accessns. £	Sub-Libs. £	Main Cat.Hall £	Campus £	R/Rs £	Reserve £	Total £
141	141	141	742	1126	1180	472	229	4172

Bibliography

G. G. Baker and Associates. A Guide to COM in the United Kingdom. 2nd. ed. October, 1971.

Business Equipment Trade Association. Microfilm: the methods and the equipment. 1971.

Chesshyre, H. A. Article on Kingston Polytechnic Library system. (Forthcoming.)

Corbett, L. and German, J. Amocs project stage 2: a computer aided integrated system using BNB MARC literature tapes. *Program*, Vol. 6, No. 1, 1-35, January, 1972. (Mentions experiments with COM output.)

Davis, D. G. Security problems in college and university libraries: student violence. *College and Research Libraries*, Vol. 32, No. 1, p. 15-22, January, 1971.

Flintshire County Library. Computer cataloguing system. Appendix: Microfilm production of catalogue. May, 1971.

Gillock, O. P. and McDonough, R. H. Spreading state library riches for peanuts. *Wilson Library Bulletin*, Vol. 45, No. 4, p. 354-357, December, 1970.

Hammond, H. I. The computer catalogue system at Shropshire County Library. *Program*, Vol. 6, No. 1, p. 74-86, January, 1972. (Includes description of catalogue production and distribution on COM fiche.)

Kozumplik, W. A. and Lange, R. T. A COM-produced library catalog. *Information and records management*, April/May 1970, p. 45-46. (An update of their 1967 article.)

Larkworthy, G. and Brown, C. G. Library catalogues on microfilm. *Library Association Record*, Vol. 73, No. 12, p. 231-232, December, 1971.

Marriott, P. An experiment in computer originated microfilm (COM). *NRCd Bulletin*, Vol. 5, No. 2, p. 39-41, Spring 1972. (Describes the system at Cornwall County Library.)

Microdoc; journal of the Microfilm Association of Great Britain. Vol. 10, Nos. 2 and 3, 1971.

NRCd Bulletin. Vols. 2-4, 1969-71.

Williams, B.J.S. Miniaturised communications; a review of microforms. 1970.

Williams, B.J.S. Progress in documentation: micrographics. *Journal of Documentation*, Vol. 27, No. 4, p. 295-304, December, 1971.

AUTOMATED ALTERNATIVES TO CARD CATALOGS: THE CURRENT STATE OF PLANNING AND IMPLEMENTATION

by Kenneth J. Bierman

Introduction

Since the beginning applications of computer technology to libraries, there has been interest in the utilization of modern technology to eliminate the card catalog as the vehicle for bibliographic control of library collections. Since 1960, several small and medium-sized libraries (less than 250,000 titles) have replaced their card catalogs with some computer-generated alternative, and work in this area has been reported in the literature.[1-4] There is little published literature, however, on replacements for the card catalog with computer-based systems intended to handle 250,000 titles or more.

In September and October 1974, a short questionnaire was sent to twenty-nine leaders in the library automation field in the United States and Canada asking which libraries were most actively working in the area of automated alternatives to card catalogs. Twenty-four responses (83 percent) were returned with thirty-four uniquely identified libraries. Concurrently, a literature search was made to determine those libraries that had published in the field in recent years. Finally, selected knowledgeable persons were telephoned to get their input. On the basis of this preliminary work, twenty-six libraries (or library-related activities such as cooperative networks, commercial vendors, etc.) were selected for personal visits. These libraries were visited between October 1974 and January 1975. In addition, fifty-one other libraries were telephoned in February and March of 1975 to get added input into the survey. The Appendix lists all libraries contacted.

Although there was great flexibility in the interviews, certain basic

Reprinted from *Journal of Library Automation*, 8: 277-98 (December 1975) by permission of the author and publisher. Copyright © 1975 by the American Library Association.

questions were always asked. These included: How long has there been serious interest in automated alternatives to card catalogs? Is there a formal committee, task force, etc., charged with the responsibility to study automated alternatives and report their findings/recommendations? What are the major reasons for interest in automated alternatives to the card catalog? What alternatives appear to be the most desirable and feasible at this time? When do you believe they will be implemented? Do you see your individual library (or institution) accomplishing the goal or will it happen cooperatively (networks, etc.)? Are there any written studies (cost projections, feasibility studies, desirability studies, user studies, etc.) as of now?

For this report, certain words will be used assuming definite and specific meanings. Library will mean a collection of primarily printed materials in the form of published monographs and serials; large collections of technical reports are, for example, generally excluded. A large library is defined as one with 250,000 titles or more in the cataloged and classified collection. An intermediate library is defined as one with less than 250,000 titles. The majority of those libraries called intermediate are between 100,000 and 200,000 cataloged and classified titles. Emphasis is placed on size in titles, not volumes, because it is the number of titles that significantly affects the size of the catalog.

The word *catalog* as it is used in this report generally refers to the union public catalog of the entire collection with the traditional access points of author, title, and subject: thus, for example, automated catalogs of serials only are excluded. Book catalogs refer to hard copy printed book catalogs that are computer printed on a line printer and reproduced or photocomposed and reproduced. Microimage catalogs refer to roll film or fiche catalogs that have been computer produced via a computer output microform or photo composed microform process; microimage catalogs that are produced by photographically filming card catalogs are not included in this study. On-line catalogs refer to stores of bibliographic data searchable by at least the same access points as the traditional card catalog via CRT, typewriter, or some other type of terminal interface.

An open catalog is one that is having new entries added to it. A closed catalog is one that is not having new entries added to it but the existing entries are being maintained (corrections and deletions are being made, etc.). A frozen catalog is a closed catalog without any maintenance of the entries in the catalog.

Why are libraries interested in automated alternatives to card catalogs? Reasons ranged from immediate and parochial, such as moving into a new building with no provision for a card catalog, to philosophical, such as wanting an information system (not just catalog) with the ability to manipulate data to meet real needs.

Reasons given by ten or more libraries were: (1) provide access to the complete (i.e., union catalog of all holdings for a particular library system including the main, branch, and departmental libraries) and up-to-date catalog from multiple places; this is referred to variously as remote catalog access, portability, and distributability; (2) provide more (beyond the usual author, title, and subject) and improved access points and search capabilities; (3) expand the availability of increased resources through the sharing of resources via union catalogs region-wide; (4) eliminate or reduce the inconsistencies and inaccuracies of card catalogs and their inhospitality to change (change in filing rules, headings, access points, etc.) as catalogs become older and larger; (5) reduce the increasing problems and costs of maintaining card catalogs as they grow in number, size, age, and complexity (presumed cost savings of an automated catalog in the future); and (6) deal with pressures and influences for change both internally (from staff and users) and externally (most especially the Library of Congress).

Two additional reasons were cited more than once and with some degree of fervor: the increasing floor space occupied by card catalogs and the increasingly serious physical deterioration of very old and heavily used card catalogs. It is reasonable that as libraries become older and larger these two reasons will increase in importance. Two particularly interesting reasons, among several others included above, were given by Ohio State University: (1) Americans have been conditioned to expect very fast response, and electronic catalogs are the only way to provide fast response; and (2) if librarianship is best served by smaller units of service, then library activities must be decentralized, including decentralized access to the most up-to-date and accurate library records.

The above reasons provide a composite picture of reasons cited by both intermediate and large libraries. There were, however, variations in frequency of reasons cited by type of library. Public libraries cited remote catalog access as the major reason for interest. This is not surprising since public libraries generally have large numbers of branches and maintain many card catalogs that have a high percentage of title overlap. University libraries, however, more often emphasized the improved catalog access through more and improved access points and searching techniques. Given the large and diversified collections of university libraries and the specificity of many of the service requests, this is again not surprising. Also not surprising is the fact that those academic libraries with highly centralized collections tended not to be as interested in remote catalog access as those academic libraries with highly decentralized collections.

There was interest in expanding the availability of resources among all types and sizes of libraries. Inconsistencies and inaccuracies of card catalogs and their rigidity and inhospitality to change were mentioned more by large libraries than intermediate. Increasing problems and costs of maintaining card catalogs were mentioned by many libraries; academic and public libraries with decentralized collections were concerned about the number of catalogs they were maintaining while large libraries were more concerned with the size and complexity of the very large union card catalogs (some having over 20 million cards).

Pressures and influence for change internally and externally were seldom mentioned by intermediate libraries but often mentioned by large libraries. The most significant external pressure cited by large libraries was the Library of Congress, but not a single intermediate library cited this as a reason. This is not surprising since many large libraries have greatly increased their reliance on LC cataloging in the last few years. Another significant factor is that the activities of the Library of Congress have been followed closely by large academic and research libraries. Several large libraries specifically cited Rather's paper, *The Future of Catalog Control in the Library of Congress*, as well as the presentations at the Association of Research Libraries eighty-fifth Membership Meeting (January 1975), *The Future of Card Catalogs*.[5, 6] Changes planned by LC of concern to large libraries included the abandonment of superimposition, revision of the LC filing rules, revision of romanization policies, and major revision of the subject heading list.

Intermediate Libraries

Twenty-eight intermediate libraries were contacted (Table 1); the majority were academic libraries (32 percent) followed closely by public libraries (29 percent), and special libraries (25 percent). State libraries, library cooperatives, and service bureaus made up the remaining libraries contacted (14 percent).

The majority (54 percent) have printed book catalogs; microimage catalogs accounted for 29 percent and on-line catalogs for 17 percent. A few of the intermediate libraries contacted did not have automated alternatives but were seriously planning for an on-line catalog through OCLC within the next three or four years, assuming OCLC adds additional access points and search capabilities as well as complete local data (holdings, locations, etc.).

The majority (80 percent) of the intermediate libraries had been interested in automated alternatives for more than two years as opposed to only 25 percent of the large libraries. All of the public libraries contacted had been interested in automated catalogs for over two years and the majority for over five years.

Unlike the large libraries surveyed, the intermediate libraries had far greater diversity of opinion on the future options. Although several (a majority of the academic and special libraries but not a majority of the public libraries) indicated that on-line catalogs were the ultimate, intermediate libraries were far more willing to seriously consider printed book and microimage alternatives. On-line catalogs seemed a long way off because of cost and, for public libraries, because of the problem of many locations and varied educational and experiential levels of users. In this regard the intermediate-sized libraries and large public libraries were in agreement.

Table 1. Summary of Libraries Contacted

Personal Visits

Type of Library	Number Contacted		
	Intermediate	Large	Total
Public	2	3	5
Academic	2	10	12
Special	0	0	0
National and State	1	3	4
Cooperatives and Service Bureaus	2	3	5
TOTAL	7	19	26

Telephone

Type of Library	Number Contacted		
	Intermediate	Large	Total
Public	6	2	8
Academic	7	21	28
Special	7	0	7
National and State	0	4	4
Cooperatives and Service Bureaus	1	3	4
TOTAL	21	30	51

Total Personal Visits and Telephone

Type of Library	Number Contacted and Percentage					
	Intermediate		Large		Total	
Public	8	28.6%	5	10.2%	13	16.9%
Academic	9	32.1	31	63.3	40	51.9
Special	7	25.0	0	0.0	7	9.1
National and State	1	3.6	7	14.3	8	10.4
Cooperatives and Service Bureaus	3	10.7	6	12.2	9	11.7
TOTAL	28	100.0	49	100.0	77	100.0

Intermediate libraries were not as insistent on authority control as were the large libraries. Several of them mentioned it as desirable and important, but not with the same emphasis as did the large academic libraries.

Like the large libraries, the intermediate academic and public libraries see cooperation and networking as essential for the economic success of automated catalogs. The special libraries were not as interested in the cooperative approach due, at least in part, to the specialized and sometimes confidential nature of their materials.

The largest number of intermediate libraries with automated alternatives had computer-generated printed book catalogs ranging in size from 160,000 titles to 75,000 titles as of January 1975 (Table 2). The majority of the intermediate-sized libraries with printed book catalogs are planning to go to microimage catalogs within three years. The reasons cited were cost and time, in that order. The recumulations and cumulative supplements rise in cost quickly as the number of titles grows because the same entries are continually reprinted. The more frequent the cumulative supplement interval and the recumulation schedule, the greater the cost. As the catalog grows in size, the time lag between cutoff date for data entry and final production of the book catalogs generally increases.

Table 2. Printed Book Catalogs

Library	Titles Jan. 1975	Titles/Year	Titles Jan. 1980
		Large Libraries	
Los Angeles Co., Calif.‡	325,000	15,000	400,000
UC/Santa Cruz, Calif.†	250,000	20,000	350,000
NYPL—Res. Libs., N.Y.‡	220,000	80,000	620,000
NYPL—Branch Libs., N.Y.‡	170,000	40,000	370,000
		Intermediate Libraries	
Fairfax Co. P L, Va.°	160,000	20,000	260,000
Orange Co. P L, Calif.°	150,000	10,000	200,000
Baltimore Co. P L, Md.°	150,000	10,000	200,000
Enoch Pratt Lib., Md.°	150,000	13,000	215,000
Bell Telephone Labs, N.J.	150,000	5,000	175,000
King Co. Lib., Wash.‡	140,000	15,000	215,000
Prince George's Co., Md.°	140,000	10,000	190,000
Hennepin Co., Minn.	100,000	5,000	125,000
Washington Network, Wash.§	75,000	50,000	325,000

° Decision to go to microimage catalog within three years.
† Decision to go to on-line or microimage catalog within three years.
‡ Seriously considering microimage or restructured printed book catalog within three years.
§ The Washington Library Network, housed at the Washington State Library, publishes the Washington Resource Directory, which is a union catalog in register/index format and is used as the only library catalog by two public library systems in Washington. The Washington Library Network includes over 120 libraries of all types. Plans include closing card catalogs within two or three years and replacing them with a combination of on-line and microform catalogs as well as converting brief records for all titles to support circulation and finding/locating functions.

Of the microimage catalogs surveyed (Table 3), nine were fiche and one was roll film. Five were at academic libraries, two were at public libraries, and three were at special libraries. The libraries previously discussed that have printed book catalogs and that plan to go to microimage catalogs were public libraries. Thus, there will be an increase in the number of public libraries with microimage catalogs in the near future. Baltimore County recently announced plans to implement a roll film catalog within a year.[7] All of the microimage catalogs are less than five years old, and the majority are less than two years old. Computer Output Microform (COM) catalogs are becoming popular; they can be produced for a fraction of the cost of a corresponding printed book catalog and in a fraction of the time (weekend turnaround time for a complete cumulation is possible). While none of the printed book catalogs had recumulations any less frequently than yearly, and several had recumulations only every other year, six of the COM catalogs are completely recumulated quarterly and one is re-cumulated every four weeks.

The three special libraries reported user acceptance as high. The public libraries have not had the microimage catalog long enough to know if and how it is being accepted by the users. The academic libraries generally reported high user acceptance with some reservations. The University of Texas/Permian Basin did a survey of user reactions and found that 9 percent of the student users and 13 percent of the faculty users complained about the microimage catalog. The most common complaints were readability (hard on the eyes) and usability (readers difficult to use). The Georgia Institute of Technology also had a partial user survey completed, and their interesting experiment with remote access microimage catalogs is the only one documented in the literature.[8-10]

Table 3. Microimage Catalogs (Computer Produced)

Library	Titles Jan. 1975	Type	Maintaining Card Catalog
Lockheed Missiles, Calif.°	175,000	fiche°	No
Boeing Co., Wash.	150,000	fiche	No
U.T./San Antonio, Tex.	130,000	film	No, but plan to create A/T card catalog
Florida Tech. U., Fla.	120,000	fiche	Yes, and plan to continue
Marin Co., Calif.	100,000†	fiche	No
U.T./Permian Basin, Tex.	90,000	fiche	No
Georgia Inst. Tech., Ga.‡	75,000	fiche	Yes‡
Tulsa City-County, Okla.§	50,000	fiche§	No
U.T./Dallas, Tex.	50,000	fiche	No
Eastman Kodak, N.Y.	50,000	fiche	No

° Previously was a roll film catalog.
† Total expected in June 1975.
‡ The remaining collection (125,000 titles) is also available in a microimage catalog that was produced by filming the card catalog. These titles are gradually being added to the data base and included in the COM catalog. When this is completed (in two or three years), the card catalog will be discarded.
§ Previously was a printed book catalog.

If microimage catalogs are new, experimental, and rare, on-line catalogs are even more so. None of the libraries contacted were relying exclusively on an on-line catalog. One academic and three special libraries contacted in the intermediate group had partial on-line catalogs. The Rochester Institute of Technology (New York) is currently converting its 150,000 titles into a locally developed on-line system; that portion of the collection converted is available on-line. The card catalog continues to be maintained. After conversion is completed in two years, the file will be available on-line as well as in microimage (roll film). The Aerospace Corporation Library (California) has 80,000 titles on-line. Subject access, which is not yet implemented, is scheduled to be available in late 1975; in the meantime, a card catalog continues to be maintained. NASA has several libraries using an on-line file of 60,000 titles to supplement their card catalogs in various ways; microimage catalogs are also planned for the future. Finally, IBM has a few libraries with small (20,000 titles or less) on-line catalogs which for the most part are in addition to existing card catalogs. Several of the intermediate libraries that are OCLC participants plan on closing their card catalogs within five years and using the OCLC system as the vehicle of catalog access after that time. They all emphasize, however, that such a decision is dependent upon developments at OCLC, particularly in the area of access points and search capabilities (subject access as well as much better author/title access is required) and availability of complete local data (local variations to the bibliographic data as well as local call numbers, holding and location statements are not now available through the on-line system).

The intermediate libraries contacted are very willing and eager to engage in experimental catalogs for future use. Many libraries in this size range have been doing so for several years, and it is clear that they intend to continue doing so. Automated catalogs provide them the flexibility, and trauma, of changing and reordering the display of the bibliographic data as desired to meet changing needs both for the using public and the library.

Large Libraries

Forty-nine large libraries were contacted (Table 1), the majority being academic libraries (63.3 percent). The remaining 36.7 percent were about evenly divided between public libraries, state and national libraries, and library cooperatives and service bureaus.

Slightly more than half of the large libraries contacted either had appointed or were preparing to appoint a formal group (committee, task force, etc.) to look into automated alternatives to the card catalog, prepare working papers, and ultimately make recommendations. Some committees are long range (such as Cornell's which has a target date for recommendations of 1978), and some are shorter range.

Almost without exception, the large academic libraries envision an on-line catalog as the successor to the card catalog. Few feel that there will be an interim period of a temporary alternative (printed book or more likely microimage) before the on-line catalog is available; rather, they will stick with the card catalog until the technology and economics of on-line catalogs are available. The majority feel that the physical and intellectual condition of their card catalogs is adequate to last at least until that time. Of the twenty-seven academic libraries that would suggest time frames, six (22 percent) feel an alternative catalog will be implemented within the next five years, ten (37 percent) feel it will be six to ten years, and eleven (41 percent) feel it will be longer than ten years. The majority of the first group have on-line experience through using their own or the OCLC on-line cataloging system, and few of the libraries that feel it will be more than ten years have on-line experience.

The large public libraries also feel that on-line catalogs will be the ultimate future but see a rather lengthy interim period of printed book or microimage catalogs. They cite the problems of multiple branches and heavy use by a great variety of people with varying educational/experiential levels as major deterrents to on-line catalogs for public libraries. In this way they are similar to the intermediate public libraries contacted.

The library cooperatives and service bureaus generally agree with the academic libraries that on-line catalogs will be the evolutionary step from card catalogs, not printed book or microimage catalogs. One felt it would be within five years, two felt five to ten years, and two felt longer than ten years.

The state and national libraries generally felt that book or microimage catalogs, perhaps along with on-line catalogs, would follow. Interestingly, they are generally more optimistic about the time frame with five of the seven suggesting that on-line catalogs might happen within five years and all seven suggesting six to ten years with some certainty.

Although the majority of the libraries envision an on-line catalog, they feel that some physical backup will be required in the form of a card file in title and/or shelf sequence, or printed book or microimage catalogs with at least brief entries. Further, the majority of the libraries feel automated authority control is essential.

Finally, virtually all of the large libraries contacted stated that the automated alternative to the card catalog would have to be a cooperative effort (i.e., networks). A few felt that they would support their own systems, with only cooperative record generation. However, a larger number felt that they would never be able to support their own data bases and hardware/software systems and that this would have to be supplied and supported in a networking operation.

Three of the large libraries (not included in the above summary) currently have an automated alternative to the card catalog. Unlike the intermediate libraries, where there was a variety of alternative forms of the catalog, all of the large libraries contacted that have alternatives have the same type: printed book. Two have no card catalogs, and the third has a closed card catalog and an open automated catalog.

The smallest of the three is the University of California at Santa Cruz. It has had a computer-generated printed book catalog since the library began in 1967, and in January 1975 the catalog contained approximately 250,000 titles. The book catalog is in two sections; author/title and subject with each section being recumulated every other year. Monthly cumulative supplements are produced. All computing is done locally and is batch processing; the record format is MARC compatible. Twenty copies of the catalog are produced by photocopying, and the catalog grows at the rate of approximately 20,000 titles a year. In addition to the printed book catalog, a shelf card catalog and main entry,card catalog, also containing in-process records for items on-order or received but not cataloged, are maintained. An interesting cost study of the computer-generated book catalog has been completed as an internal report.[11]

The library is experiencing some difficulty with the book catalog due to its increasing size. Specifically, the cumulations are taking six months and longer to get the required twenty copies photocopied. The library has done a study of microimage (COM) and on-line alternatives and has recommended that the library go to an on-line catalog with printed book backup containing brief bibliographic data.[12] If this is funded, they hope to be operational on-line in 1976 or 1977 at the latest. Although the entire operation is now done locally, they do not rule out the possibility of a cooperative effort at a later time.

The Los Angeles County Public Library has had a computer-produced printed book catalog since 1969. Prior to that, they had printed book catalogs produced by various means including unit record equipment and photographic processing. Thus, no public card catalogs are in use and none have been in use for over twenty years. In January, the catalog contained approximately 325,000 titles and grows at the rate of approximately 15,000 titles a year. The catalog is recumulated annually and is kept up to date with cumulative supplements. The last cumulation (1974) was 30,000 pages long and was printed in 400 copies. The catalog and supplements are produced by a commercial firm (General Research Corporation, Santa Barbara, California). The pages are photocomposed, the bibliographic data is complete with extensive annotations, and the record format is non-MARC but will likely become MARC compatible in 1976.

Primarily because of cost ($325,000 in 1974/75), the library is very interested in other alternatives. They are considering alternatives to reduce the book catalog production costs including increasing the cumulation period, eliminating the annotations and/or fiction subheadings, going to a register/index arrangement, and going to microimage. Microimage seems the most promising at this point, but the library is waiting to see the performance of other microimage catalogs. Because of the size of the collection, they are particularly interested in the possibility of an ultrafiche format. Although no definite plans have been made, the library is taking steps to plan a unified approach to microimage catalogs with other libraries in the region.

The third large library visited that has a computer-generated catalog is the New York Public Library (NYPL). Both the branch libraries and the research libraries closed their public card catalogs on December 31, 1971, and initiated computer-generated printed book catalogs effective on January 1, 1972. With some exceptions (non-Roman alphabets, etc.), all cataloging since 1972 is in machine-readable form and is displayed in printed book catalogs. Cataloging done prior to 1972 is available through the frozen, but still accessible, public card catalogs. A number of publications describe the reasons for this major step (primarily physical deterioration of the public card catalogs) and the printed book catalog system.[13-15]

Two book catalogs are produced. The branch libraries book catalog contained approximately 170,000 titles as of January 1975 and the research libraries approximately 220,000 titles. The branch libraries catalog grows at the annual rate of 40,000 titles and the research libraries catalog at the annual rate of 80,000 titles. Thus, in less than two years the research libraries printed book catalog will surpass in size the catalog of Los Angeles County Public Library and in three years will more than double its present size. The computing is all batch mode and is done locally. The book catalogs are produced via photocomposition and contain complete bibliographic data; the record format is MARC compatible and the bibliographic data generally Library of Congress compatible.

When the book catalogs were started in 1972, it was thought that they would have a viable economic life of seven to ten years. Since that time, due to unanticipated increases in costs, most particularly paper costs, the viable life has been reduced to five to seven years. Within the next two to four years one or more of the following choices will be made: (1) reduce the cumulative supplements from monthly to quarterly; (2) go to an index/register approach; (3) split the catalog on the basis of subject, language, etc., and not recumulate that portion; or (4) go to microform cumulations and/or supplements. No decisions have been made, but there has been some experimentation with microimage catalogs and with COM service bureaus capable of handling diacriticals and perhaps nonroman alphabets.[16] The NYPL will have a mixture of printed book, microimage, and on-line catalogs in the future. Exclusively on-line catalogs are not acceptable to the research libraries because of the difficulty of patron use. A number of possibilities will be considered (on-line register with indexes in book form, microimage register with printed indexes, etc.), and it is possible that the branch libraries and research libraries will have different solutions. The possibilities of ultrafiche are also seriously being considered.

The Boston Public Library has accepted the results of the basic research done at the New York Public Library, and as of January 1, 1975, closed and froze its General Libraries (corresponding to the branch libraries at the NYPL) card catalogs. The General Libraries union card catalog has been revised and is being published in book form using a photographic process; the expected publication date is July 1975. New titles added to the General Libraries after January 1, 1975, and changes (updates) to the "old" catalog are being processed through a computer-based system with the intention of beginning publication of printed book catalogs (using a commercial vendor, Inforonics, Inc., Maynard, Massachusetts) later in 1975. The expected growth rate is 30,000 titles a year. In the meantime, a temporary supplementary union card catalog is being maintained for the General Libraries. A team is now revising the catalog of the Research Library with tentative plans for closing, freezing, and publishing it and continuing with computer-produced printed book catalogs sometime in the next few years.

No large libraries have microimage catalogs that replace the main public card catalog. However, two large libraries (New York State Library and the University of British Columbia) have announced a date when they plan to close their card catalogs and implement a microimage catalog and several other large libraries are seriously considering it. Two of the three large libraries (New York Public and Los Angeles County) that now have printed book catalogs are considering microimage catalogs for the short-range future. The Illinois State Library is actively doing research in microimage catalogs and the National Library of Canada has preliminary plans for maintenance of an on-line union catalog with microimage (COM) distribution throughout Canada.[17-19]

The New York State Library planned to close its main card catalog in the summer or fall of 1975 and implement a microimage (roll film) catalog. They further plan to convert brief records into machine-readable form for all titles to support the finding/locating function of the catalog, and film the closed public catalog to provide a frozen microimage retrospective catalog of the base holdings supporting the bibliographic function of the catalog. The University of British Columbia plans to begin converting to machine-readable form bibliographic data for 1975 and later imprints for creation of a COM finding list catalog beginning in September 1975. A great deal of research has been done on the data elements to be included in the microimage catalog.[20] It has been proposed, but not finally approved, that beginning with 1976 imprints cards will no longer be filed in the author/title and subject files of the public catalog. Cards for earlier imprints would continue to be filed in all files and cards for all imprints (containing full bibliographic description to support the bibliographic function of the catalog), and would continue to be filed in the classed (a finding or locating catalog arranged in call number order) and shelflist files. A current survey of British Columbia needs may alter these plans.

Although no large libraries have on-line catalogs that replace the card catalog, there is a great deal of interest in this alternative. Plans at the University hopes to stop filing cards in its card catalogs by July 4, 1976. New titles (post-1975) will be available exclusively from on-line and microimage catalogs; older titles (pre-1976) will be available in the card catalog with brief records for all older titles also available on-line by author and title. All of the titles cataloged through the OCLC system will be available in both the card catalog and the on-line and microimage catalogs, providing several years of overlap between the two major catalogs. The mechanics and costs are yet to be worked out in detail. The Ohio State University Libraries have a brief record available on-line with author/title and title access for each cataloged title in the collection showing holdings, locations, and current status (in circulation, at bindery, etc.) as a by-product of its on-line circulation system; this "catalog" can be used to support the locating or finding function of the catalog, and a limited number of terminals are available for general public use.[21, 22]

Several other large libraries have partially operational on-line systems and are in some stage of experimentation with on-line catalogs for public use; a great deal of significant work has been done at these libraries. The entire collection of Syracuse University Library is available on-line by author, title, and series—no subject access is yet available. CRT's are available throughout the building and are available for internal use and for assisting users. Terminals for public use are planned soon. Stanford University, through BALLOTS, has over 90 percent of its recently cataloged collection available from CRT terminals. The entire collection of the undergraduate library (80,000 titles) is available from both a printed book catalog and an on-line catalog, and a few terminals are available for reference and public service use. Similarly, the University of Toronto produces a book catalog for the science library (125,000 titles) and is experimenting with an on-line partial catalog. They have almost completed their retrospective conversion and have one million machine-readable records in a non- MARC format.

Both the University of Chicago and Northwestern University have operational on-line systems. The University of Chicago is implementing a library data base system which, among other functions, will provide catalog access to titles cataloged since 1968.[23] Closing of certain departmental and area catalogs is planned as soon as possible, possibly within the next year. Northwestern University Library presently has an operational on-line technical services system. Work is under way to add "browsable" author/title and title/author indexes and provide other refinements which will permit the system to serve as a true on-line catalog for use by the public as well as library staff. By fall 1976 they expect to begin acceptability testing of user- operated terminals. If the test results are favorable and if it can be determined that the savings in technical services costs will offset the cost of the additional terminals and the increased disc storage, they expect to close their author/title card catalog by late 1977.

Both the National Library of Medicine (NLM) and the National Agricultural Library (NAL) are experimenting with on-line catalogs. The National Library of Medicine ran an experiment in parallel with continuing use of the public card catalog for a short period of time early in 1974. CRT terminals to the on-line catalog file (CATLINE; 150,000 titles) were placed in card catalog areas. Problems associated with public use of on-line terminals quickly became apparent and the experiment was discontinued. The NLM recognizes that many advantages exist for on-line catalogs and is presently searching for methods to overcome the problems associated with public accessibility to on-line data bases. The National Agricultural Library recently completed an internal study of the feasibility of closing its card catalog by January 1976 in favor of on-line access to the CAIN (Cataloging and Indexing) data base.[24] For a number of reasons, it was decided that it was not feasible to take this step by January 1976, but that a plan might be developed which would make it possible by 1960. NAL closed its dictionary card catalog in 1965 and began a new divided card catalog using

AACR and LC classification. The catalogs are also available in book form, computer-generated since January 1970.

The Library of Congress has suggested the possibility of closing its card catalogs as early as 1980 and beginning on-line, printed book, and micro-image catalogs from that point forward.[25] An interesting feature of their suggestion is the concept that the on-line file would be considered sufficient for all cataloging decisions (forms of entry, subject headings, etc.).

Large libraries indicate that they will consider and experiment with a variety of alternatives in terms of separating the finding and the bibliographic functions of the catalog as suggested by the University of British Columbia.[26] Each function may have a different form of catalog. For example, the on-line file could be brief index records to support the finding or locating function, with complete description to support the bibliographic function available only from a card file (in shelf and/or author and/or title sequence) or a microimage or printed book catalog. Perhaps the full data will be available on-line for heavily used items while less used items might have only brief data on-line with full data off-line (microimage or printed book or card file). Perhaps the on-line system will be a cumulative supplement to a printed book (or microimage) catalog that is recumulated infrequently (perhaps every two or three or five years). Perhaps the author/title catalog will be on-line but the subject catalog will be microimage or printed book. The large libraries seem to feel that a variety of options should be explored and that heavy, but not exclusive, emphasis will be placed on on-line systems.

The vast majority of libraries have not committed their thoughts to writing up to this time. Three libraries, however, have prepared several outstanding publications which deserve special mention: the Library of Congress, the University of California/Berkeley, and the University of California/Los Angeles. These libraries have done studies of their existing card catalogs which are both fascinating and serve as excellent beginning models for other libraries that might wish to do the same.[27-32] The Library of Congress has prepared a provocative position paper on the future of catalog control in the Library of Congress.[33] The University of California/Berkeley has prepared a study of desuperimposition and the future of the catalogs in which it recommends that the card catalogs not be closed until a suitable on-line alternative is implemented, which it estimates will be in ten or more years.[34] UCLA and UCB have each written outstanding studies of alternative physical forms for library catalogs which consider technical aspects, user aspects, and major cost aspects.[35,36] UCLA has also completed a preliminary user survey and published its recommendations for the future of the catalogs in the fall of 1975.[37]

Comments and Predictions

Several individuals expressed concern about confusion in the definition of a library catalog. Most often there was no clear understanding or statement of the definition or purpose(s) of the library catalog. The issue of the finding or locating functions of the catalog versus the collocating, coalescing, and syndetic functions was mentioned by several people. Generally, the smaller the library, the more emphasis was placed on the former functions, and the larger the library, the greater the emphasis on the latter. The University of Chicago defined a catalog as a file of bibliographic records that is under authority control and provides the locating and collocating functions incorporated in the Paris Principles. Thus, a file of bibliographic records, even if available on-line, which does not have careful name and subject authority control, is simply that—a file of records, not a catalog. Smaller libraries, however, seemed not to place great importance on this, and a few seemed willing to give up authority control to a significant extent. A clear understanding and statement of what a library catalog is would seem to be essential before major changes are planned.

Many libraries are thinking and planning in terms of automating the card catalog; that is, using the computer as the vehicle or carrier of the traditional card catalog with the implied assumption that no major changes or improvements were in order. A few libraries, however, stressed that the facilities of the computer are not the same as the facilities of a card catalog and that classical cataloging rules and bibliographic descriptions, designed for card catalogs, are inappropriate for automated (particularly on-line) catalogs of the future. A majority felt that no major changes in the bibliographic record were appropriate; a minority felt that major changes were very much needed. A majority felt that cataloging would remain essentially a human operation with some aids from the computer. A minority stressed that much of "classic" cataloging (such as assigning name and subject access points) will be done automatically through computer-structured indexes from title page information. To think in terms of automating the card catalog or the traditional cataloging functions without giving serious consideration to other possibilities for major improvements is to fall far short of what might be possible.

Related to the question of the definition and purpose(s) of library catalogs, and an integral part of it, is the question of how catalogs are used and how they might be used if they were structured and could be accessed differently. In short, what should, as well as what does, a catalog do? Many libraries mentioned this as a major unknown and a major impediment to their future planning. The majority of libraries had done no user surveys of catalog use and planned to do none; rather they were relying and planned to rely in the future on user studies done elsewhere. Lack of knowledge about how library catalogs are used (or might be used) seemed to be a major reason for making the automated catalog as nearly like the card catalog as possible on the assumption that the "new" catalog will then at least be as satisfactory as the "old" catalog, which is assumed to be at least adequate.

Although a minority of large libraries plan to implement automated alternatives to their card catalogs in the near future (within three or four years), the majority do not for several reasons. First, there is the matter of economics. Although many of the libraries acknowledge that card catalogs will eventually be replaced with a computer system because as the costs of card catalogs continue to rise and the costs of computers continue to decline, economic pressures and other factors will force libraries to switch to computer-based catalogs, they do not feel that this has yet occurred, nor do they feel it will occur before 1985. In short, while the economics of computer catalogs for large libraries may be coming, the majority of large libraries believe the time has not yet arrived nor will it arrive for several years. Second, there is the matter of the Library of Congress. Many large libraries stated emphatically that any major change from a card catalog toward an automated catalog would and should wait for LC to take the leadership role. Many large libraries stated that the Library of Congress must determine for certain what it will do, and that other large libraries would follow. Since LC is obviously not going to be in a position to move for several years, their library would also not move. Third, and perhaps most important, several libraries mentioned the lack of significant, meaningful, or useful research in the area of automated catalogs for large libraries as a major factor in their "go slow" approach. Based on this study, there appears to be little significant research occurring at the majority of the libraries visited, and there is a noticeable lack of long-range planning, much less research, at least as represented by written documents. In light of the above and many other factors, large libraries for the most part do not intend to move too fast to close their card catalogs and implement automated alternatives in the belief that the time is not yet right.

The following predictions are based on the survey results. These predictions are for large libraries only; a different set of predictions, based on an intensive study of intermediate libraries, would be appropriate for small to intermediate-sized libraries.

1. There is considerable and growing interest among large libraries in automated alternatives to card catalogs; however, most of the serious planning is relatively recent (within the last two years). This interest will increase greatly in the next few years and will be exhibited by the creation of an increasing number of formal committees or task forces which will write an increasing number of reports.

2. Although a few more large libraries will close their card catalogs and implement alternative automated catalogs during the next decade, the majority will continue to rely on card catalogs as the primary access to the collections through at least 1985.

3. When a significant number of automated alternatives to card catalogs are implemented by large libraries, they will be done so cooperatively. The majority of large libraries will not have their own hardware/soft-

ware systems and data bases. The bibliographic systems will be extremely flexible and will not be exclusively tied to any particular medium (card, book, microimage, etc.).

4. As automated alternatives are implemented, the card catalogs will be first closed and then, within five to ten years, frozen and committed to microimage through photographic processes. Large libraries will have two catalogs at least for the next twenty-five years: a frozen retrospective catalog in card or microimage form and an open ongoing catalog in machine-readable form.

5. The majority of automated alternatives to card catalogs for large libraries will be on-line catalogs, supplemented (in the sense of being in addition to) with hard copy catalogs in card and/or microimage and/or printed book form. Exclusively printed book catalogs for large collections will not be acceptable because they are slow to appear and expensive to print and cumulate. Exclusively microimage catalogs for large collections will not be acceptable because of the user interface and acceptance problems and because they offer no significant improvement over card catalogs in improved searching capability. Because of the automated catalog's ability to be responsive to change, large libraries will be in a constant state of alternative "mixes" of on-line, hard copy, and microimage catalogs to meet changing situations, needs, and financial conditions in the future.

Acknowledgments

I wish to thank

1. the Council on Library Resources for supporting this fellowship project by paying the direct costs for travel and communications;
2. the university and library administration of Virginia Polytechnic Institute and State University who provided the released time, with pay, required to complete this project;
3. Dr. Gerald A. Rudolph for suggesting the topic, and Mr. H. Gordon Bechanan for patiently supporting the project during my released time.

References

(Items with an * preceding them are recent reports completed by individuals, committees or task forces working on the future of the card catalog for their library or are items of special interest.)

1. ALA-RTSD Book Catalogs Committee, "Book Form Catalogs: A Listing Compiled from

Questionnaires Submitted to the Book Catalogs Directory Subcommittee, ALA, 1968," *Library Resources & Technical Services* 14: 341-54 (Summer 1970).

2. Helen J. Waldron, *Book Catalogs: A Survey of the Literature on Costs* (Santa Monica, Calif.: Rand Corp., 1971), 27p. (ED 953 775).

*3. Nancy H. Lewis, "A Literature Survey on On-Line Access Versus Card Access to Library Catalogs," (Internal report, National Agricultural Library, Beltsville, Md., January 1975), 27p.

*4. University of California, Los Angeles. Working Group on Public Catalogs, Subgroup B, "Literature Survey" (University of California, Los Angeles, Library, April 1975), 35p.

*5. John C. Rather, *The Future of Catalog Control in the Library of Congress* (Revised; Washington, D.C.: Library of Congress, Technical Processes Research Office, 1975), 9p.

*6. Association of Research Libraries. *The Future of Card Catalogs; Report of a Program Sponsored by the Association of Research Libraries, 18 January 1975* (Washington, D.C.: Association of Research Libraries, 1975). (Available from ARL for $3.00 a copy.)

7. "Microfilmed Catalog Slated for Baltimore County," *Library Journal* 100: 802 (May 1, 1975).

8. Robert J. Greene, *Faculty Acceptance and Use of a System Providing Remote Bibliographic and Physical Access to an Academic Library* (Ph.D. dissertation, Florida State University, 1973), 190p. (Available from University Microfilms, Ann Arbor, Michigan, Order No. 73-30, 283.)

9. Robert J. Greene, "Microform Library Catalogs and the LENDS Microfiche Catalog," *Microform Review* 4: 30-34 (January 1974).

10. Edward Graham Roberts and John P. Kennedy, "The Georgia Tech Library's Microfiche Catalog," *Journal of Micrographics* 6: 245-51 (July/August 1973).

11. Luke Howe, "Cost Analysis of Present UCSC Book Catalog Supplement System" (Internal report, University of California, Santa Cruz, n.d.), 12p.

*12. Luke Howe, "Future Library Catalogs (22 October 1974)"; "Beyond the Book Catalog at U.C. Santa Cruz: COM and On-Line Alternatives (15 January 1975)" (In-house reports, U.C. Santa Cruz Library, California).

13. James W. Henderson and Joseph A. Rosenthal, *Library Catalogs: Their Preservation and Maintenance by Photographic and Automated Techniques* (Cambridge, Mass.: M.I.T. Press, 1968), 267p.

14. Thomas Parr, "Library Automation and the New York Public Library," *LARC Reports* 3, no. 3: 1-103 (Fall 1970).

15. Michael Malinconico and James A. Rizzolo, "The New York Public Library Automated Book Catalog Subsystem," *Journal of Library Automation* 6: 3-36 (March 1973).

16. New York Public Library, Research Libraries, *The Use of Microfilm in Relation to the Retrospective and Prospective Catalogs of the Research Libraries of the New York Public Library: A Report to the Council on Library Resources* (New York: New York Public Library, Research Libraries, 1972), 39p. (ED 067 107)

17. Canadian Union Catalogue Task Group, "The Canadian Union Catalog Task Group: First Report and Interim Recommendations," *National Library News* (January 1974), p. 3-12.

18. National Library of Canada, "Statement by the National Librarian on the First Report and Interim Recommendations of the Canadian Union Catalogue Task Group," *National Library News* (January 1974), p. 13-19.

19. Roderick, M. Duchesne, *Canadian National Bibliographic Data Base Study: The Report* (Ottawa, Ontario: National Library of Canada, March 1974), 60p. plus 3 appendixes and 8 annexes.

20. University of British Columbia, Catalogue Project Task Group, *Basic Bibliographic Data (For Diaplay in a COM Catalogue)* (Vancouver, British Columbia: Univ. of British Columbia, 1974), 53p.

21. Hugh C. Arkinson, "The Ohio On-Line Circulation System," in University of Illinois, Graduate School of Library Science, Clinic on Library Applications of Data Processing, 9th, Urbana, Illinois, 30 April-3 May 1972, *Proceedings: Applications of On-Line Computers to Library Problems*; Edited by F. Wilfrid Lancaster, University of Illinois, Graduate School of Library Science, Urbana, Illinois, 1972, p. 22-28.

22. Irene Braden Hoadley and A. Robert Thorson, eds. *An Automated On-Line Circulation System: Evaluation, Development, Use* (Columbus, Ohio: Ohio State Univ. Libraries, 1973), 85p.

23. Charles T. Payne, "The University of Chicago Library Data Management System," in University of Illinois, Graduate School of Library Science, Clinic on Library Applications of Data Processing, 11th, Urbana, Illinois, 28 April-1 May 1974, *Proceedings: Applications of Minicomputers to Library and Related Problems*; edited by F. Wilfrid Lancaster, University of Illinois, Graduate School of Library Science, Urbana, Illinois, 1974, p. 105-19.

*24. Jeanne M. Holmes, ed. "On-Line Catalogs for NAL by January 1976: Conclusions and Rec-
ommendations," (Internal report, National Agricultural Library, Beltsville, Maryland, 22 January
1975), 3p. plus 3 exhibits.
 25. Rather, *The Future of Catalog Control*, 9p.
*26. Robin W. MacDonald and J. McRee Elrod, "An Approach to Developing Computer Cata-
logs," *College & Research Libraries*, 34: 202-208 (May 1973).
 27. John C. Rather, *The Main Catalog: An Examination of a Critical Problem* (Washington,
D.C.: Library of Congress, Technical Processes Research Office, 1969), 6p.
 28. Richard S. Angell and John C. Rather, *The Library of Congress Card Catalog: An Analysis
of Problems and Possible Solutions* (Washington, D.C.: Library of Congress, Technical Processes
Research Office, 1972), 20p. (Not available for distribution.)
 29. Library of Congress, Technical Processes Research Office, *The Library of Congress Card
Catalog: Problems and Possible Solutions* (Washington, D.C.: Library of Congress, 1973), 3p.
*30. Janice Knouse, *Main Library Catalogs [of the University of California Library, Berkeley]
prepared for the Subcommittee on the Future of the Catalogs* (University of California, Berkeley,
1974), 144p. (Not for distribution. Available on interlibrary loan only.)
*31. Carol Snyder, "Bibliographic Control in UCB Branch Libraries" (University of California,
Berkeley, July 1974), 13p. (Not for distribution. Available on interlibrary loan only.)
*32. University of California, Los Angeles. Working Group on Public Catalogs, Subgroup A,
"UCLA Public Catalogs" (University of California, Los Angeles, Library, April 1975), 40p.
 33. Rather, *The Future of Catalog Control*, 9p.
*34. University of California, Berkeley. Subcommittee on the Future of the Catalogs, "To Close
or Not to Close: Desuperimposition and the Future of the Catalogs" (General Library, University
of California, Berkeley, February 1975), 38p. (Available for purchase at $5.00 per copy from
Library Photographic Service, University of California Library, Berkeley, California 94720.)
*35. Barbara A. Nozik, "Alternative Physical Forms for Library Catalogs: Card, Book, Micro-
form, On-Line" (University of California, Berkeley, July 1974), 32p. (Not for distribution. Available on interlibrary loan only.)
*36. University of California, Los Angeles. Working Group on Public Catalogs, Subgroup B,
"Alternative Catalog Formats" (University of California, Los Angeles, Library, April 1975), 11p.
*37. University of California, Los Angeles. Working Group on Public Catalogs Subgroup C, "User
Survey" (University of California, Los Angeles, Library, April 1975), 100p.

Appendix A — Libraries Contacted

The following libraries and individuals were visited (V) or telephoned (T) on the dates indicated.

British Columbia. University of British Columbia Library, Vancouver. V: December 11, 1974.
    Basil Stuart-Stubbs, Librarian. Robin MacDonald, Assistant Librarian/Technical Services.
    William Watson, Assistant Librarian/Planning. J. McRee Elrod, Cataloging.
California. Aerospace Corporation Library, El Segundo (Los Angeles). T: March 24, 1975. Edythe
    Moore, Manager, Library Services.
California. California State Library, Sacramento. V: January 27, 1975. Gerald Newton, Chief of
    Technical Services. Liz Gibson, Systems Analyst.
California. IBM Library, San Jose. T: March 7, 1975. Marjorie Griffin, Library Manager.
California. Lockheed Missiles and Space Company Library, Palo Alto. T: March 19, 1975. Art
    Fried, Library Supervisor.
California. Los Angeles County Public Library, Los Angeles. V: January 30, 1975. Robert C.
    Goodwell, Chief, Technical Services.
California. Los Angeles Public Library, Los Angeles. V: January 30, 1975. Mary Fischer, Automa-
    tion Coordinator.
California. Orange County Public Library, Orange. T: March 7, 1975. Harry M. Rowe, Jr., County
    Librarian.
California. Stanford University Libraries, Stanford. V: January 29, 1975. Allen B. Veaner, Assistant
    Director for Bibliographic Operations.
California. University of California, Berkeley. V: January 28, 1975. Joseph A. Rosenthal, Associate
    University Librarian/Technical Services. Virginia Pratt, Chairperson, Subcommittee on the
    Future of the Catalogs. Susan K. Martin, Head, Systems Office.

California. University of California, Los Angeles. V: January 31, 1975. Judith Corin, Assistant University Librarian.

California. University of California, Santa Cruz, V: January 29, 1975. Luke T. Howe, Head, Library Systems Office.

California. University-Wide Library Automation Program (ULAP), Berkeley. V: January 28, 1975. Jay Cunningham, Director. Brian Aveney, Manager, Bibliographic Center. Mike Berger, Associate Manager-Operations, Bibliographic Center.

Connecticut. Yale University Library, New Haven. T: March 5, 1975. David Weisbrod, Library Development Officer.

District of Columbia. Library of Congress, Washington, V: December 9, 1974. John Rather, Chief, Technical Processes Research Office. William J. Welsh, Director, Processing Department. Henriette D. Avram, Chief, MARC Development Office.

District of Columbia. National Aeronautics and Space Administration Libraries, Washington. T: March 14, 1975. Madeline Losee, Program Coordinator for Libraries.

Florida. Florida Technological University Library. Orlando. T: November 6, 1974. Lynn W. Walker, Director of Libraries.

Georgia. Georgia Institute of Technology Library, Atlanta. V: October 17, 1974. Edward Graham Roberts, Director.

Illinois. Illinois State Library, Springfield. T: March 7, 1975. Tony Miele, Assistant Director, Technical Services.

Illinois. Northwestern University Library, Evanston. V: November 7, 1974. Velma Veneziano, Library Systems Analyst. Karen Horny, Assistant University Librarian for Technical Services. Betty Furlong, Coordinator of Automation Procedures for Technical Services.

Illinois. University of Chicago Library. V: November 8, 1974. Charles Payne, Systems Development Librarian. Helen Schmierer, Library Systems Analyst, Herman Fussler, Professor, Graduate Library School.

Illinois. University of Illinois Library, Urbana. T: March 11, 1975. Robert Talmadge, Director of Technical Services.

Indiana. Indiana University Library, Bloomington. T: February 24, 1975. William J. Studer, Associate University Librarian.

Maryland. Baltimore County Public Library, Towson. T: February 25, 1975. Charles W. Robinson, Director.

Maryland. Enoch Pratt Free Library, Baltimore. T: March 4, 1975. Marian Sanner, Assistant Director.

Maryland. National Agricultural Library, Beltsville. T: March 26, 1975. Richard Farley, Director. Jeanne Holmes, Chief, Analysis Division.

Maryland. National Library of Medicine. Bethesda. T: March 17, 1975. Joseph Gant

Maryland. Prince George's County Memorial Library, Hyattsville. T: February 24, 1975. Elizabeth Hage, Director. Walter Shih, Assistant Director for Datamation.

Maryland. University of Maryland Libraries, College Park. T: March 4, 1975. Walter Hamner, Assistant Director, Automation Services.

Massachusetts. Boston Public Library, Boston. T: March 19, 1975. Liam M. Kelly, Assistant Director.

Massachusetts. Harvard University Library, Cambridge. T: March 4, 1975. Colin McKirdy, Associate Librarian for Data Processing.

Massachusetts. Inforonics, Inc., Maynard. T: March 18, 1975. Larry Buckland, Head.

Massachusetts. Massachusetts Institute of Technology Libraries, Cambridge. T: March 7, 1975. Patricia Sheehan, Library Systems Designer.

Massachusetts. NELINET (New England Library Information Network), Wellesley. T: March 12, 1975. Ruth Tighe, Assistant Director.

Massachusetts. University of Massachusetts Library, Amherst. T: March 5, 1975. Richard Talbot, Director.

Michigan. University of Michigan Libraries, Ann Arbor. T: March 7, 1975. Frederick Wagman, Director.

Minnesota. Hennepin County Public Library, Edina. V: November 11, 1974. Jerry Pennington, Head, Technical Services.

Minnesota. Minneapolis Public Library, Minneapolis. T: March 11, 1975. Lillian Wallis, Head of Technical Services.

Minnesota. University of Minnesota Libraries, Minneapolis. V: November 11, 1974. Glenn Brudvig, Assistant Director for Research and Development.

Missouri. University of Missouri Libraries, Columbia. T: March 7, 1975. Dwight Tuckwood, Director.

New Jersey. Bell Telephone Laboratories Library, Murray Hill. T: March 18, 1975. W. Kenneth Lowry, Director.

New Jersey. Princeton University Library, New Haven. T: March 5, 1975. R. E. Utman, Data Processing.

New York. Columbia University Libraries, New York City. T: March 5, 1975. Jerome Yavarkovsky, Assistant University Librarian for Planning.

New York. Cornell University Libraries, Ithaca. T: February 25, 1975. Ryburn Ross, Assistant Director for Technical and Automated Services.

New York. Eastman Kodak Company Research Library, Rochester. T: March 18, 1975. Wilma Kujawski, Librarian.

New York. FAUL (Five Associated University Libraries), Syracuse. T: March 5, 1975. John Aubry, Coordinator.

New York. IBM Library, Yorktown Heights. T: March 1, 1975. Gordon Randell, Librarian.

New York. New York Public Library, New York City. V: December 10, 1974. Maurice Friedman, Head of Technical Services, Branch Libraries. Paul Fasana, Head of Preparation Services, Research Libraries. Sam Membert, Systems Analysis and Data Processing Office (SADPO).

New York. New York State Library, Albany. T: March 12, 1975. Peter Paulson, Director.

New York. Research Libraries Group, New York City. T: March 7, 1975. James E. Skipper, Executive Director.

New York. Rochester Institute of Technology Library, Rochester. T: March 12, 1975. Gary MacMillan, Director.

New York. State University of New York, Albany. T: February 25, 1975. Glyn Evans, Head of Systems Planning.

New York. State University of New York, Binghamton. T: March 18, 1975. Ron Lewis, Card Catalog Manager.

New York. Syracuse University Libraries, Syracuse. T: March 4, 1975. Gregory N. Bullard, Assistant Director for Processing and Computer Based Operations.

Ohio. Cleveland State University Libraries, Cleveland. T: March 11, 1975. Raymond Collins, Acting Director.

Ohio. Kent State University Libraries, Kent. T: March 12, 1975. Hyman Kritzer, Director.

Ohio. Ohio College Library Center, Columbus, V: October 30, 1974. Fred Kilgour, Director.

Ohio. Ohio State University Libraries, Columbus. V: October 31, 1974. Hugh C. Atkinson, Director. Betty J. Meyer, Assistant Director for Technical Services. Larry X. Besant, Assistant Director for Public Services. Bernard Bayer, Acting Head, Mechanized Information Center.

Ohio. University of Akron Libraries, Akron. T: March 7, 1975. Paul Schrank, Director.

Ohio. University of Toledo Libraries, Toledo. T: March 7, 1975. Al Hogan, Acting Director.

Oklahoma. Tulsa City-County Library. V: February 3, 1975. Ruth Blake, Head, Technical Services.

Ontario. College BiblioCentre, Don Mills (Toronto). V: January 16, 1975. Gordon H. Wright, Director. Valentina DeBruin, Manager, Bibliographic Services.

Ontario. Council of Ontario Universities. Library Cooperative System. V: January 16, 1975. Ralph E. Stierwalt, Director.

Ontario. National Library of Canada, Ottawa. V: January 17, 1975. Hope Clement, Director, Research and Planning Branch. Louis Forget, Assistant Director (Systems), Research and Planning Branch. R. Penner, Assistant Director (Systems), Public Services Branch. R. M. Duchesne, Assistant Director (Networks), Research and Planning Branch. Edwin Buchinski, Chief, Canadian MARC Office.

Ontario. University of Toronto Library, Toronto. V: January 16, 1975. Everet Minett, Director, Library Automation Systems. Jean Heathcote, Acting Manager of Operations, Library Automation Systems. Robin Braithwaite, Manager of User Services, Library Automation Systems.

Oregon. Richard Abel and Company. (Now Blackwell North America), Portland. V: December 13, 1974. John Knapp, Head, Automated Systems.

Pennsylvania. Indiana University of Pennsylvania, Indiana. T: February 25, 1975. Daniel C. Shively, Coordinator, Catalog Department.

Pennsylvania. University of Pennsylvania Libraries, Philadelphia. T: February 24, 1975. Richard DeGennaro, Director.

Texas. University of Texas, Austin. T: March 3, 1975. Vandolyn Savage, Head, Automated Systems.

Texas. University of Texas, Dallas. V: February 4, 1975. James Dodson, Librarian. Richard Meyer, Head, Technical Services.

Texas. University of Texas, Permian Basin. T: February 25, 1975. Richard Jenson, Librarian.

Texas. University of Texas, San Antonio. T: February 24, 1975. Michael Kelly, Director.

Utah. Brigham Young University Library, Provo. T: March 7, 1975. Donald Nelson, Director.

Virginia. Fairfax County Public Library, Springfield. T: February 24, 1975. William Whitesides, Director. Jay Watson, Associate Director.

Washington. King County Library System, Seattle. T: February 24, 1975. Erma Jean Morgan, Head, Technical Services.

Washington. Washington Library Network, Washington State Library, Olympia. V: December 12, 1974. Mary Jane Reed, Associate Librarian, Planning and Research. Gene Bismuti, Head, Public Services. Jackie Rudeen, Head, Technical Services.

Wisconsin. University of Wisconsin Libraries, Madison. T: March 7, 1975. Joseph Treyz, Director.

MICROFORM LIBRARY CATALOGS AND
THE *LENDS* MICROFICHE CATALOG

by Robert J. Greene

Early American libraries listed the contents of their collections in manuscript or book catalogs.[1] As library collections increased in size, these book catalogs were supplanted by the card catalog. Recent advances in computer technology and reprography, coupled with the increasing cost of maintaining large catalogs, have revived the book catalog as a tool for bibliographic access to library collections.

A logical step from the printed-book catalog is the book catalog in microform. It is possible to store catalogs in microform at less cost than in book or card form. In addition, microform catalogs can be easily and cheaply duplicated. The microform catalog has many of the advantages and disadvantages of the book catalog when compared with the card catalog. These are summarized by Tauber and Feinberg; some of the disadvantages of the book catalog these authors note follow:

1. Book catalogs are less current than card catalogs.

2. The cost of producing book catalogs is higher.

3. Limited cataloging is often used in book catalogs.

4. The book catalog is inflexible. To make changes or deletions requires defacing the catalogs.

5. The book catalog is susceptible to wear, mutilation, and theft.

6. The book catalog volumes may be large and heavy, creating binding and handling problems.[2]

There is evidence indicating that a microform catalog, updated by the COM process, can either eliminate or reduce many of the above cited disadvantages of book catalogs. The COM process allows updating at *frequent*

Reprinted from *Microform Review*, 4: 30-34 (January 1975) by permission of the publisher. Copyright © 1975 by Microform Review Inc.

intervals at reduced cost and without limiting the length of entries. Additions and deletions can be made in each update. Microfiche and cartridge-protected microfilm are reasonably durable. Microforms take up less space than volumes of a printed book catalog, and binding costs are eliminated.

On the other hand, there are two major disadvantages of microform catalogs: equipment is necessary to review or use the catalog, and microforms have not attained the user acceptance enjoyed by printed media.

Review of "Traditional" Library Microform Catalogs

Librarians have resisted the use of catalogs in microforms. Until recently, catalogs have been microfilmed for two reasons: as back-up records in case of destruction or mutilation of the card catalog and as an intermediate step in the production of catalog cards or book catalogs. In neither of these applications is the microform used as the public catalog.

There have been only a few reported examples of microfilmed card catalogs used as public catalogs. Matsumiya and Bloomfield described one used at Hughes Aircraft Company (California). When a new branch was opened some five miles away from the main company library, and additional copy of the card catalog was needed. Several methods of duplicating the 160,000 cards in the catalog were considered, but copying the card catalog on microfilm was judged to be the least expensive method. Projected costs for a ten-year period were $30,000 for a book catalog, $48,000 for a card catalog, and $22,000 for a periodically updated microfilm catalog. The Hughes catalog was microfilmed and placed in thirty-three 16mm cartridges. Experience with the catalog has indicated two disadvantages of the system. First, it is impossible for more than one person to use the catalog at one time; second, it takes longer to find an entry in the microfilm catalog than in the card catalog (twenty seconds for the card catalog versus forty seconds for the microfilm catalog). Both of these drawbacks were not considered significant for this small branch and were outweighed by the advantages of lower cost and space savings of the microfilm catalog.[3]

Gaines has described a second example of a microform catalog serving as a public catalog. In this application, remote subject access provided by multiple copies of the subject catalog and cost savings over a comparable book catalog were the chief reasons for selecting a microform catalog. Microfiche was used for the catalog instead of roll microfilm because it was believed that sheet film would cause fewer problems for users. The microcatalog was produced for the Ramapo (N.Y.) Catskill library system and distributed to forty-five of its branch libraries. The following cost comparison for the book and microfiche catalogs were given: one hundred

copies of the 1967 book catalog of 51,000 entries cost $11,264; fifty-five
sets of the 1970 microfiche catalog of 60,000 entries cost $2,758. In addi-
tion, it was necessary to provide microfiche readers and microfiche storage
files for each of the branches at a total cost of $6,032. Even considering
the costs of the reading and filing equipment, which were nonrecurring,
the microfiche catalog was less expensive than the book catalog. A questionnaire answered by branch librarians provided data indicating that the
catalog was considered useful by 84 percent of the respondents; however,
the catalog was used fewer than ten times per week in all but two of the
branches.[4]

A third microfilmed catalog serving as a public catalog was produced
by the New Jersey State Library. The Micro-Automated Catalog system
(MAC) has provided copies of the state library's 600,000-entry dictionary
catalog to nine libraries to aid in the state library's interlibrary loan activities. The total cost of filming the catalog and providing the nine duplicate
copies and nine reader-printers was less than $25,000.[5]

It is evident from the reports about these three working microform catalogs that this catalog format has considerable potential where the low cost
of production, duplication, and provision of remote access are important;
however, the problem of updating, a major disadvantage of book catalogs,
still remains when the microform catalog is produced by filming a card
catalog. Updating requires rephotographing the entire card catalog at periodic intervals (as in the Hughes Aircraft catalog) or providing a supplement
to the main catalog (as in the New Jersey State Library catalog). The first
option is expensive, and the second option lengthens the time required to
find an entry in the catalog. In addition, both methods of updating require
that a card catalog (to be photographed) be maintained.

Role of COM—A New Approach
to the Microform Catalog

The problem of updating catalogs on microfilm shows promise of being
solved with the help of computers and COM (computer-output microfilm)
devices. The computer can be programmed to interfile catalog entries
quickly and without error. COM devices have the ability to output computer-produced magnetic tapes directly onto microfilm instead of the
usual paper printout. Such microfilm (or microfiche) output is both faster
and cheaper to produce than conventional printout. Thus, the library catalog can be updated at regular intervals by outputting the entire recompiled
catalog in microform.

One of the first attempts to employ a COM device to generate a library
catalog has been described by Kozumplik and Lange of Lockheed Missiles
and Space Company (California):

The catalog's 1,051,060 look-up points or entries are organized in six sections; source, title, authors, contract number, subjects, and report numbers, call numbers. . . . The 16mm microfilm comprising these million plus retrieval points are loaded into 40 cartridges (replacing 720 card catalog drawers); each cartridge contains 100 ft. of film which is exposed in 1,800 two-column pages of computerized catalog text processed by the SC4020 Stromberg Carlson COM device.[6]

These six sections are updated and corrected quarterly. The catalog is supplemented by a listing of new acquisitions using the key-word-in-title format. The microfilm catalog operates at a net savings of $13,000 annually (over the previously used card catalog) because "(1) card filing costs are avoided; (2) there are no catalog cases to purchase; and (3) there is a 200% savings in space to house the microfilm installation."[7] The system has been accepted by both the scientists and the librarians because "look up time was greatly reduced and the system was easy to operate."[8] The catalog can be easily duplicated and used at remote locations and multiple locations within the library.[9]

Three other examples of COM-generated catalogs have been briefly noted in the literature. One is being used at a small, recently established junior college, El Centro College, in Dallas, Texas, in place of the traditional card catalog. The approximately 100,000 author, title, and subject entries fill about three-fourths of one microfilm cartridge. Six copies of the catalog are available for viewing on readers or reader-printers.[10]

The second example of a COM-produced microfilm catalog is a short-title catalog developed at Tulane University in New Orleans as a by-product of records made for a computer-based circulation system. The catalog covers about 80 percent of the library holdings and can be viewed at two locations remote from the card catalog. Three conclusions are drawn from experience with this catalog:

1. A microfilm catalog per se is acceptable to most users. In fact, many users during this experiment were enthusiastic about the technique and urged that it be further developed.
2. Existing microfilm reading equipment is, at best, marginally durable for use by the public with little or no instruction or supervision.
3. A catalog with limited bibliographic data is not an acceptable guide to the library; library staff and other knowledgeable users are frustrated by its incompleteness, and the bibliographically unsophisticated are unaware of its limitations.[11]

Despite these limitations, the principal investigator still considers microform catalogs a promising area for investigation.[12]

Larkworthy and Brown have reported on a COM catalog in use at the Westminister City Libraries in England. The authors compared the COM catalog with a computer-produced book catalog. Over a projected ten-year period, the COM catalog offered considerable savings because of the high cost of cumulating the printed catalog. The reaction of the public to the COM catalog was noted as "encouraging."[13]

The *LENDS* Microfiche Catalog

Remote physical and bibliographic access to the Georgia Tech Library are provided by a system named LENDS (Library Extends Catalog Access and New Delivery Service). Remote physical access is provided by a telephone request and book delivery service. Remote bibliography access is provided through the distribution of the library catalog to thirty-five locations on the campus. The LENDS microfiche catalog is in two parts; the basic catalog containing all entries filed in the card catalog through September 1971, and a supplement containing all entries added to the catalog after this date.

The basic catalog was produced by microfilming the main card catalog using a 16mm rotary camera. The film was slit to a 5mm width and taped to 4 x 6 acetate sheets to form microfiche masters. Appropriate eye-legible headings were also filmed and taped to the masters. With a packing density of approximately 1,100 card images per fiche, the basic catalog consisted of 717 microfiche. Fifty duplicate sets of the basic catalog were reproduced from these masters by the diazo process.

The supplement to the basic catalog is produced by the COM process. All cataloging since 1966 at Georgia Tech has been converted to machine-readable form and is used as the data base for the supplement. Approximately 6,000 machine-based entries can be reproduced on each of the 4 x 6 microfiche, in contrast to 1,100 card images. The entire supplement is recompiled and reissued on a bimonthly basis.

Each of the LENDS remote catalog installations consists of a microfiche reader, a copy of the basic catalog, and a copy of the supplement catalog. These catalog installations have been placed in almost all the academic, research, and administrative departments at Georgia Tech. A detailed description of the development and implementation of the LENDS microfiche catalog has been provided by Roberts and Kennedy.[14]

Faculty Use of the *LENDS* Microfiche Catalog

The author investigated faculty use and acceptance of the LENDS remote access system shortly after its implementation.[15] Data were gathered concerning faculty use of the microfiche catalog during this study. Sixty-three faculty members who had used the LENDS catalog and thirty-seven faculty members who had not used it were interviewed.

The 100 subjects were asked to complete a microform attitude questionnaire. It was found that 59 percent of the microfiche catalog users
were classified as having above-average (positive) attitudes toward the use
of microforms in libraries. Only 41 percent of those faculty who had not
used the LENDS catalog were classified as above average in microform
attitude. Although this difference indicated a fairly strong relationship between microform attitude and use of the microfiche catalog, this relationship was not found to be statistically significant.[16]

Some comments made by faculty may indicate why the relationship between microform attitude and use of the LENDS catalog is not stronger.
Faculty reported that they did not like to read microfilmed reports and
books, but they did not mind using the microfiche catalog. This was because catalog use required use of microforms for only a few minutes at a
time while reading other library materials required a much longer time.
Therefore, it is suggested that the use of microform catalogs by libraries
may not encounter the user resistance that has been experienced in the
use of other microforms in libraries.

Access to the *LENDS* Catalog and Its Use

The departmental LENDS microfiche catalogs were located in rooms that
varied greatly in ease of faculty access. Catalogs were placed in departmental offices, storage rooms, conference rooms, reading rooms, and
faculty offices. Some of these locations were locked at all times, and some
were unlocked at all times. Departmental LENDS catalogs were classified
as having good or poor access based on their locations and whether a
faculty member needed a key to use them.

Nine of the LENDS catalogs were classified as having poor access.
Twenty-three of the faculty interviewed were members of these nine
departments. Only eight (29 percent) of these faculty were LENDS catalog users. On the other hand, fifty-five (71 percent) of the seventy-seven
faculty who were members of the departments providing good access to
the LENDS catalog were users of this catalog. Therefore, it was concluded
that ease of access to LENDS microfiche catalog was a significant factor
in determining its use.

Problems and Advantages of the *LENDS* Catalog

Fifty LENDS users were asked to cite problems they encountered in using
the system. Below is a list of the problems faculty had in using the LENDS

catalog, together with the number of faculty who cited the problem.

1. Could not find the correct microfiche from the author/title, subject, or serials file (4).
2. Could not load the microfiche correctly in the reader (1).
3. Did not understand the arrangement of entries ("cards") on the microfiche (1).
4. Had difficulty using the transport mechanism to shift the fiche position (1).
5. Had difficulty reading the information on the screen (out of focus, brightness, contrast, or dust) (15).
6. Someone else was using the microfiche catalog when I wanted it (1).
7. Microfiche catalog is not in a convenient location for me (1).

The high number of faculty citing reason number 5 was attributed to difficulty some users had locating the focus control knob on the reader. This knob was not readily visible, and it was not labeled. Very few users reported any difficulty in using the LENDS catalog after their first attempt, however.

The fifty LENDS users were asked to cite any advantages they saw in the LENDS catalog over the card catalog. These advantages (with the number of faculty citing) are given below:

1. The LENDS catalog provides me with a knowledge of the library collection without leaving my department (11).
2. It is easier to browse through or scan the microfiche catalog than the card catalog (6).
3. Books (entries) are easier to locate in the microfiche catalog (5).
4. I can sit down while using the microfiche catalog (4).
5. By using the microfiche catalog, I can make students aware of library materials (1).

Findings of the Study Concerning the *LENDS* System

The LENDS microfiche catalog was only one component of the LENDS system. Most of this study was concerned with faculty acceptance of the LENDS system as a whole and not just the microfiche catalog. Some of the more important findings concerning the LENDS system are given below.

1. Faculty library book circulation increased because of the availability of LENDS.

2. LENDS was sued by faculty primarily to request books already known to them. It was not used extensively to locate books by the subject approach.

3. The lack of library browsing capability provided in LENDS was not a significant deterrent to its use.

4. A much higher proportion of faculty with offices located farther from the library were LENDS users than faculty with offices located closer to the library.

5. Library use patterns of many faculty were changed due to presence of LENDS. LENDS also affected the work patterns of some of the library staff.

Summary

Georgia Tech's experiment with the LENDS microfiche catalog has demonstrated a successful method for reproducing a large card catalog in microform. This method involves microfilming the basic card catalog and updating the catalog with a COM-produced cumulative supplement. Multiple copies of the microform catalog can be distributed to provide remote bibliographic access to a central library collection.

The LENDS microfiche catalog was accepted and used by many Georgia Tech faculty. Existing faculty attitudes toward microform did not prove to be a major deterrent to use of this microfiche catalog. Catalog use was enhanced by combining it with a book delivery system. The combination of the microfiche catalog and the delivery system was especially useful to faculty located some distance from the library. The increased access provided by LENDS resulted in a significant increase in the number of books circulated to faculty.

References

1. For a history of early printed book catalogs, see Jim Ranz, *The History of the Printed Book Catalog in the United States* (Ann Arbor, Mich.: University Microfilms, 1960).

2. *Book Catalogs*, ed. Maurice Tauber and Hilda Feinberg (Metuchen, N.J.: Scarecrow, 1971), pp. 22-23.

3. H. Matsumiya and M. Bloomfield, "Working Microfilm Catalog," *Special Libraries* 55 (March 1964): 157-59.

4. Katherin Gaines, "Undertaking a Subject Catalog in Microfiche," *Library Resources & Technical Services* 15 (Summer 1971): 297-308.

5. Oliver P. Gillock, and Roger H. McDonough, "Spreading State Library Riches for Peanuts," *Wilson Library Bulletin* 45 December 1970): 354-57.

6. William A. Kozumplik and R. T. Lange, "Computer Produced Microfilm Library Catalog," *American Documentation* 18 (April 1967): 68.

7. Ibid., p. 68.

8. Ibid., p. 67.

9. Ibid., p. 77.

10. "Microfilm Claimed Tops for Library Catalog," *Library Journal* 94 (May 15, 1969): 1936.

11. Council on Library Resources, *14th Annual Report: For Period Ending June 30, 1970* (Washington, D.C.: Council on Library Resources, Inc., 1970), pp. 30-31.

12. Ibid., p. 31.

13. Graham Larkworthy and Cyril G. Brown, "Library Catalogs on Microfilm," *Library Association Record* 73 (December 1971): 231-32.

14. Edward Graham Roberts and John P. Kennedy, "The Georgia Tech Library's Microfiche Catalog," *Journal of Micrographics* 6 (July 1973): 245-51.

15. Robert John Greene, "Faculty Acceptance and Use of a System Providing Remote Bibliographic and Physical Access to an Academic Library" (Ph.D. diss., Florida State University, 1973).

16. The 0.05 level of significance using the chisquare test was adopted as the level to indicate statistical significance for this study.

MICROFILM CATALOGS IN A
BRITISH PUBLIC LIBRARY SYSTEM

by Jill C. Le Croissette

The Westminster City Libraries in London are among the growing number
of British libraries that have successfully introduced microform catalogs
for public use. Westminster is a large metropolitan library system that includes numerous branches, a main reference library, and a medical library.
Its adult loan collection totals approximately 750,000 volumes, of which
about 75 percent are nonfiction. The computer-produced catalog at Westminster was begun in April 1970 as a union list of nonfiction holdings and
was initially produced by photocopying pages of computer printout. The
excessive costs and delays involved in this method soon led Westminster
to adopt Computer Output Microfilm (COM) reproduction techniques.
Microfilm cassettes containing catalog information were introduced for
public use in June 1971. Westminster's experience with computer-produced catalogs and microfilm readers, which has proved very satisfactory,
is described in greater detail by Larkworthy and Brown.[1] Because of this
successful experience with COM, Westminster is now planning to start
separate catalogs for the children's collection of ten thousand titles and
the Central Music Library stock of sixty-thousand titles. As yet, no commitment has been made about the adult fiction holdings because of pro-
cedural problems caused by decentralized acquisition of these materials
within the system.

Content of the Catalog

All current nonfiction acquisitions since 1970, including materials on order and in process, are recorded only in the computer-produced catalog, which now contains more than sixty-nine thousand titles. Conversion of pre-1970 holdings is being undertaken as time permits. When all nonfiction lending and reference works have been converted, the catalog will contain approximately two hundred thousand titles.

Because the public must still refer to the card catalog for earlier titles, the microfilm readers containing the catalog of recent acquisitions are located near the card file, so that patrons can go from one to the other if necessary. The computer-produced entries are similar in content to the earlier card records and are in fixed-field format. The data file contains a bibliographic record for each title, with a supplementary record for each copy in the system. The bibliographic record includes the International Standard Book Number (ISBN), or a locally generated substitute number, the Dewey Decimal Classification number, author, title, and imprint. At the Westminster libraries, subject access is provided through a classified catalog, not through a subject catalog, so the file record also provides for two additional classification numbers to be recorded, if required. The individual copy record contains processing and control information, including the branch location and special shelving symbol, if any.

A classified listing and an author listing are provided for public use and are completely updated each month. A printed index of subject terms referring users to the appropriate classification number is available as a subject guide, but this requires updating much less frequently than the catalogs. All data are in upper-case characters. Although some entries, such as corporate names, must be truncated to fit the fixed-field format, it is considered that sufficient information is given to allow the user to identify and retrieve the item. There is reported to be no immediate demand by either the public or the library staff for a catalog arranged by title. Subsidiary outputs include statistical reports for staff use and overdue order notices, which are sent to vendors, but the main emphasis is presently upon catalog listings for public use.

For current acquisitions, catalog input data are prepared on a paper-tape typewriter as part of the ordering process. Corrections, additions, and changes made to the record after the initial input, as well as pre-1970 holdings and withdrawals, are usually input on a keypunch machine, which is also used as a back-up input device.

Catalog Format

Evaluation of the advantages and disadvantages of fiche, roll film, and cassette film led Westminster to choose cassette microfilm. Roll film was quickly eliminated from consideration because catalog use is normally distributed over the entire record, and patrons and staff want information quickly. The time and cumbersome procedures required to thread and re-wind roll films were felt to be a deterrent to use.

The size of the Westminster catalog, when completed, is expected to reach the equivalent of approximately twenty thousand pages of computer printout, which, if reproduced on microfiche, would also result in a sizable file. The anticipated difficulty of maintaining a large file of microfiche in correct sequence, while making it readily accessible for consultation by patrons, was one of the reasons Westminster chose microfilm cassettes. An additional reason for preferring cassettes over microfiche is that they are much less vulnerable than microfiche to undetected vandalism or loss. It is relatively easy to determine whether cassettes are missing from the file or to rearrange misfiled cassettes in the correct sequence, but the loss or mis-placement of individual fiche may be harder to detect. No significant prob-lems resulting from vandalism have been reported at Westminster. The potential difficulties with microfiche are cited as a strong justification for cassettes by the London Borough of Camden, which is developing a similar computer-produced catalog for its library system.

Use of cine-mode format is preferred to comic-mode because the former makes it easier for patrons to scan the file and find a given record. As the film is wound, it can be stopped periodically to check the location on what is effectively one continuous page. The information being checked (author, classification number, etc.) always appears in the same relative location on the screen, making it simple for the user to find the items he or she is look-ing for.

Equipment Considerations

A major factor in selecting microfilm readers for public use was ease of operation. Motorized machines were originally considered unsuitable for public use because of their tendency to "run away" with all but experi-enced operators. As the cassettes increase in size, however, the time re-quired to wind manually through a full cassette in search of the desired information may become a problem for users, although it currently takes only about fifty seconds for each hundred feet of film. Westminster has recently begun to use motorized microfilm readers in the five principal lending libraries, where two cassettes containing the author catalog are now held in motorized readers with push-button controls. The machines have proved so simple to operate and are so clearly preferred by the public that the staff at Westminster now feels that they are highly desirable for use in public departments.[2]

Both the author and the classified listings have now expanded to two cassettes. The staff at Westminster has always hoped it would prove possi-ble to allow the user to select the appropriate cassette from the catalog file and insert it in the machine, rather than dedicating a reader to each cassette. Experience with allowing the public to change the two cassettes of the classified catalog has so far been quite successful.[3]

The machines are installed at standing height to discourage patrons from using the catalog consultation tables for other purposes. Simple instructions are provided. The level of ambient light around the readers, which are in an open public area, is rather too high for users' comfort, and some method of reducing this lighting level is desirable.

Although the machines are used by the public without staff supervision or assistance, relatively few routine maintenance problems have been reported. This is believed to be because the machines were originally selected for simplicity of operation and because cassette-loading machines avoid many of the problems that occur during loading and unloading of roll film. More detailed information about the criteria for selection of the original readers is given by Larkworthy and Brown.[4] Day-to-day maintenance and cleaning of the lenses are required, and it was found advantageous to train library staff to perform these functions.

System Development

The detailed development of the catalog was carried out by Cyril Brown, systems analyst for Westminster City Council, in consultation with library staff at Westminster and Kensington, led by Graham Larkworthy, the head of the Bibliographical Services Division for the Westminster City Libraries. Mr. Brown was assigned half-time to this project from February 1967 to August 1969 and full-time from then until April 1970. Mr. Larkworthy estimates that library staff time spent on developing this project was approximately half that of the systems analyst.[5] No outside consultants were involved, although some equipment manufacturers were consulted on technical matters. As of 1973, documentation was not sufficiently complete to be available for distribution.

User Acceptance

Acceptance of the computer-produced microfilm catalogs by the public has been exceptionally good, due in large part to the careful preliminary planning and investigation on which the system design was based. Continued experimentation with new techniques and equipment has also helped to make the system responsive to user needs. All types of users have adapted quickly to the new format, and some consider it an improvement over the card catalog. Copies of the microfilm catalogs are also available in the technical services area, where the staff uses them as part of their daily routine. Westminster plans to investigate the feasibility of listing the complete contents of the data file to facilitate the checking of processing details, but, for the present, the library staff considers the output adequate for its needs and is generally in favor of the new format.

Other Installations in Britain

The Borough of Camden catalog mentioned above is to be implemented as a replacement for hard copy printout, which was used previously in the system. The new catalog will be in microfilm cassette form, and lists will be produced in classification number, author, and title, sequences. All data will be in upper-case characters because the librarians at Camden prefer this format for microform listings. The data file is being planned for multipurpose use, including cataloging, acquisitions, and circulation applications, and will contain fuller information than the initial output listings.

A discussion of some other British library systems using microform catalogs is given by Stuart-Stubbs in a study undertaken on behalf of the Canadian Union Catalogue Task Group.[6] Buckle and French describe the complete microfilm catalog to be implemented at Birmingham University Library.[7]

Conclusions

For libraries in the United States that are faced with the problems of preparing and distributing union lists of holdings or multicopy catalogs, there seem to be many advantages in the kind of microform catalogs now in use in British libraries. Patrons of these libraries have readily accepted the new format, and library staffs are delighted with the frequent updating, which becomes financially feasible with COM catalogs. With careful selection of equipment, maintenance problems with microform readers can be kept to a minimum, although further improvements in simplicity and reliability are still desirable for machines designed to be used by the public.

Cost figures for installations in Britain, even when they are available, are not directly applicable in the United States, but Larkworthy and Brown provide exemplary data for libraries wishing to make their own estimates.[8] Libraries using COM are convinced that it is substantially less expensive to produce and replace microfilm catalogs than hard copy printouts.

One reason for the success of these installations may be the deliberate limitation upon the amount of data provided for public use. The inclusion of a standard identification number in the data file, however, does provide the potential for accessing more extensive machine-readable data from other sources, should the need arise in the future. In Britain, the ISBN or the British National Bibliography (BNB) number is almost always available for currently published works; libraries in the London area are reporting their holdings by ISBN only to the London and South East Library Region union catalog.

Comparatively little use of COM techniques has been reported in the United States so far.[9] The successful experience with microform catalogs in Britain should be encouraging to those libraries presently struggling with the mounting costs and inconveniences involved in the use of conventional computer printout to display bibliographic information.

Acknowledgments

The information on which this paper is based was obtained during a consulting assignment for Information Design, Inc. The author would like to thank Cyril Brown of the Westminster City Council Management Services Unit, Graham Larkworthy of the Westminster City Libraries, Kate Oram of the Borough of Camden and Laurie Jefferson of Scottish Instruments Ltd. for their assistance. Any errors and omissions are the responsibility of the author.

References

1. Graham Larkworthy and Cyril G. Brown, "Library Catalogues on Microfilm," *Library Association Record* 73 (December 1971): 231-32, and their "A Library Catalogue for Public Use," *NCRd Bulletin* 5 (Summer 1972): 78-80.

2. Graham Larkworthy, personal letter to the author. (The machines used are the Caps "Mercury.")

3. Ibid.

4. Larkworthy and Brown, "A Library Catalogue for Public Use."

5. Larkworthy, personal letter.

6. Basil Stuart-Stubbs, *Developments in Library and Union Catalogues and the Use of Microform in British Libraries* ([Vancouver?] National Library of Canada, 1973). (Mimeographed)

7. D. G. R. Buckle and Thomas French, "The Application of Microform, to Manual and Machine-Readable Catalogues," *Program* 6 (July 1972): 187-203.

8. Larkworthy and Brown, "Library Catalogues on Microfilm."

9. Stuart-Stubbs, *Developments*, p. 12; Mary L. Fischer, "The Use of COM at Los Angeles Public Library," *Journal of Micrographics* 6 (May 1973): 205-10; Edward G. Roberts and John P. Kennedy, "The Georgia Tech Library's Microfiche Catalog," *Journal of Micrographics* 6 (July 1973): 245-51.

COM CATALOG BASED
ON OCLC RECORDS

by Richard W. Meyer and John F. Knapp

The production of a COM catalog using OCLC records on magnetic tape is outlined. Standards developed within the library community as represented in the MARC format have made this catalog possible. A brief overview of the procedures involved and of the catalog is presented.

Introduction

This article reports on the successful use of currently available computer technology in support of cataloging and processing at the University of Texas at Dallas. The experience at UT-Dallas suggests to libraries interested in seeking alternatives to the card catalog that there are options open to them in developing and maintaining a machine-readable data base without requiring local access to a computer and systems staff.

The UT-Dallas Library is maintaining its catalog on data bases in two remote locations and integrating these records regularly to produce a microfiche catalog for its patrons. The bibliographic data communications between two cataloging centers—Ohio College Library Center (OCLC) and Blackwell North America (formerly Richard Abel and Company)—using the MARC format as the medium of exchange are described below.

Background

Under arrangements with the three new campuses of the University of Texas located in Dallas, San Antonio, and the Permian Basin, Richard Abel and Company developed a set of computer programs which maintain a machine-readable data base and produce catalogs in a variety of formats. Using the same software, catalogs can be produced on a computer line

Reprinted from the *Journal of Library Automation*, 8: 312-21 (December 1975) by permission of the author and publisher. Copyright © 1975 by the American Library Association.

printer, on a COM device, or on photocomposition equipment. The records may be combined to produce either dictionary or divided catalogs. To date, the system has been used for the three University of Texas libraries to produce catalogs on microfiche and microfilm using COM technology. UT-Dallas is currently undertaking to install this batch software system on its local computer facility; however, in the meantime, the system is being maintained by Blackwell North America (B/NA).

Initially for its current acquisitions, UT-Dallas developed its bibliographic data base by using Abel cataloging services, which included the production of catalog cards and labels and the retention of a machine-readable record in the MARC format. Retrospective cataloging for the library was concurrently converted by systematically working through its shelflist, at that time containing 12,000 titles. Cataloging was ordered from Abel by LC card number for 1969 and later imprints. For titles with imprints earlier than 1969, the library searched the Abel data base title index and ordered those found by Abel record number. For those titles not found on the Abel data base, the shelflist card was photocopied, and the copy was sent to Abel to keyed and converted to machine-readable form. This 12,000 title collection consisted of mostly English-language books with emphasis in science and technology. The current and retrospective records were merged into a separately identified UT-Dallas cataloging data base, which now contains records for approximately 48,000 titles growing at a rate of 20,000 titles per year. Similar procedures were used to assemble cataloging files for the other two campuses.

In 1973, when it became apparent that UT-Dallas would be joining the Ohio College Library Center network under the aegis of the Inter-University Council of North Texas (IUC), it was conjectured that the OCLC terminals could be used to support current cataloging activities and that OCLC records on tape could be added to the UT-Dallas data base maintained by Abel. Since both centers use the MARC data definition and can produce records in the MARC structure, would it be possible to keep records from both sources on a single file? In practice, this is essentially what happened.

System Operation

All present cataloging operations at UT-Dallas are centered around production of catalog copy via the UT-Dallas link to OCLC. Current imprints as well as retrospective titles and continuing shelflist conversion of a recently purchased library collection are processed routinely with a pair of CRT terminals in the manner used by many libraries linked with OCLC. Each title is searched in the OCLC data base prior to ordering as a preorder bibliographic check, and, if not found, is searched again subsequent to receipt.

When the search or re-search is made with book in hand and the corresponding OCLC catalog record is located, copy is produced immediately if no significant bibliographic editing is required. When significant editing or original cataloging is needed, a work sheet is prepared by the cataloging staff. The data are then entered into the OCLC data base using a terminal and catalog copy is produced.

Because UT-Dallas relies on a microfiche catalog, only two catalog cards are produced by OCLC—one for the card shelflist which continues to be maintained and one for a temporary title catalog, which was intended to provide access to recently cataloged books between supplements to the microfiche catalog. However, the latter file has been discontinued since B/NA has started biweekly supplementation to the catalog. UT-Dallas currently uses the second card as a feedback card for error correction when necessary and discards the rest. OCLC maintains an archival record of all catalog production which includes any local modifications made to the basic bibliographic records, e.g., added notes and call numbers. The only significant difference between these records and those supplied by the Library of Congress MARC Distribution Service is that OCLC uses the 001 field for its own record number and puts LC card number in the 010 field (which is according to specification in the MARC format).[1] The UT-Dallas archival file is written onto magnetic tape in the ASCII character set and sent from Columbus to Dallas biweekly.

When the tape arrives, the records are processed on a local computer to prepare a tape to be sent to B/NA. This processing consists primarily of error checking and conversion to an EBCDIC character set. For example, the presence of an 050 or 090 field is checked to assure that there is a call number in the record. In addition, the OCLC record number is moved into a fixed field position, and the records are sorted to insure that they are arranged in ascending record number order (they arrive from OCLC unsorted).

When the records are received by B/NA in Portland, they are added to the UT-Dallas data base. In addition to OCLC records, records for non-monographic cataloging produced by the UT-Dallas cataloging staff and sent to B/NA for conversion and inclusion (as with OCLC production two main entry cards are produced) are merged into the data base. These new records plus any older records which might have been modified (e.g., a change of call number or location) appear on a biweekly cumulating catalog supplement on microfiche which supports a yearly master cumulation of the catalog. Therefore, in actual use, the patron is required to search no more than two catalog alphabets. The biweekly producton schedule appears to be an adequate compromise between keeping the catalog up-to-date and the cost of frequent catalog production. It is interesting to note that an economic biweekly supplementation schedule can be maintained with a COM catalog; this has not usually been possible with printed book catalogs. The average time delay between the production of the cataloging at the terminal and the appearance of those records in the catalog is eight weeks, which compares favorably with typical card production and filing schedules in most medium-sized academic libraries.

UT-Dallas has divided its microfiche catalog into author, title, subject, and shelflist arrangements. This division seems to be in line with current trends and follows the practice formerly used in the card catalog. Within the four divisions, several different approaches to the display of the data are used. Selection of the page formats and the content of each catalog entry were based on an analysis of search strategy and on a user survey. The first catalog cumulation was produced in a variety of formats with differing content, and a survey of user experience with this catalog was used as a basis for format selection in future catalogs.

The author catalog (Figure 1) contains very brief entries which consist of author, title statement, date of publication, and call number. This catalog is viewed only as a finding list by author. For detailed information or citation verification, the user is required to access the title catalog.

The title catalog (Figure 2) contains full entries which show the complete bibliographic record arranged in single paragraph style. Imprint, collation, notes, and other parts of the record are slightly harder to distinguish here than in a typical unit card because of the lack of indention, but this is not a significant problem. The more compact format permits more entries to be displayed on a page, an offsetting user benefit.

The subject catalog (Figure 3) contains truncated records which are subsorted by author under the appropriate subject heading. The computer programs generating the catalog are flexible enough to allow for different approaches, such as subsorting under headings chronologically rather than by author. The subject catalog also contains subject cross-references. The subject entry consists of author, title, edition, date of publication, subject tracings, and call number. The subject tracings are shown in order to accommodate the user's search strategy which might look for more pertinent subject headings under the heading being perused, thereby augmenting the "see also" structure in the catalog.

The shelflist (Figure 4) contains complete records which are arranged by call number. The records are internally sorted in MARC tag order. The MARC tags are shown to allow the library to track down problems. For instance, the reason for the lack of a series entry in the catalog may be pinpointed by noting that the MARC series field has been tagged as an untraced series (490 instead of 400-440). The OCLC and B/NA control numbers are also shown here to facilitate error correction.

The indentions, spacing, and arrangement of all entries have been organized to optimize readability of the catalog without wasting space. In most of the catalogs the entries are displayed in three columns within a page—the page fills the screen of the microfiche readers used at UT-Dallas. The records are blocked into rectangular paragraphs which are visually comfortable and easy to scan. The heading, the body, and the call number are printed on different indentions in order to make scanning easy and to make the call number stand out. Should extended use prove the page layout or the entry format and contents to be ineffective, simple tables driving the computer program logic can be altered so allow alternatives without modifying the programs themselves.

As mentioned above, the subject catalog contains a full cross-reference structure. This structure includes all the relevant see references and see also references (with blind see also's eliminated) found in the *Subject Headings Used in the Dictionary Catalogs of the Library of Congress*, 7th edition.[2] The provision of cross-references is one feature of the batch processing system which includes subject authority control. The authority file

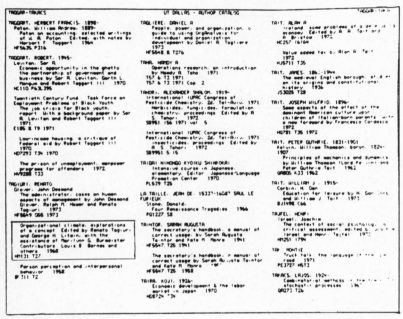

Fig. 1. Author Catalog.

which supports this part of the system uses the *Subject Headings Used in the Dictionary Catalogs of the Library of Congress*, 7th edition as its base, but it has been considerably enhanced with updates from several supplements and additions of headings not included in the LC list, e.g., personal names, geographic names, new combinations of heading and subheadings, etc. The current file contains over 130,000 headings (the original LC file had 60,882).

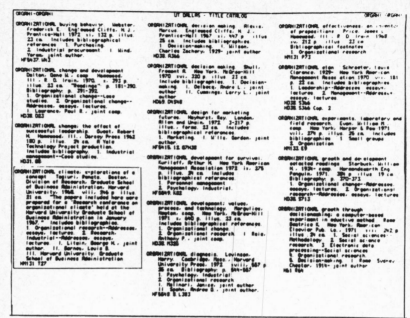

Fig. 2. Title Catalog.

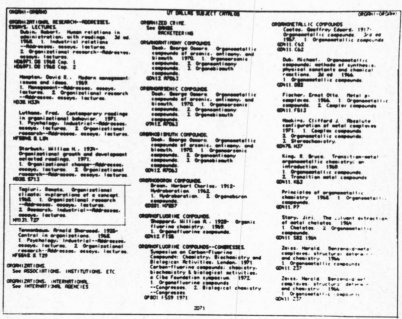

Fig. 3. Subject Catalog.

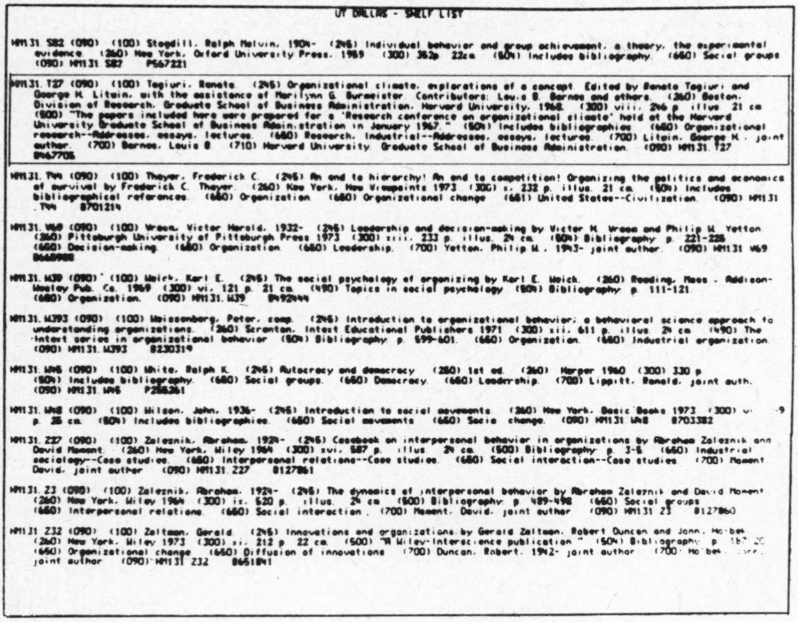

UT DALLAS - SHELF LIST

HM131.S82 (090) (100) Stogdill, Ralph Melvin, 1904- (245) Individual behavior and group achievement, a theory, the experimental evidence. (260) New York, Oxford University Press, 1959 (300) 352p. 22cm (504) Includes bibliography. (650) Social groups (090) HM131.S87 P567221

HM131.T27 (090) (100) Tagiuri, Renato. (245) Organizational climate, explorations of a concept. Edited by Renato Tagiuri and George H. Litwin, with the assistance of Marilynn G. Burmeister. Contributors: Louis B. Barnes and others. (260) Boston, Division of Research, Graduate School of Business Administration, Harvard University, 1968. (300) viii, 246 p. illus. 21 cm (500) "The papers included here were prepared for a 'Research conference on organizational climate' held at the Harvard University Graduate School of Business Administration in January 1967." (504) Includes bibliographies. (650) Organizational research--Addresses, essays, lectures. (650) Research, Industrial--Addresses, essays, lectures. (700) Litwin, George H., joint author. (700) Barnes, Louis B. (710) Harvard University. Graduate School of Business Administration. (090) HM131.T27 B467706

HM131.T44 (090) (100) Thayer, Frederick C. (245) An end to hierarchy! An end to competition! Organizing the politics and economics of survival by Frederick C. Thayer. (260) New York, New Viewpoints 1973 (300) x, 232 p. illus. 21 cm. (504) Includes bibliographical references. (650) Organization. (650) Organizational change (651) United States--Civilization. (090) HM131.T44 B701214

HM131.V69 (090) (100) Vroom, Victor Harold, 1932- (245) Leadership and decision-making by Victor H. Vroom and Philip W. Yetton (260) Pittsburgh University of Pittsburgh Press 1973 (300) xiii, 233 p. illus. 24 cm. (504) Bibliography p. 221-226 (650) Decision-making. (650) Organization. (650) Leadership. (700) Yetton, Philip W., 1943- joint author. (090) HM131.V69 B660900

HM131.W39 (090) (100) Weick, Karl E. (245) The social psychology of organizing by Karl E. Weick. (260) Reading, Mass., Addison-Wesley Pub. Co. 1969 (300) vi, 121 p. 21 cm. (490) Topics in social psychology (504) Bibliography p. 111-121. (650) Organization. (090) HM131.W39 B492444

HM131.W393 (090) (100) Weissenberg, Peter, comp. (245) Introduction to organizational behavior; a behavioral science approach to understanding organizations. (260) Scranton, Intext Educational Publishers 1971 (300) xii, 611 p. illus. 24 cm (490) The Intext series in organizational behavior (504) Bibliography p. 599-601. (650) Organization. (650) Industrial organization. (090) HM131.W393 B230319

HM131.W46 (090) (100) White, Ralph K. (245) Autocracy and democracy (250) 1st ed. (260) Harper 1960 (300) 330 p. (504) Includes bibliography. (650) Social groups. (650) Democracy. (650) Leadership. (700) Lippitt, Ronald, joint auth. (090) HM131.W46 P288261

HM131.W48 (090) (100) Wilson, John, 1936- (245) Introduction to social movements. (260) New York, Basic Books 1973 (300) v... 9 p. 25 cm. (504) Includes bibliographies. (650) Social movements (650) Socia change. (090) HM131.W48 B703382

HM131.Z27 (090) (100) Zaleznik, Abraham, 1924- (245) Casebook on interpersonal behavior in organizations by Abraham Zaleznik and David Moment. (260) New York, Wiley 1964 (300) xvi, 587 p. illus. 24 cm. (500) Bibliography p. 3-6. (650) Industrial sociology--Case studies. (650) Interpersonal relations--Case studies. (650) Social interaction--Case studies. (700) Moment, David, joint author (090) HM131.Z27 B127861

HM131.Z3 (090) (100) Zaleznik, Abraham, 1924- (245) The dynamics of interpersonal behavior by Abraham Zaleznik and David Moment (260) New York, Wiley 1964 (300) ix, 520 p. illus. 24 cm (500) Bibliography p. 489-498 (650) Social groups (650) Interpersonal relations. (650) Social interaction. (700) Moment, David, joint author (090) HM131.Z3 B127860

HM131.Z32 (090) (100) Zaltman, Gerald. (245) Innovations and organizations by Gerald Zaltman, Robert Duncan and Jonn. Holbek (260) New York, Wiley 1973 (300) xi, 212 p. 22 cm. (500) "A Wiley-Interscience publication." (504) Bibliography p. 187-20[illegible] (650) Organizational change. (650) Diffusion of innovations (700) Duncan, Robert, 1942- joint author (700) Holbek, [illegible] joint author (090) HM131.Z32 B651841

Fig. 4. Shelflist.

The subject authority control system has three purposes in addition to the provision of cross-references: (1) to verify headings on all current cataloging to reduce error in the catalog; (2) to convert obsolete headings on all retrospective cataloging as they are added to more current terminology (*Aeroplanes* is now *Airplanes*, at last); and (3) to maintain the subject headings in the catalog over time and make changes as the terminology and structure of the authority file are made more current. The latter capability provides an important advantage over the card catalog. One change to a heading in the authority file automatically changes all like headings in the catalog. Therefore, when the Library of Congress recently changed *China (People's Republic of China, 1949-)* to *China* and *Formosa* to *Taiwan*, all records on the UT-Dallas catalog were changed accordingly. Likewise, when the Library of Congress releases the *LC List of Subject Headings*, 8th edition, in machine-readable form, this file will be used to update the current authority file, and those changes will be reflected in subsequent cumulations of the catalog.

Conclusions

The approach to cataloging at UT-Dallas has been successful. It has made effective use of limited staff resources during a period of intensive collection development for a new institution. The UT-Dallas cataloging staff has never exceeded four nonprofessionals and 25 percent of one professional's time. In addition, the microfiche catalog allows much more flexibility in catalog maintenance because entry formats, catalog organization, and record content can be readily changed over time. The catalog is easily reproducible and portable, allowing the library to distribute copies around the campus. The use of the OCLC cataloging service has facilitated the inclusion of new titles in the catalog. It is interesting to note that UT-Dallas is not using OCLC primarily as a source for catalog cards but as a source for customized machine-readable records. This raises some interesting questions about the future of OCLC: Will OCLC's role as a card production service diminish as more libraries use machine-readable alternatives to the card catalog just as UT-Dallas has? Will OCLC undertake to maintain the customized cataloging data base of each of its member libraries, which is quite a different service than now offered?

The example of UT-Dallas highlights the importance of standards developed within the library community which, because this library was willing to adopt them, created the opportunity described above. The relevant standards are the *Anglo-American Cataloging Rules* as practiced by the Library of Congress and the MARC record format, which includes both a data structure and a data definition.[3,4] It is hoped that those individuals within the profession involved in the development and maintenance of these standards will take inspiration from this example and use it to replenish some of the personal expenditure of emotional energy necessary to reach accord on the various issues.

References

1. Library of Congress, MARC Development Office, *Books: A MARC Format* (5th ed., Washington, D.C.: 1972).

2. Library of Congress, *Subject Headings Used in the Dictionary Catalogs of the Library of Congress* (7th ed., Washington, D.C.: Library of Congress, 1966).

3. *Anglo-American Cataloging Rules*. North American Text. (Chicago: American Library Assn., 1967).

4. Library of Congress, MARC Development Office, *Books: A MARC Format*.

COM (COMPUTER OUTPUT MICROFILM) AND
LIBRARY CATALOGS

Additional Readings

Aschenborn, H. J., "South African UNICAT: The Union Catalogue of Monographs in South African Libraries on Microfiche," *South African Libraries*, 41:53-57 (October 1973).

Avedon, Don, *Computer Output Microfilm*. 2nd ed. Silver Springs, Md.: National Microfilm Association, 1973.

Butler, Brett, and Van Pelt, John, "Microphotocomposition—A New Publishing Resource," *Journal of Micrographics*, 6:7-13 (September 1972).

Cooke, L. R., "Computer-Produced Library Catalogue on Microfilm Project," *NRCd Bulletin*, 3:40 (Spring 1969).

Fischer, Mary L., "The Use of COM at Los Angeles Public Library, *Journal of Micrographics*, 6:130-35 (May 1973).

Hammond, Hilary I., "The Computer Catalogue System at Shropshire County Library," *Program*, 6:74-86 (January 1972).

Horner, W. C., "Use and Economics of Computer Generated Microfiche Catalogs," *North Carolina Libraries*, 33:31-33 (Winter 1975).

Kozumplik, W. A., and Lange, R. T., "A COM-Produced Library Catalog," *Information and Records Management*, 5:45-46 (April/May 1970).

Larkworthy, Graham, and Brown, Cyril G., "A Library Catalogue for Public Use," *NRCd Bulletin*, 5:78-80 (Summer 1972).

Sargent, Charles W., and Lindberg, Donald, "Computer-based Union Catalog Project for the University of Missouri," *Special Libraries*, 63:121-29 (March 1972).

Schleifer, Harold B., and Adams, Peggy A., "Books in Print on Microfiche, a Pilot Test," *Microform Review*, 5:10-24 (January 1976).

Spaulding, Carl, "A Primer on COM (Computer Output Microfilm), An Alternate to Computer Printout," *American Libraries*, 7:468-70 (July/August 1976).

Williams, B. J. S., *Microform Applications in Library Catalogues: Supporting Paper K4 to the National Libraries ASP Study*. Hertfordshire, England: National Reprographic Centre for Documentation, 1972.

INDEX

INDEX